A Genius of Industrial En

EDWARD WADSWORTH

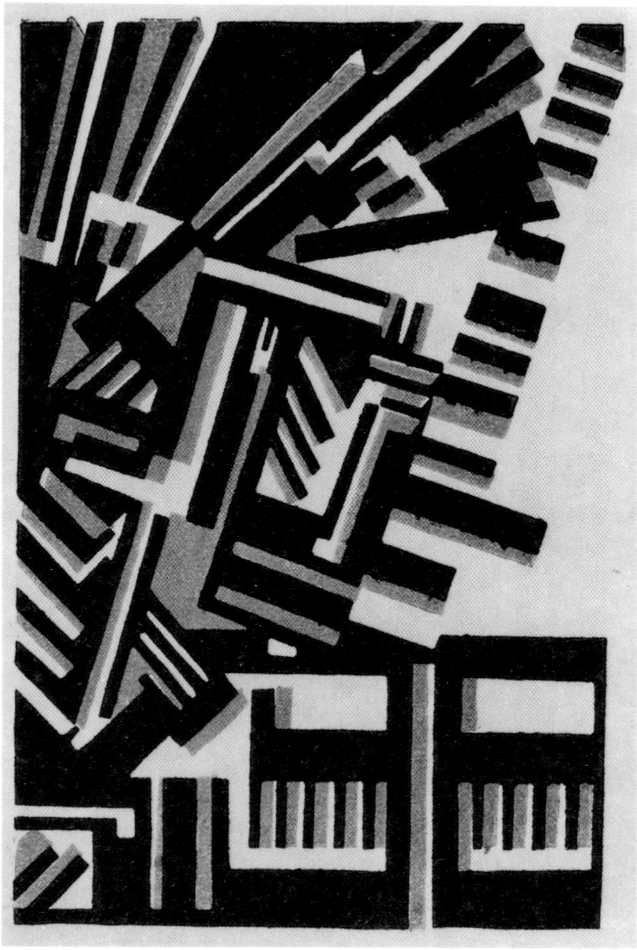

20. *The Port/Untitled Vorticist Composition* 1914-15

All I can say … is that Wadsworth was an important artist: that as much as Old Crome was a genius of agricultural England, Wadsworth was a genius of industrial England (deflected, so I think, into nautical channels).
Wyndham Lewis

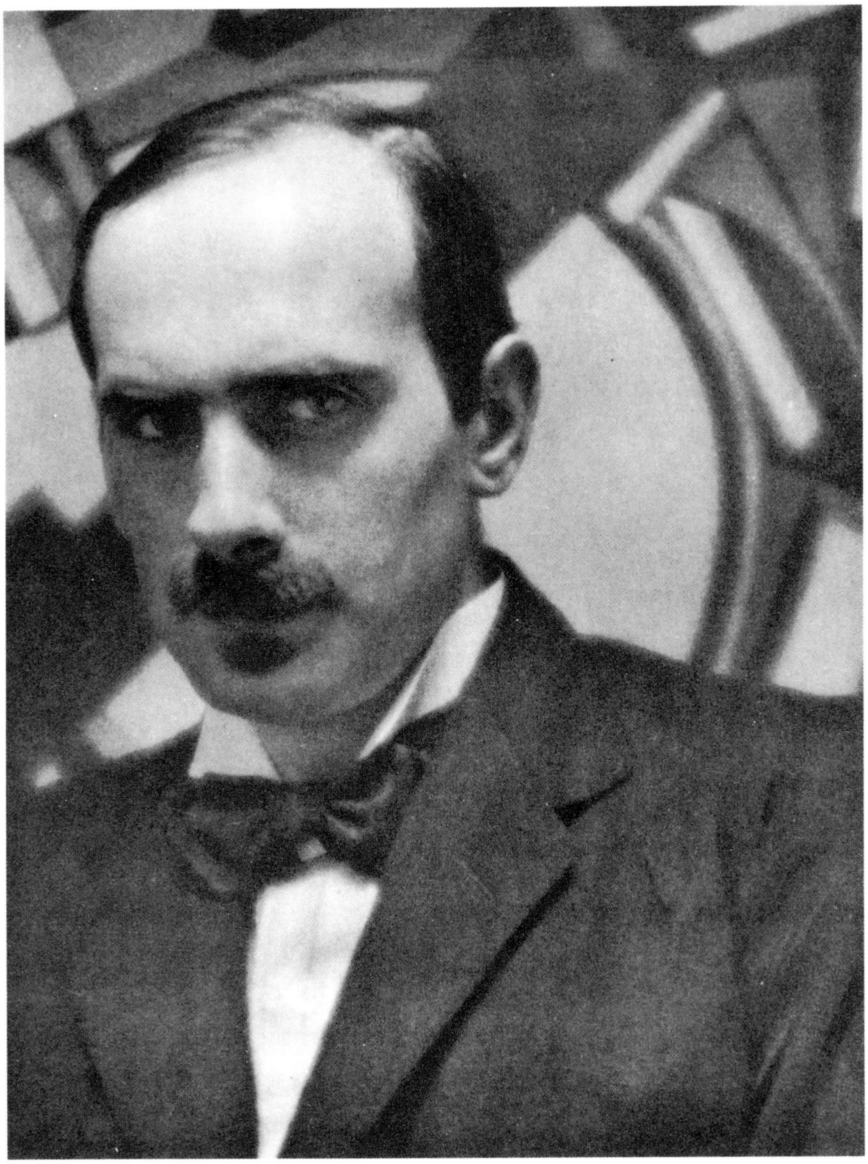

6.95

A Genius of Industrial England

Edward Wadsworth 1889-1949

Edited by Jeremy Lewison with essays by Andrew Causey, Richard Cork, Serge Fauchereau and Jeremy Lewison

Published by the Arkwright Arts Trust
and Bradford Art Galleries and Museums

Published by the Arkwright Arts Trust
and Bradford Art Galleries and Museums
to accompany the exhibition Edward Wadsworth 1889-1949
organised by Bradford Art Galleries and Museums
to celebrate the centenary of the birth of
Edward Wadsworth ARA

Exhibition dates
Cartwright Hall, Bradford 12 October 1989 – 14 January 1990
Camden Arts Centre, London 14 March – 22 April 1990

Photography
Richard Littlewood, Huddersfield
Tate Gallery
Prudence Cuming Associates
Charles A H Pickard and Son, Leeds

British Library Cataloguing in Publication Data is available

ISBN 0 9505532 7 1

Produced for the publishers by
John Taylor Book Ventures
Hatfield, Herts

Distributed to the book trade worldwide by
Lund Humphries Publishers Ltd, 16 Pembridge Road, London W11

Designed by Alan Bartram
Made and printed in Great Britain by
BAS Printers Limited, Over Wallop
Stockbridge, Hampshire

Fig. 1 FRONTISPIECE
Edward Wadsworth by Alvin Langdon Coburn 1916
(National Portrait Gallery)

Contents

Numbers in parentheses appearing in each text after the titles of works by Wadsworth refer to catalogue numbers in this publication.

Numbers in parentheses with the prefix W/A or W/D in the captions to illustrations in the text refer to the list of paintings and drawings in Barbara Wadsworth, *Edward Wadsworth: A Painter's Life*, Wilton 1989.

Numbers in the margin indicate pages on which colour reproductions of the work cited may be found.

All works by Edward Wadsworth are tempera on linen stretched over board unless otherwise indicated.

All measurements are in centimetres, height precedes width.

Full titles for all works may be found in the List of Works beginning on page 123.

Foreword

This is the first Wadsworth retrospective exhibition to have taken place in a public gallery since the Memorial Exhibition held at the Tate Gallery in 1951. It is therefore long overdue. With the exception of a show mounted at Colnaghi's in 1974, which included works from throughout his career, Wadsworth's representation in exhibitions has been confined to particular periods. Emphasis has traditionally been laid on his Vorticist works and the marine paintings of the twenties but this exhibition shows the variety of expression Wadsworth achieved throughout a career cut short by illness. Furthermore it indicates the degree to which Wadsworth was alive to avant-garde developments and the central role he played, alongside artists such as Paul Nash and Ben Nicholson, in English modernism.

The proposal to organise this exhibition was Robert Hopper's, who as City Arts and Museums Officer in the City of Bradford invited John Sheeran, then the Assistant Keeper, Fine Art, to select and administer it. When John Sheeran left the museum service halfway through the project the task of organising the exhibition fell to Christine Hopper.

The essays for the catalogue have been written by Andrew Causey, Richard Cork, Serge Fauchereau and Jeremy Lewison, the latter kindly acting as editor of the publication at very short notice with the kind permission of Nicholas Serota, Director of the Tate Gallery. We are grateful to them for their pioneering and stimulating contributions. The chronology has been compiled by Richard Humphreys.

The production of the catalogue has been made possible by generous support from the Henry Moore Foundation, the Annely Juda Foundation, Sotheby's, Waddington Galleries and the Piccadilly Gallery and it has been published to coincide with the mounting of the exhibition at Camden Arts Centre. An extensive amount of photography has been executed by Richard Littlewood and the photographic department of the Tate Gallery, to whom we offer our thanks. Rosemary Harris at the Tate Gallery has also provided assistance. We are grateful to Mark Glazebrook and Andrew Murray for providing useful information at all points of our research and for the loan of many photographs. John Taylor has overseen the production of the catalogue.

An exhibition such as this would not have been possible without the help and co-operation of many lenders, both public and private, to whom we extend our thanks. Their names appear in the list of works. We are also grateful to Jeremy Lewison and Richard Morphet for their help in negotiating further key loans for the London showing of the exhibition. Financial assistance has been provided by the David Cohen Family Charitable Trust, Grob Gallery and Mr & Mrs Edward Lee for the showing at Camden Arts Centre.

Finally, Barbara Wadsworth, the artist's daughter and biographer, deserves considerable thanks for her enthusiastic help in locating works and for her co-operation in the publication of this catalogue which, we hope, will further the understanding and enjoyment of the work of her father.

ARKWRIGHT ARTS TRUST
BRADFORD ART GALLERIES AND MUSEUMS

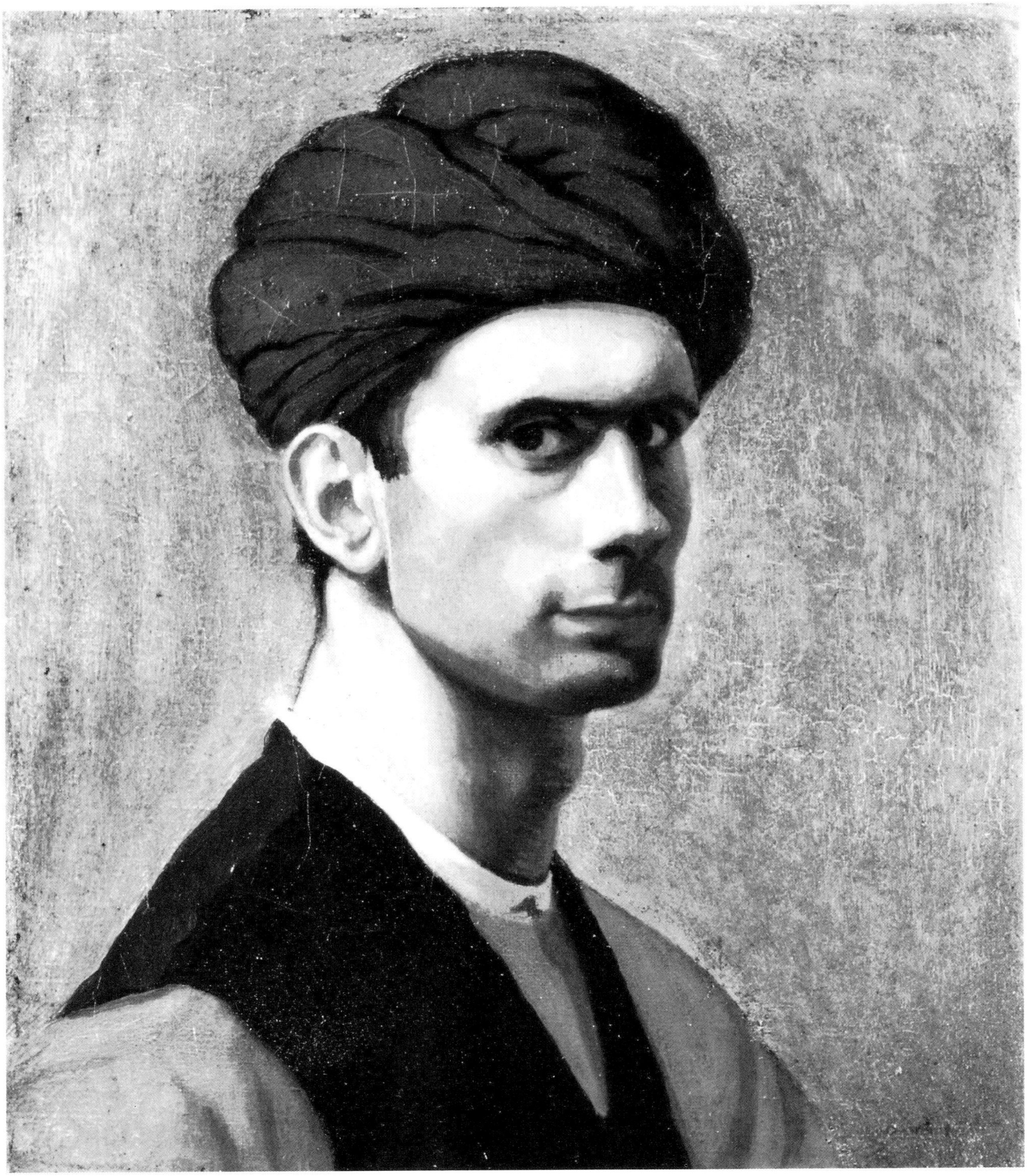

6. Self-portrait 1911

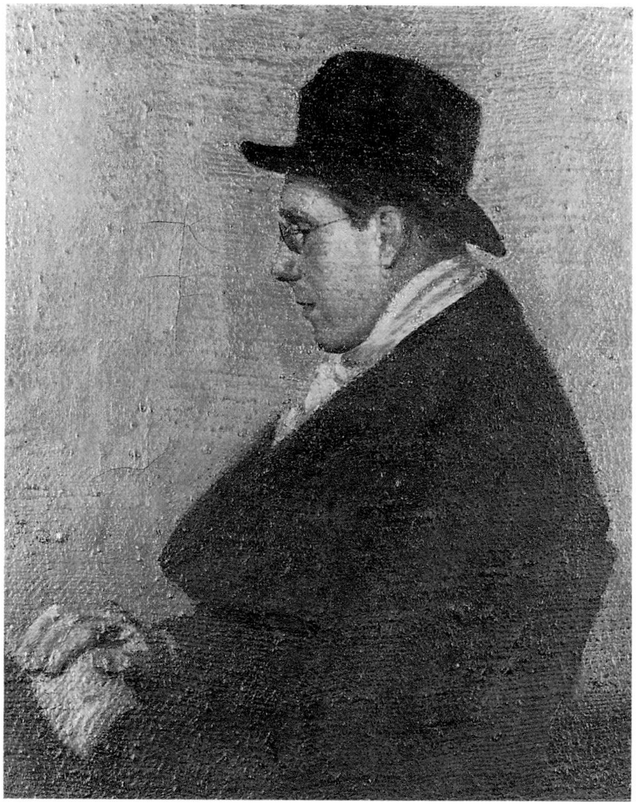

4

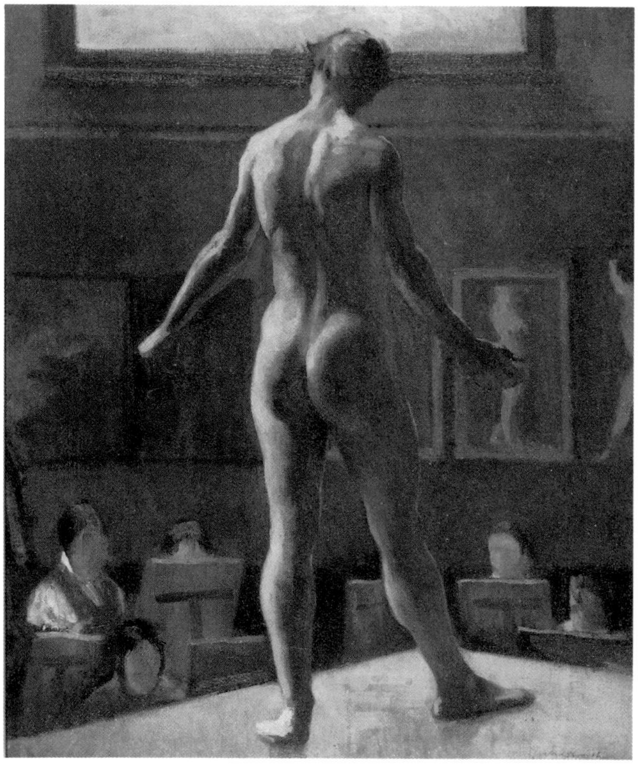

5

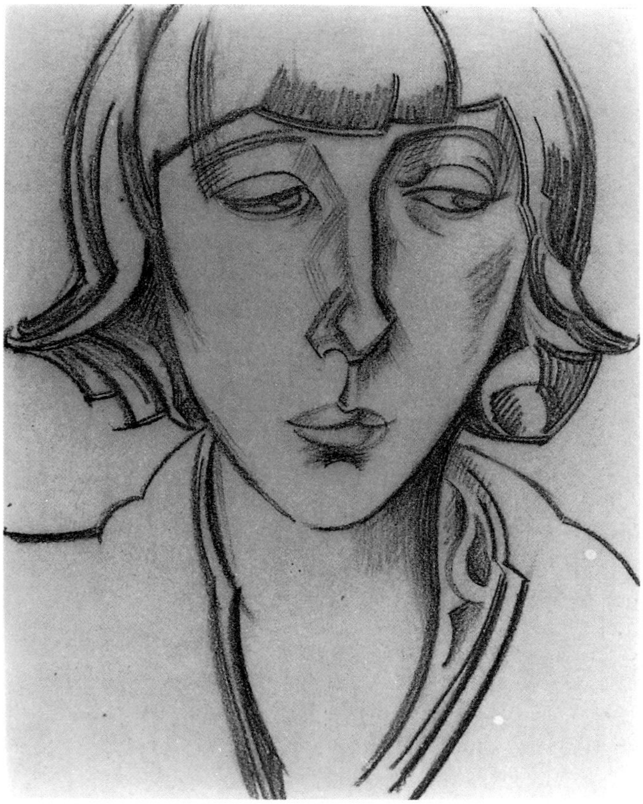

7

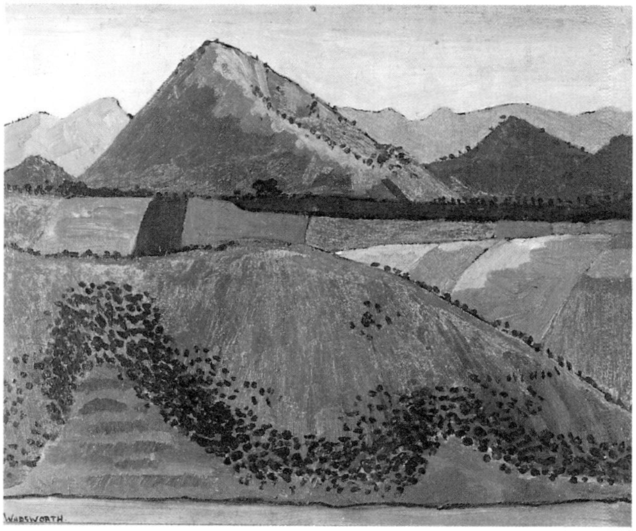

8

4. Portrait of Cuthbert Kelly 1910
5. Nude in the Life-room 1911
7. Portrait Drawing of Violet Wallis 1911
8. Landscape, Grand Canary 1912

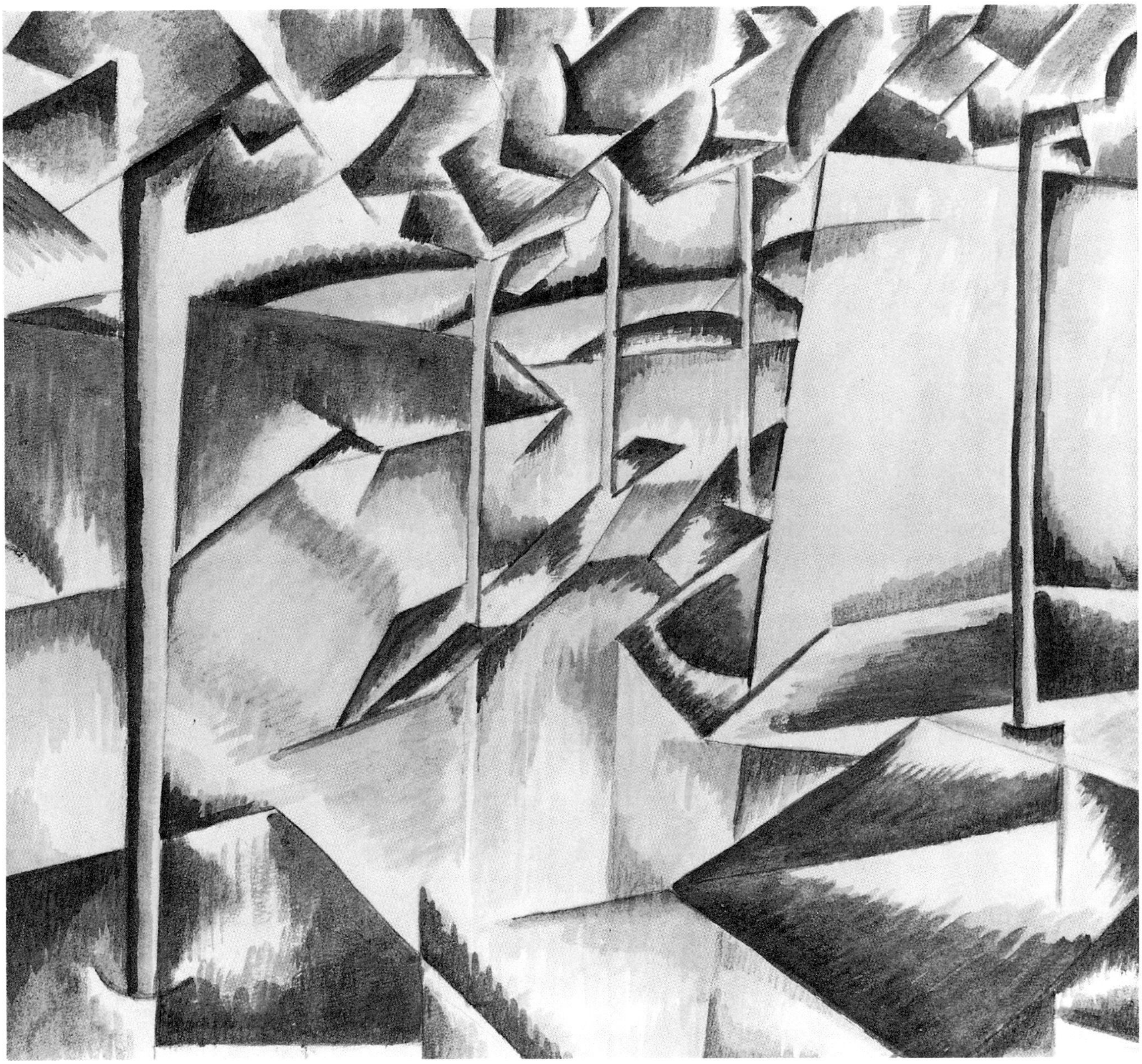

10

10. *Landscape* 1913
9. *Pool with Trees and Punt* 1913
11. *Trees beside River* 1913

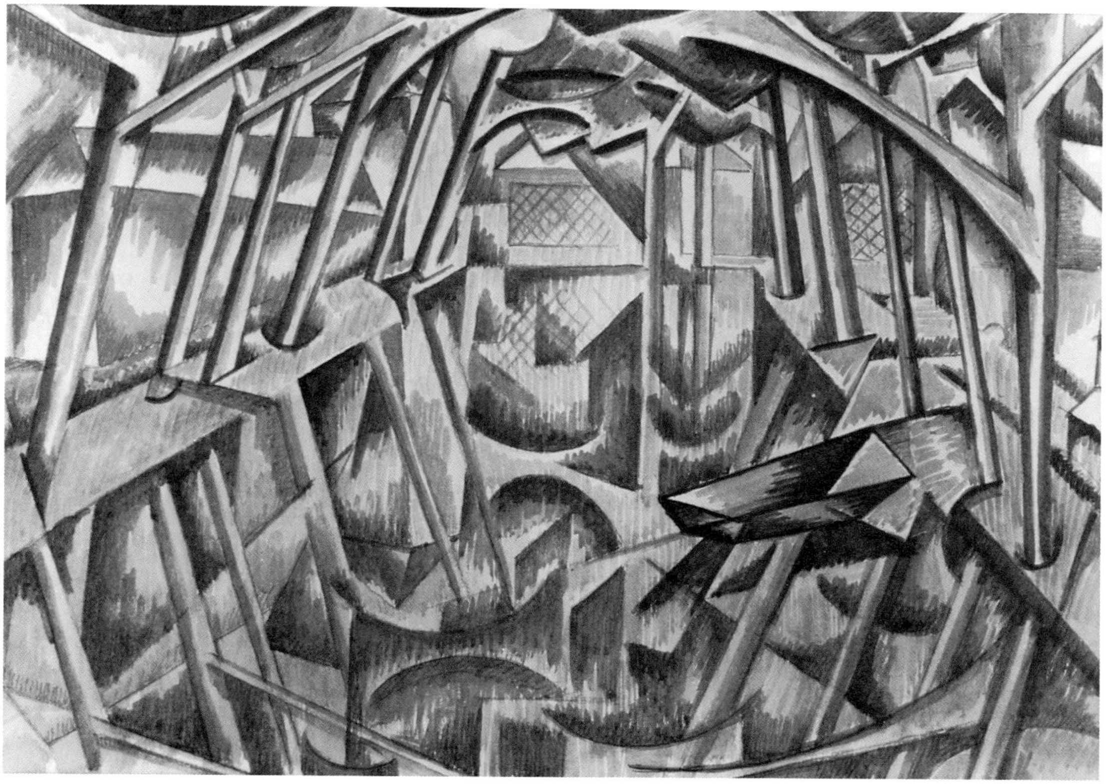

9

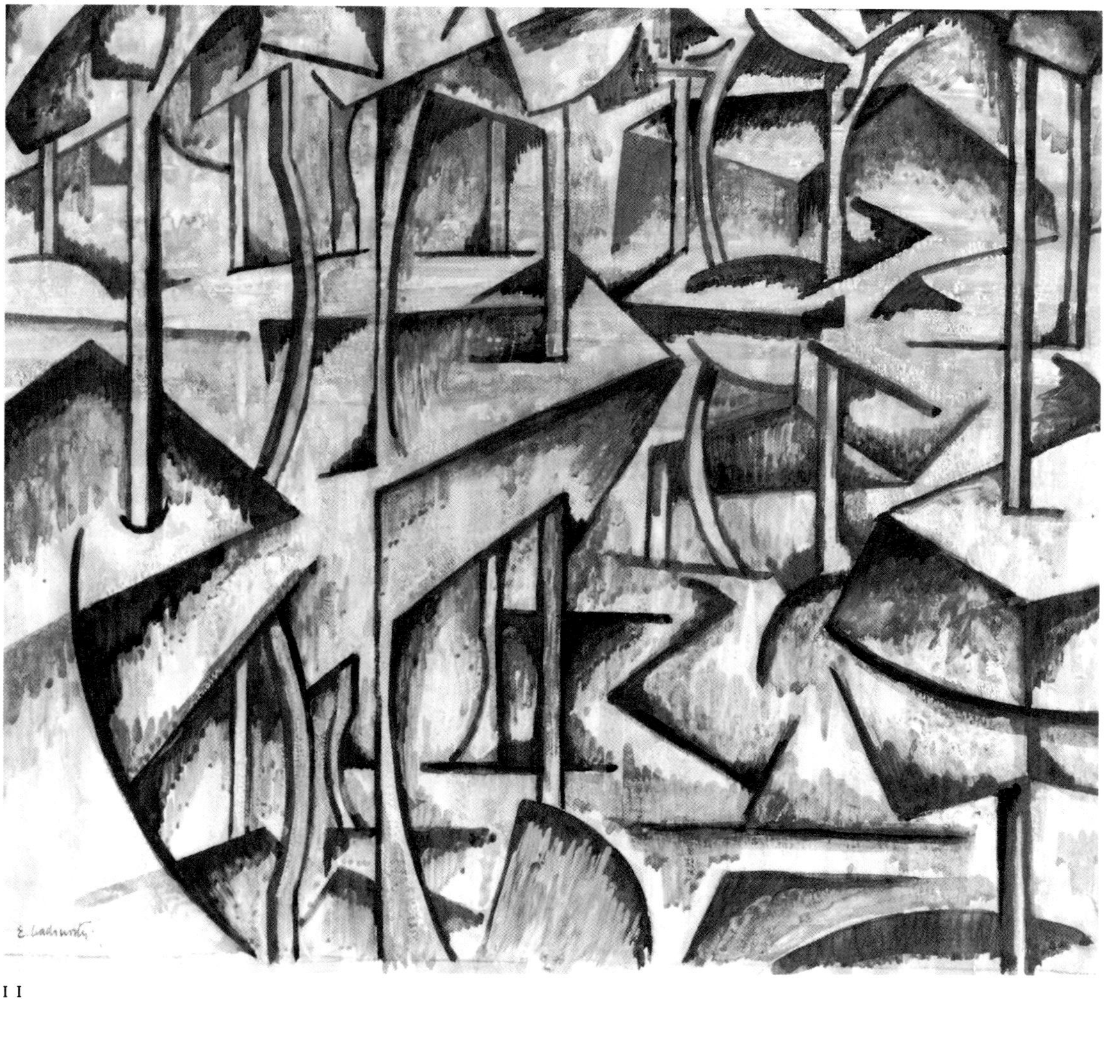

11

Richard Cork

Wadsworth and the Woodcut

By the time Wadsworth discovered the satisfaction of working with the woodcut medium, he had transformed himself into an innovative artist keenly aware of the most experimental initiatives in European art. The swiftness with which this metamorphosis took place, in the latter half of 1913, comes as a surprise after the work he produced during his student period. For the years Wadsworth spent at the Slade had given little hint of the radicalism to come. 'Nude in the Life-Room' 1911 (5), still preserved in the Slade's collection, is a fluent performance containing nothing calculated to upset the prejudices of his teachers. At a time when Tonks railed against Cubism and warned his students to avoid its influence, Wadsworth contented himself with far less extreme sources of inspiration. The 'Portrait of Mrs Violet Wallis' 1911, one of his most satisfying and resolved Slade paintings, shows a sympathy with the Camden Town Group while preserving a fundamentally Whistlerian tonality.[1] 'Plage au Havre', executed the same year, comes close to the flat, decorative patterning found in Marquet's earlier Fauvist work.[2] Wadsworth was searching for a direction and his abrupt stylistic changes show how restless he must have felt. The small landscape panels produced at Grand Canary (8) and Brittany in 1912 are modest exercises, where Fauvism merges with the influence of a lyrical landscapist like Innes. They display no sign of a desire to overhaul the language of painting, and even when Fry included Wadsworth in the final month of the *Second Post-Impressionist Exhibition* in January 1913, Wadsworth's 'Viaduct' (now lost) was described by one reviewer as 'novel only in [its] unaffected simplicity'.[3]

Fry's support doubtless encouraged Wadsworth to explore the implications of Cézanne's work, particularly in its relationship with the early stages of Cubism. The 1913 watercolours, executed in a woodland location near Lewes in Sussex, declare for the first time a singleminded involvement with structure. The reflections cast in the water by the punt and overhanging trees in 'Pool with Trees and Punt' (9) are almost as solid and sharply defined as the objects themselves. Once he had savoured the pleasures to be derived from this severe formal interplay, Wadsworth pursued them with relish. At the same time, however, he moved rapidly away from the pastoral inspiration of the Sussex watercolours, exchanging it for a preoccupation with urban themes which owe a great deal, in terms of style and subject-matter alike, to the example of Futurism.

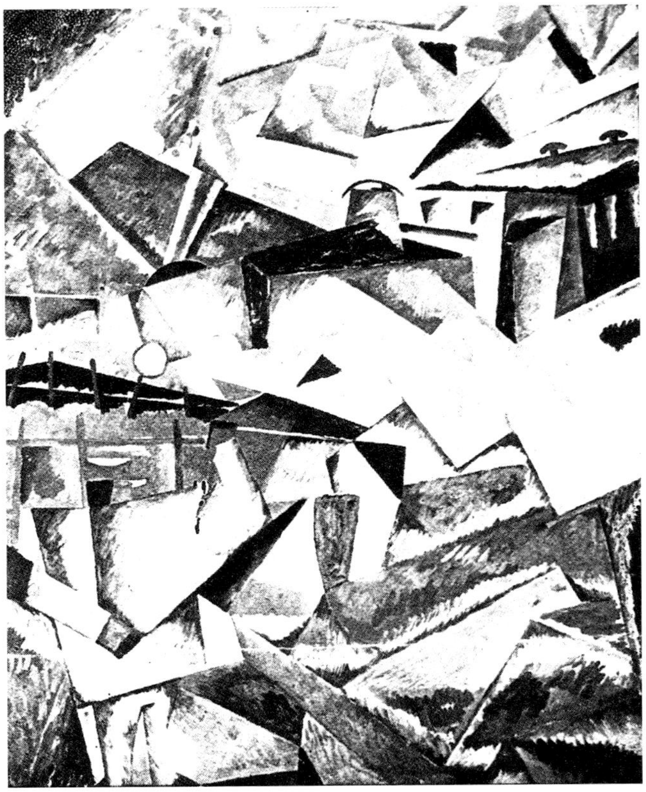

Fig.2 *L'Omnibus* 1913 (W/A 19), oil on canvas, 127 × 101.6 (whereabouts unknown)

Although he appears to have been unaffected by the Futurists' first London exhibition in March 1912, a photograph of his lost painting 'L'Omnibus' 1913 (fig.2) proves that Wadsworth had become impressed by Severini's work the following year. He probably saw it when Severini staged a one-man show at the Marlborough Gallery in April 1913. The Italian insurgent announced in a British newspaper interview that 'the elements of nature are being overtaken by inevitable destruction, and must give place to the mechanical ingenuity of man'.[5] While Wadsworth was too gentle an artist ever to share the Futurists' enjoyment of 'destruction', he would certainly have been in sympathy with a movement dedicated to stressing the central importance of machine-age dynamism. 'L'Omnibus' rejoices in the hectic energy of the vehicle's progress through the planar unrest of the city

12. Study for 'Cape of Good Hope' 1914
13. Newcastle 1913
14. Mytholmroyd c.1914

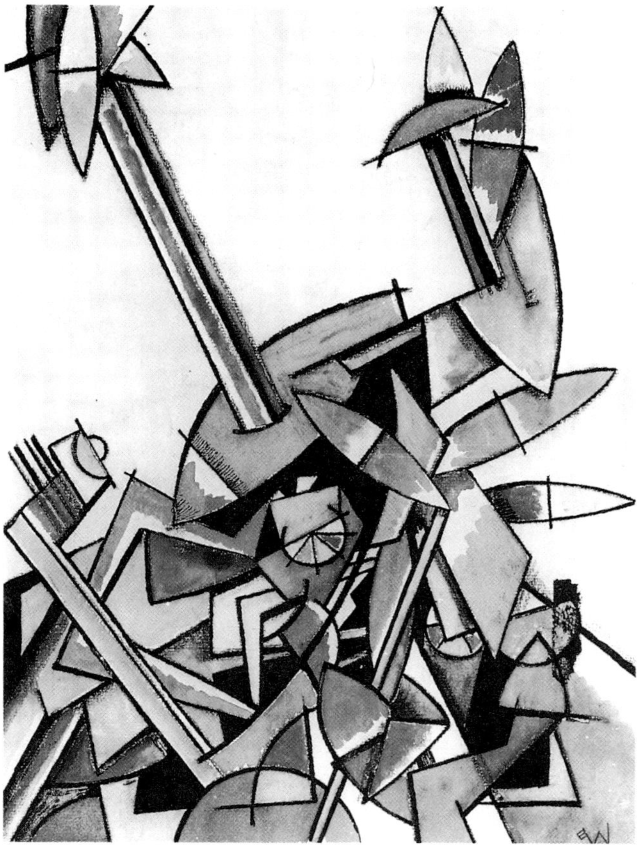

12

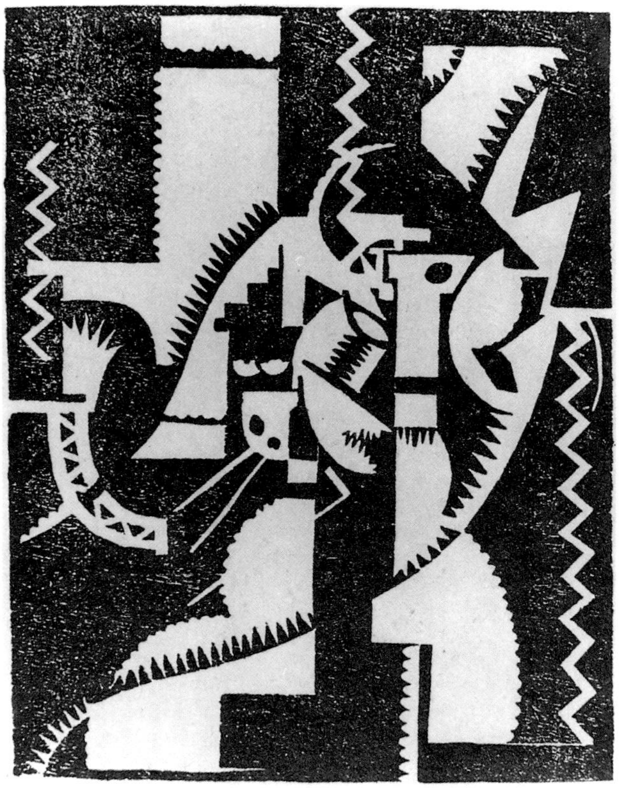

13

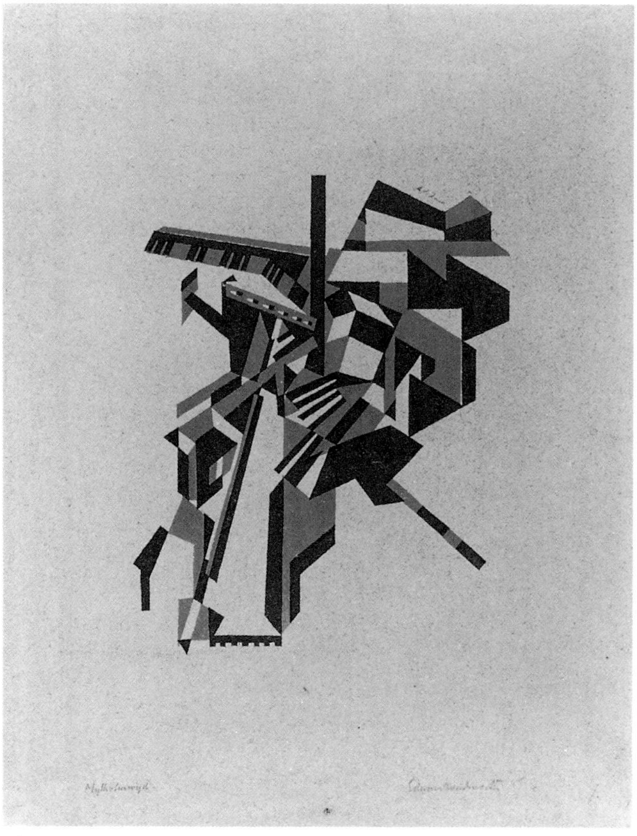

14

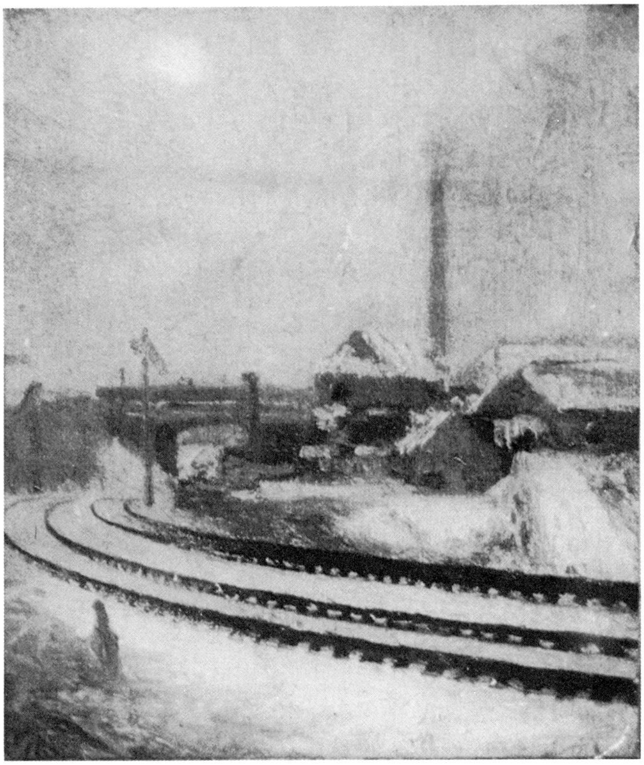

Fig.3 *Harrogate Corporation Brick-Works* 1908 (W/A 1), oil on canvas, 40.6 × 35.5 (whereabouts unknown)

around it, thereby faithfully echoing Severini's own description of how the motor bus in his painting of that name 'pursues its headlong career from Montmartre to Montrouge along the crowded streets of Paris, dashing across the path of other motors, grazing their very wheels and hurling itself in the direction of the houses'.[6]

Futurism's insistence on a wholehearted engagement with twentieth-century urban life helped the twenty-four year-old Wadsworth to identify his true interests at last. Far from passively reflecting the impact of yet another avant-garde group, he now began to connect Futurist ideas with his long-standing knowledge of northern England's industrial prowess. Although he had resisted his father's invitation to join the family worsted spinning business, Wadsworth retained considerable affection for the Yorkshire town of Cleckheaton where he was born. Wadsworth and Sons' mill was situated there and its presence ensured that he grew up in an environment which valued the power and efficiency of mechanisation. After school he was sent to Munich in order to learn German and study engineering draughtsmanship. Wadsworth soon found himself more attracted to the classes at the Knirr Art School, where his fascination with painting, drawing and, significantly, woodcutting began in earnest. Life in Munich also gave him an international perspective rather than a parochial view of art, and this cosmopolitanism spurred his readiness to take continental developments seriously later on. However, the time he spent in Germany making blueprints for engineers and cultivating the virtues of absolute precision paid significant dividends once he started making woodcuts. His innate feeling for even the most uningratiating aspects of the machine-age north fuelled his print-making as well. It is significant that one of his earliest landscapes concentrates, without any equivocation, on the railway tracks and smoking chimney of Harrogate Corporation Brick-Works (see fig.3).[7] Even if snow softens the scene which Wadsworth painted on the spot in December 1908, he clearly cherishes its underlying industrial harshness.

Meeting Wyndham Lewis in the summer of 1913, when both men worked for a while at Fry's newly-established Omega Workshops and became firm allies, must have fortified Wadsworth's interest in Futurist ideas. Unlike Fry, who shunned Marinettian precepts, Lewis at this stage was as fascinated by the Italian movement as Wadsworth.[8] But neither of them ever became an outright Futurist disciple like Nevinson, who had been a contemporary of Wadsworth's at the Slade and may well have introduced him to Severini.[9] In spite of Marinetti's forceful attempts to enlist the English avant-garde in his belligerent ranks, Lewis and Wadsworth retained their independence. The differences separating their work from Futurism were substantial, and in Wadsworth's first surviving woodcut his vision is already removed from the hectic animation of 'L'Omnibus'. Although 'Newcastle' (13) shares Futurism's fascination with machine imagery, there is no trace of the excitable, blurred movement favoured by the Italians. Instead, Wadsworth opts for a calmer and more clearly defined design, where even the zigzags and saw-tooth edges are not allowed to disrupt the essential stability of his vision. The industrial power of Newcastle is certainly celebrated here: in the first issue of the Vorticist magazine *Blast*, where this print was reproduced as a full-page illustration, 'the great PORTS'[10] of Bristol, Glasgow, Hull, Liverpool, London and Newcastle itself were hailed with reverence. However, the coldness and hardness of the machine age are also conveyed in this woodcut, which refuses to brandish any romantic Futurist excitement about its raw material. Industrialisation had come to Italy long after Britain, and when Wadsworth signed the Vorticist manifesto in *Blast* he proclaimed his agreement with Lewis's view that 'machinery, steam-ships, all that distinguishes externally our time, came far more from here than anywhere else.'[11]

The approach adopted by Wadsworth in 'Newcastle' helps to explain why he soon became one of the most loyal members of the Vorticist group. This eruptive alliance, which broadcast its official birth with the publication of the rum-

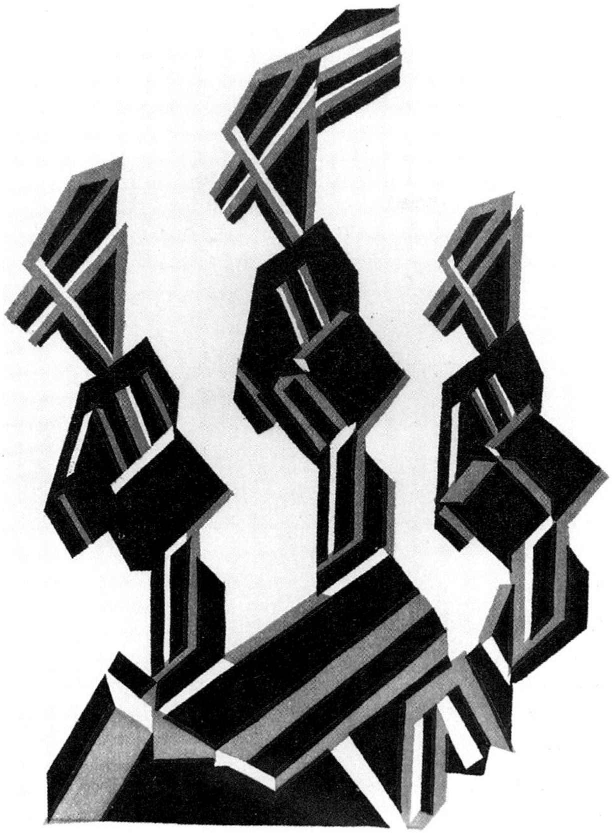

17

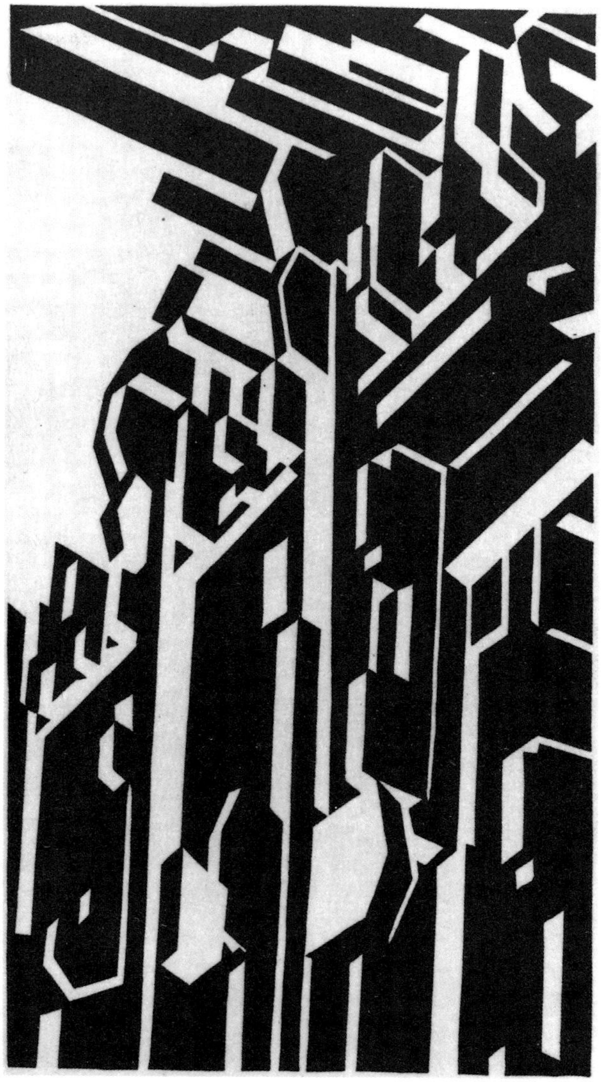

16

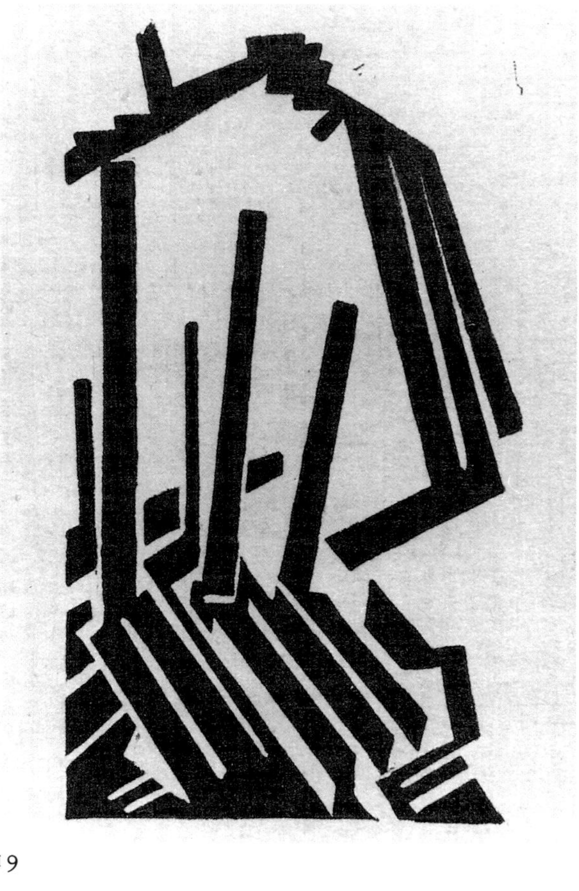

19

17. *Street Singers* 1914 (state a)
19. *Fustian Town – Hebden Bridge* 1914-15
16. *Façade* c. 1914-15

bustious *Blast* in July 1914, conveyed its involvement in the machine age with unwavering starkness and rigorous clarity. The Vorticists wanted to confront the modern industrial world on its own bleak terms and, in this respect, their art had something in common with the rasping attack of German Expressionism. In the spring of 1914 an exhibition of *Modern German Art* was held at the Twenty-One Gallery in London, which staged a simultaneous show of Wadsworth's early woodcuts.[12] Lewis was impressed by the exhibition, declaring that 'the quality of the woodcut is rough and brutal, surgery of the senses, cutting and not scratching: extraordinarily limited and exasperating.' He decided that 'it is one of the greatest tests of fineness' and concluded: 'Where the Germans are best – disciplined, blunt, thick and brutal, with a black simple skeleton of organic emotion – they best qualify for this form of art'.[13]

Wadsworth's presence in the same gallery implied an affinity between his woodcuts and their German counterparts. But these connections can easily be exaggerated. Although Wadsworth shared the Germans' love of vigorous impact, he did not permit any roughness of handling or rampant emotionalism to disturb his partiality for cool precision. He prepared himself with characteristic thoroughness for print-making, according to a letter written in the Vorticist period where he informs Lewis that 'I have done one or two drawings for woodcuts ... I hope to do several while I am here so that I can occupy myself in the winter with cutting them.'[14] 'Harbour of Flushing', probably the next print he made after completing 'Newcastle', is notable for its refusal to admit any evidence of personal 'handwriting'. It remains as clean-cut and severe in organisation as the forms it depicts. In spite of the compressed energy of the ships gathered so tightly in the harbour's mouth, Wadsworth uses the woodcut to cleanse his art of anything which might detract from its razor-sharp exactitude. A few years later he explained why the woodcut 'appeals to me more than any of the other mediums (etchings, lithographs, mezzotints etc)', declaring that 'it leaves nothing at all to accident'.[15]

This emphasis on total control and refinement meant that his prints swiftly became more sophisticated in their technique than 'Newcastle' had been. Incorporating more and more of the intricately constructed properties of machines, the woodcuts draw much of their strength from his familiarity with the factory looms of his childhood. 'Cleckheaton', which marks the moment when Wadsworth formally acknowledged his birthplace's nourishing effect on his imagination, marshals the distant hills into a sequence of gaunt pyramids, and silhouettes most of the blackened chimney-shafts thrusting above the crowded mills below. The unusual agitation of this woodcut, which would soon give way to a more classical stillness, probably reflects Wadsworth's close emotional involvement with a townscape he knew so intimately. However, he eagerly admired other northern centres, for Lewis recalled 'Wadsworth taking me in his car on a tour of some of Yorkshire's cities. In due course we arrived on the hill above Halifax. He stopped the car and we gazed down into its blackened labyrinth. I could see he was proud of it. "It's like Hell, isn't it?" he said enthusiastically.'[16]

The pride Wadsworth took in the area may have prevented him from dealing with this 'Hell' in an openly disturbing manner. Rather than descending into the streets and viewing industrial centres at close quarters, he preferred to appraise them from a distance. He emphasises the interlocking, geometric beauty of 'Mytholmroyd' (14), a small Yorkshire manufacturing town, with the clarity of an artist who strives for an understanding of his subject's totality. No one appears to inhabit the Yorkshire village Wadsworth depicted in a particularly lucid, eponymous two-colour woodcut. Just as he sliced into the woodblock with unerring finesse, so the light carves the houses on the hillside into segments, which assert their own identity as independent units of form. They still retain a representational function but their hard-edged purity also recalls a passage from Kandinsky's *The Art of Spiritual Harmony*, which Wadsworth included in his selection of translations from the book in *Blast No. 1*. Kandinsky discusses 'a square, a circle, a triangle, a rhombus, a trapezium, and the other innumerable forms which become ever more complicated and possess no mathematical significance. All these forms are citizens of the abstract empire with equal rights.'[17]

The further Wadsworth removed himself from a representational account of his subject, the more he asserted the abstract elements in his woodcuts. Although 'Semaphore' still contains suggestions of roofs, chimneys and windows, it claims the right to depart very radically from any dependence on mimesis. The composition deploys forms which evoke pistons and levers, cranking out their mechanistic movements. Real semaphore uses an alphabet of succinct, jerking signals to relay its meanings and Wadsworth must have wanted his woodcut to rely on an equally terse sequence of signs. However, he never wanted to sever his work completely from its connections with the visible world. In 1914 he painted a picture called 'A Short Flight', fusing the components of the machine with glimpses of the ground far below. The image suggests that Wadsworth may have gone on a flight at this period, and as early as 1912 his lost 'bird's-eye-view' of Long Acre already suggested to one critic that it had been painted 'from an aeroplane'.[18] Whatever the truth of the matter, he certainly made use of aerial views to help him arrive at the imagery in his most simplified woodcuts. 'New Delight' looks like a cluster of railway-lines and factory roofs seen from a plane; its title, the name of a pub he would

21

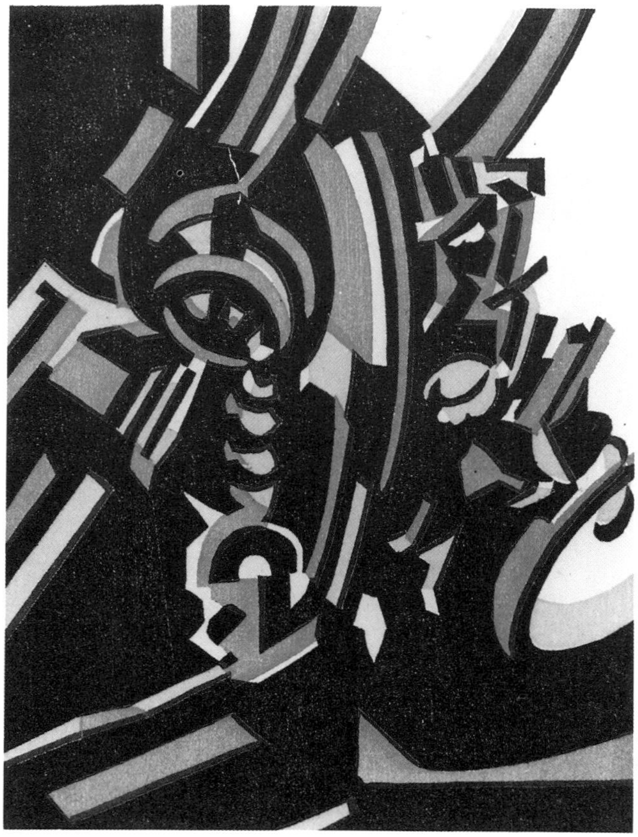

23

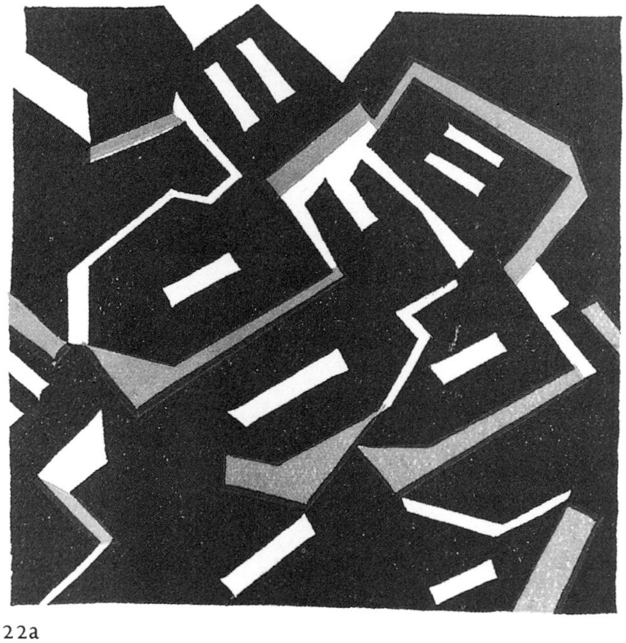

22a

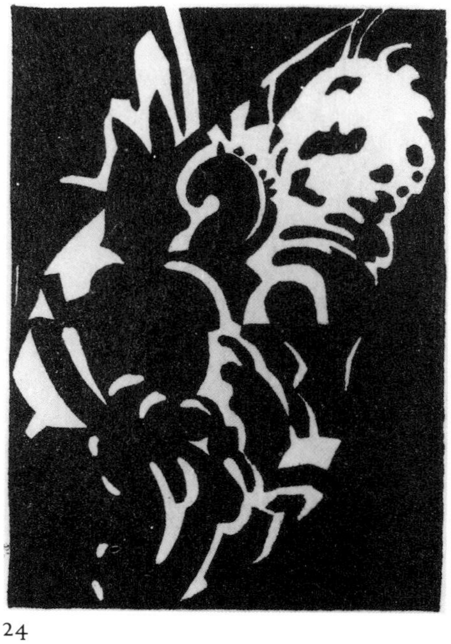

24

21. Illustration (Typhoon) 1914-15
22a. Top of the Town 1916-17
23. Invention/Mudros 1917 (state a)
24. Kt X B 1917

have known near Hebden Bridge, probably refers to the excitement Wadsworth derived from the new way of seeing provided by air travel.

Delight, in fact, is the principal emotion running through Wadsworth's Vorticist work. Although Lewis later declared that 'Wadsworth was the painter most closely associated with my Vorticist activities',[19] the two men were in many respects very different. Ezra Pound, who gave Vorticism its name and became its principal theoretical supporter, was struck by the contrast between them. Pointing out that Lewis's restless and satirical temperament was far removed from Wadsworth's sensibility, Pound wrote in August 1914 that 'the vorticist movement is not less unanimous because its two best known painters, Mr Lewis and Mr Wadsworth, are quite different, both in their works and in their modus vivendi. I can not recall any painting of Mr Wadsworth's where he seems to be angry.' Pound decided that his differentiation between the two men 'arranges itself almost as a series of antitheses. Turbulent energy : repose. Anger : placidity, and so on.'[20] Pound owned some of Wadsworth's woodcuts and he responded to them above all on an abstract level. Singling out the 'Harbour of Flushing', he praised it as 'a very fine organisation of form' and then went on to equate it with music. In his 'Vortex' article in *Blast No. 1*, Pound had listed at the head of a section called 'Ancestry' the celebrated assertion by Pater that 'all arts approach the condition of music'.[21] Wadsworth's woodcuts bore out this dictum in Pound's view, for he claimed that in 'Harbour of Flushing' 'there is a definite, one might say a musical or a music-like pleasure for the eye in noting the arrangement of the very acute triangles combined like "notes in a fugue"'. The analogy made absolute sense to Pound when he attempted to account for the pleasure Wadsworth's woodcuts gave him: 'One is much more at ease in comparing this new work to music. I recall a black and white of Mr Wadsworth's, a thing like a signal arm or some other graceful unexplained bit of machinery, reaching out, and alone, across the picture, like a Mozart theme skipping an octave, or leaving the base for the treble.'

Pound was right to emphasise the musical strain in Wadsworth's art. Married to a violinist, he often worked on the woodcuts with the sound of his wife's rehearsals to sustain him in the neighbouring room. These affinities, however, were not the only reason why Pound found Wadsworth's prints so eloquent. He also admired the woodcuts because they reminded him of Eastern art. Writing about a picture called 'Khaki', he asserted that it 'does not "look like" anything, save perhaps a Chinese or Japanese painting with the representative patches removed. The feeling I get from this picture is very much the feeling I get from certain eastern paintings, and I think the feeling that went into it is probably very much the same as that which moved certain

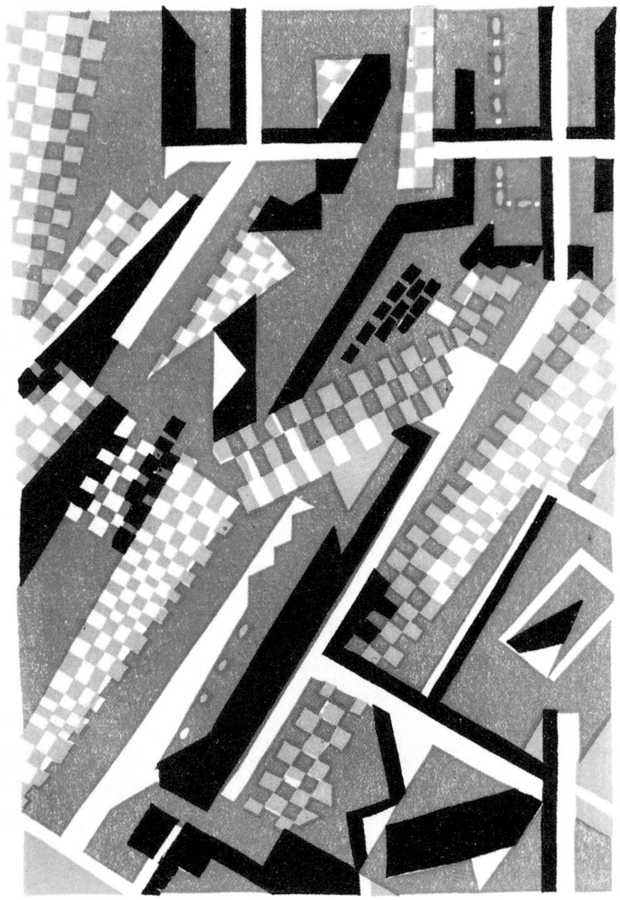

Fig.4 *The Open Window* c.1915, woodcut, 18.4 × 13.3, The Trustees of the Tate Gallery

Chinese painters.'[22] With his enthusiasm for Chinese poetry and the *haiku* tradition, Pound would have been more ready to identify this influence than the Vorticist artists themselves. But Wadsworth did admit, in 1914, that one of his pictures 'is more like a Chinese painting or Japanese print, I think'.[23] A clear debt to the taut economy and dynamism of Japanese print-making can likewise be found in Lewis's work, and the Vorticist artist Frederick Etchells later praised the 'Korinesque treatment'[24] of a Wadsworth woodcut called 'Dock Scene' (36).

Throughout his Vorticist period, which lasted until the end of the First World War, Wadsworth continued to exploit the flat, impersonal quality of the woodcut as well as pushing its capacity for precision to an extreme limit. He persistently used the medium to stress the machine-like character of his art, and in several prints explored the metamorphosis which images undergo when they are printed in different colour combinations. As many as six versions of 'The Open Window' (fig.4) exist and they bear witness to Wadsworth's

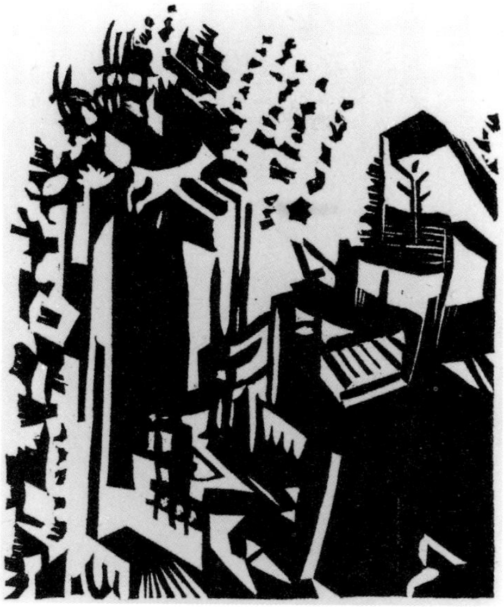

27

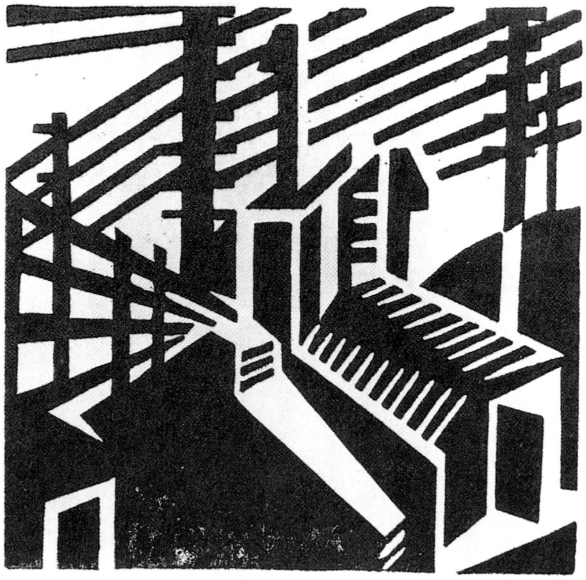

30

26

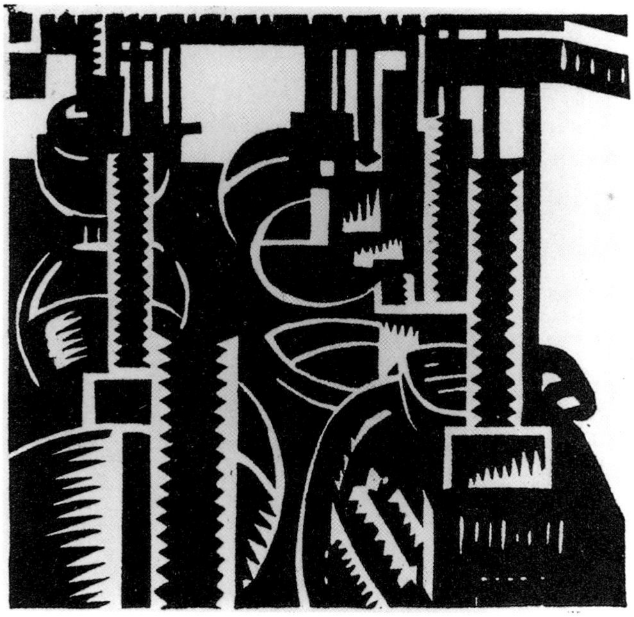

31

28

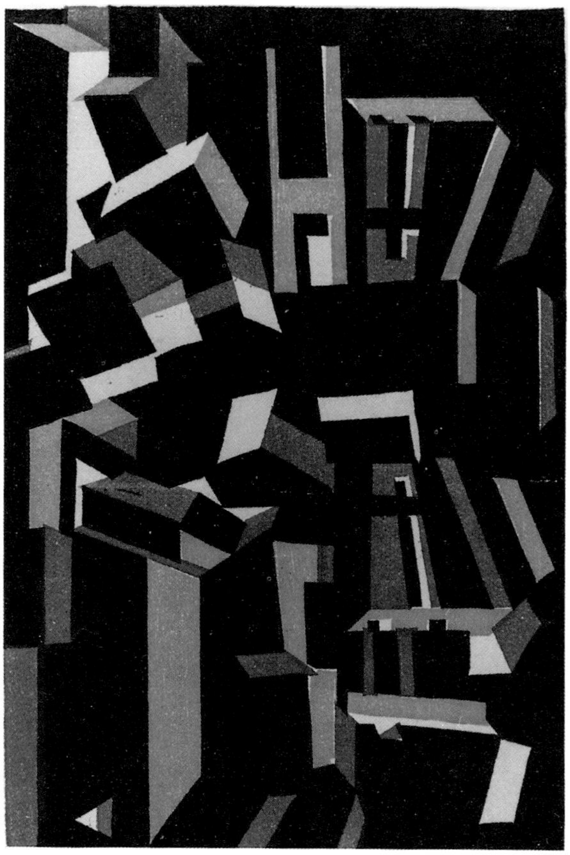

27. *Scene for a Fairy Tale* 1916
26. *Greek Village with Windmills* 1916
28. *Interior/Mudros* 1917
30. *Railway Embankment/Platelayers' Sheds* 1918
31. *Tugs* 1918

involvement with the transformations which changes of colour can engender. Ranging from the austere restraint of grey and black to the fierce exuberance of scarlet and green, the abundant and resourceful variations on 'The Open Window' theme suggest that Wadsworth's fascination with woodcuts reached its height no more than a year after he began experimenting with them.[25] He expressed his enthusiasm for two-colour prints in a 1915 letter to Lewis, declaring that 'they are much more effective than using a single block – more than twice as effective in fact'.[26]

Most of his Vorticist prints are modest in size but Wadsworth soon felt ready to attempt larger woodcuts. Restricting himself to black and white for the purpose, possibly because he felt unsure about deploying colour on this scale, Wadsworth executed two of his most commanding prints. One of them, 'Illustration (Typhoon)' (21), looks at first glance like an uncompromisingly abstract image. But Wadsworth inscribed the British Museum's copy of this woodcut with a quotation from Joseph Conrad's *Typhoon*: '... the iron walls of the engine room. Painted white, they rose high into the dusk of the skylight, sloping like a roof: and the whole resembled the interior of a monument, divided by floors of iron grating, with lights flickering in the middle, within the columnar stir of machinery.'[27] It is one of Wadsworth's most rigid and awesome woodcuts, enclosing the viewer in the very heart of the machine world which the Vorticists placed at the centre of their art. By calling the print 'Illustration', Wadsworth also appears to be insisting that even the most apparently abstract of his works takes as its starting-point a specific, observable aspect of modern life.

If 'Illustration (Typhoon)' shows Wadsworth at his most severe, the other large woodcut, 'Rotterdam', displays the most energetic side of his art. It is a vigorous image, exulting in the wind-buffeted animation of ships moored in harbour. Wadsworth simplifies their hulls and striped funnels so radically that they are difficult to distinguish from the other forms in the design, and he gives the monochromatic elements a hard-hitting optical dazzle as well. For all its reductive concentration on essentials, this woodcut arose directly from Wadsworth's visit to Rotterdam in July 1914. It is the most lively of the prints of industrial ports he made during his Vorticist period and provides the most satisfactory visual parallel to the verbal celebration published in the opening manifesto of *Blast No. 1*, where the Vorticists praise 'scooped out basins, heavy insect dredgers, monotonous cranes, stations, lighthouses blazing through the frosty starlight, cutting the storm like a cake, beaks of infant boats, side by side, heavy chaos of wharves, steep wall of factories'.[28] Of all his 1914 woodcuts, 'Rotterdam' is the one which best helps to explain why Wadsworth became so readily involved in the dazzle-camouflage of ships four years later. It also elicited particular admiration from his Vorticist ally Henri Gaudier-Brzeska, who wrote to Wadsworth from the trenches of the Western Front thanking him for sending a group of 'tender' woodcuts. 'I have some preference for "Rotterdam"', he told Wadsworth, before admitting that 'I do not know why, as the same qualities persist through them all, at the same degree. When you send me some more, as I am greedy to see much vorticism just now, print them on the thin. The reason is this, I have room for them in my knapsack and the less weighty the individuals are, the more I shall be able to stuff in.'[29]

In view of Wadsworth's partiality for maritime themes, it was appropriate that he served during the war in the Eastern Mediterranean as an Intelligence Officer for the Royal Naval Volunteer Reserve. But the island of Mudros, where he was stationed, provided surroundings far removed from the urban harshness of northern England. A work of 1916, 'View of a Town', proves that his Mudros woodcuts remained, at first, close to the character of his previous work. A year later, however, 'Invention/Mudros' (23) displays a new interest in curvilinear arabesque which suggests that the rhythms of the sea around the island had begun to affect his art. The former angularity disappears for a while, swept away by a preoccupation with maritime flow which culminates in 'Disruption' (25)[30]. Mechanistic imagery has here been replaced by the surge and swell of the water, and the influence of Kandinsky's most dream-like abstractions dominates the orchestration of the design. Wadsworth never pursued the enticing possibilities of this remarkable woodcut in his other 1917 woodcuts. But the six different colour versions of 'Riponelli: A Village in Lemnos' (29) show how he revelled in the transformations achievable by moving from a subdued grey and black combination to mauve, pale blue and, finally, an almost incandescent red-purple variation. Etchells was right to praise 'the Ægean group' of prints for Wadsworth's 'richness and fluidity in the use of his medium'.[31] Colour p.49

Opportunities for making art on active service were inevitably limited, but he was fortunate enough to find an occupation close to his own concerns after returning from Mudros. Wadsworth became employed to supervise the dazzle-camouflage of over two thousand ships, largely at Bristol and Liverpool. He probably owed this congenial task to Lieutenant-Commander Norman Wilkinson, an academic marine painter with no interest in experimental art. Wilkinson masterminded the spectacular development of dazzle-painting on ships after coming to the conclusion that invisibility offered no escape from submarine attack. The crucial question was whether the vessel's course could be accurately determined by the enemy and he saw dazzle-painting as the most reliable way of frustrating a submarine's aim. In a paper delivered to the Newcastle Victory Meeting

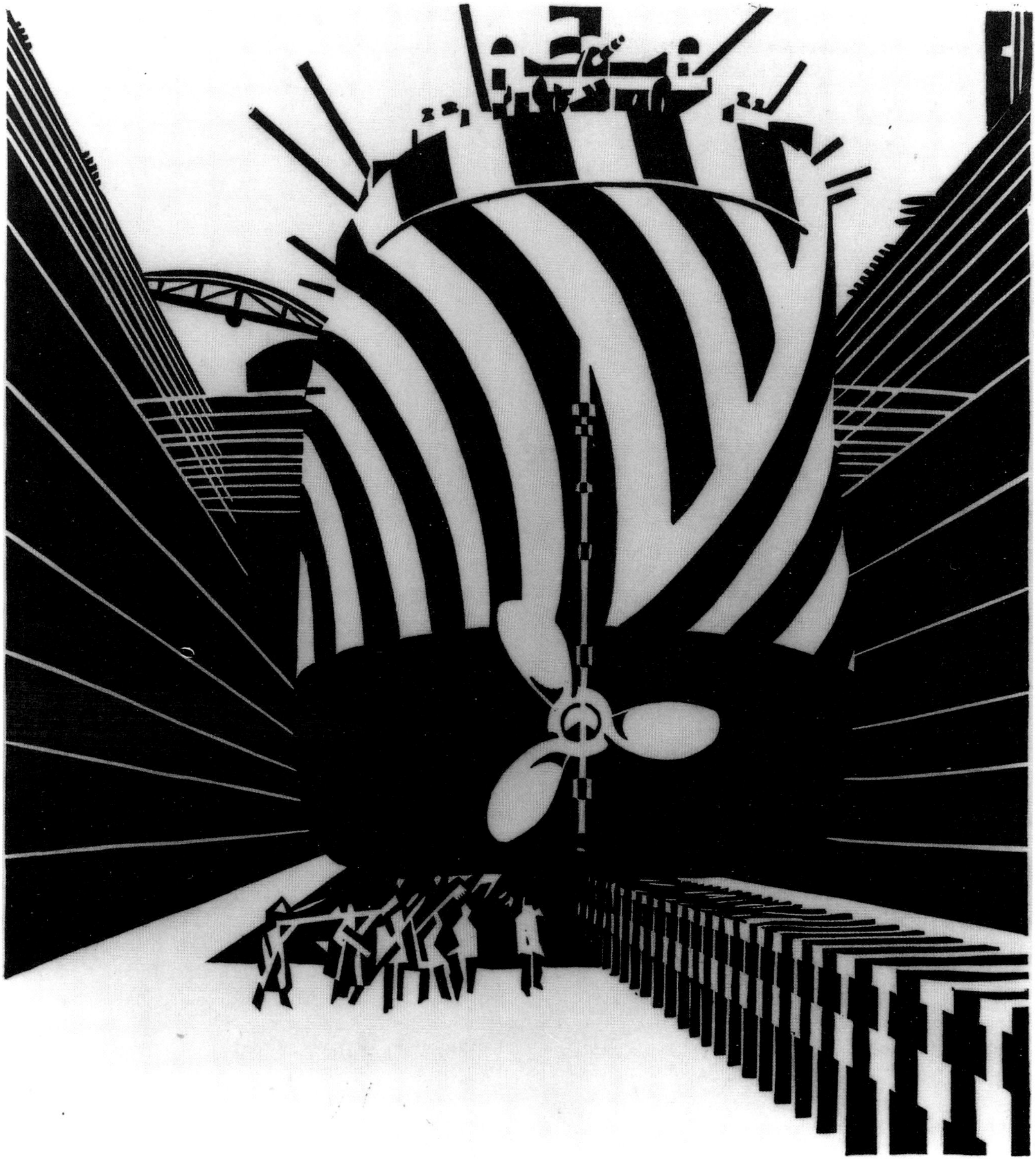

32. Drydocked for Scaling and Painting 1918

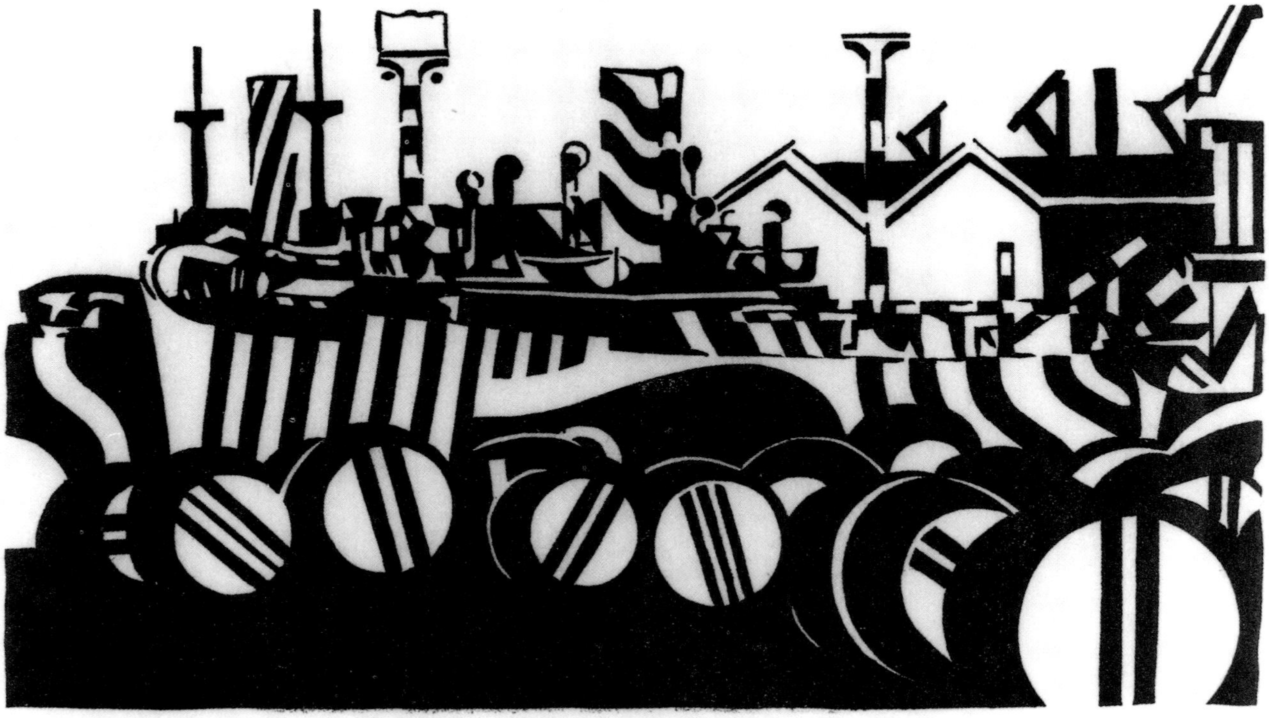

33

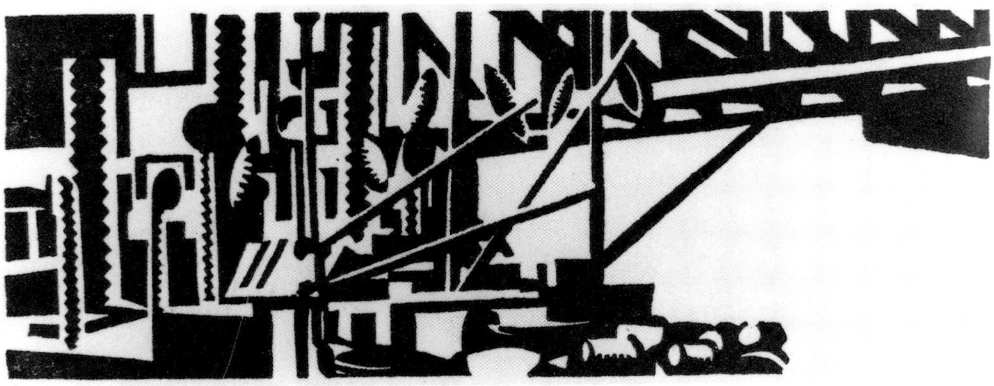

35

33. *S.S. Jerseymoor* 1918
35. *Minesweepers in Port* 1918 (state a)
34. *Dazzled Ship in Drydock* 1918
36. *Dock Scene* 1917

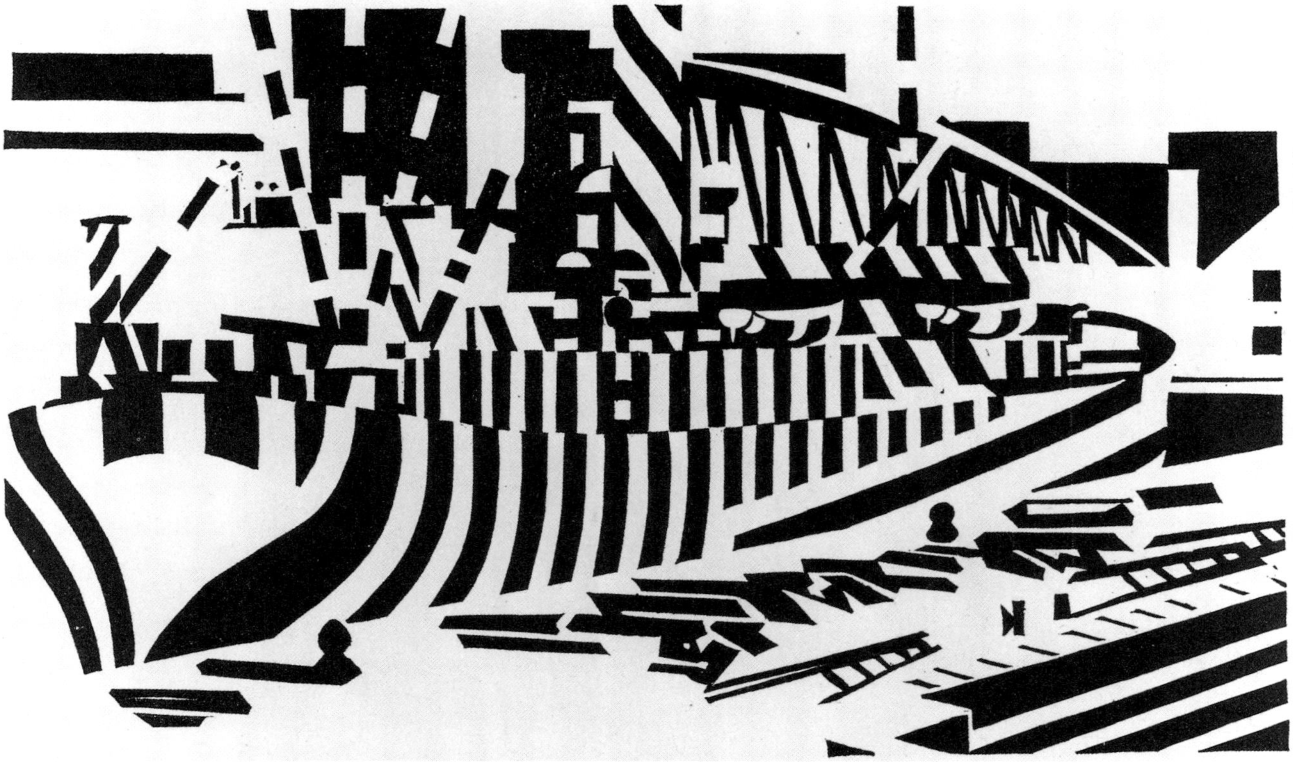

34

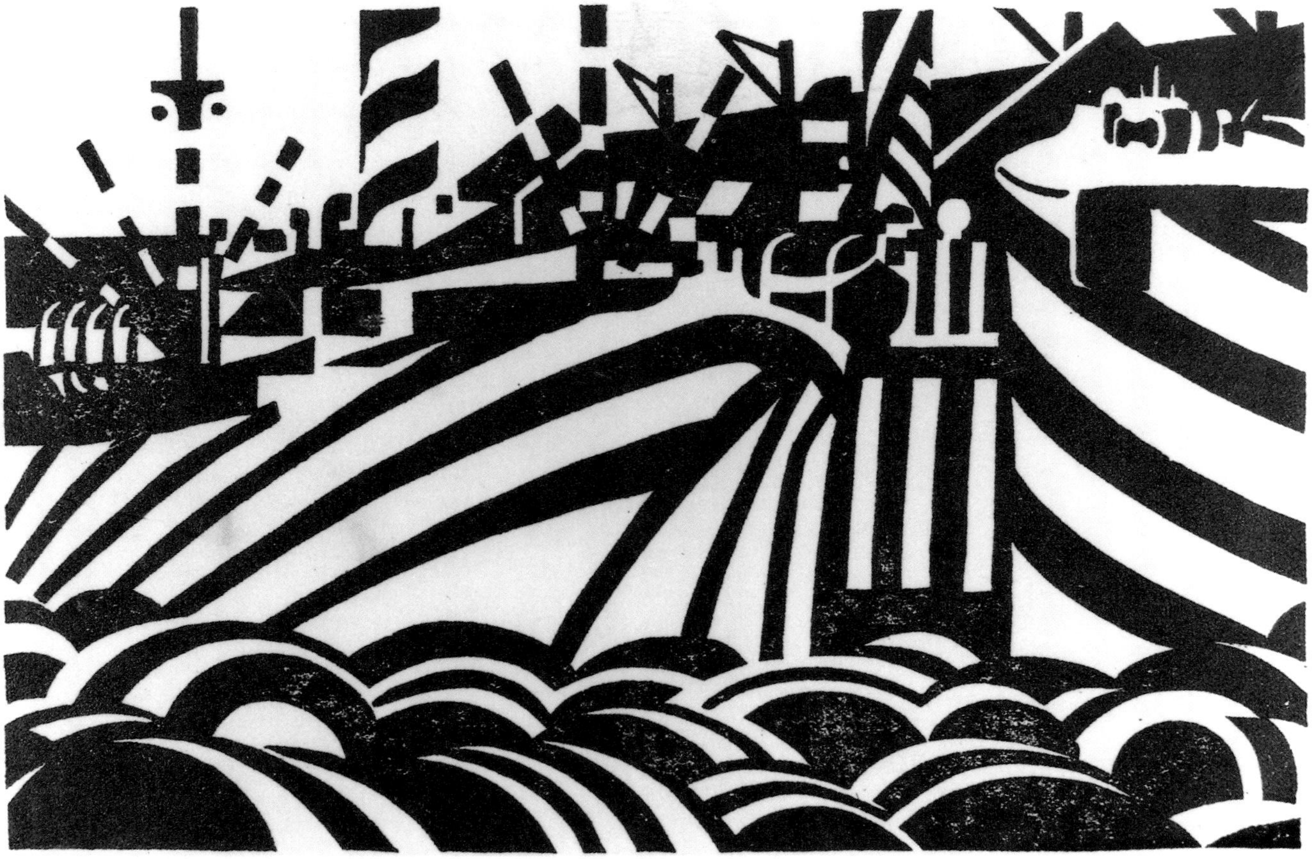

36

in 1919, he defined dazzle as 'a method to produce an effect (by paint) in such a way that all accepted forms of a ship are broken up by masses of strongly contrasted colour'.[32]

After tests in a studio, the approved designs were sent to the major British ports where ten Lieutenants, Wadsworth among them, supervised the painting of the ships themselves. Surviving photographs testify to the extraordinary boldness of the applied patterns. The explosive diagonal and zig-zag bands had a wild, ragtime impact. Hulls and funnels alike were transformed into crazily festooned apparitions, intended to disorientate any U-boat Commander scrutinising them through his periscope. Far from turning the vessels into instant targets, these delirious exercises in optical deception were deemed effective. Wilkinson reported that dazzle saved many ships from destruction. Although a number of camouflaged vessels were hit by torpedoes, 'a far larger percentage of these made port than ships painted light grey, owing to the submarine making an erratic shot, and so injuring the vessel in a less vital spot'.[33]

As might be expected, the sight of the *Aquitania* or the great white star liner *Olympia* covered in dizzying, hard-edged stripes proved irresistible for artists. The sight of the mighty vessels receiving their patterns in drydock provided Wadsworth with ready-made subjects for his own art. During 1918 he found time to produce an outstanding series of woodcuts, each one of which revelled in the optical bite of the bands surging their way across the ship's surface. When he held an exhibition of these stark, energetic prints in 1919, Etchells claimed in the catalogue that dazzle-camouflage 'would probably never have developed as it did had it not been for the experiments in abstract design made by a few modern artists during the years immediately prior to 1914'.[34] This assertion is hard to justify in view of Wilkinson's role as the originator of dazzle. But he might, conceivably, have been influenced on a subliminal level by the work of the avant-garde, and his decision to involve Wadsworth surely implies an awareness on Wilkinson's part of Vorticist work. Over in Paris, Picasso had already been amazed by the sight of some large cannon rumbling down the boulevard Raspail. His companion Gertrude Stein recalled that he stopped to stare at their painted camouflage patterns and 'was spellbound. C'est nous qui avons fait ça, he said, it is we that have created that.'[35]

At all events, the connections between camouflage and the avant-garde were evident enough to persuade the *Illustrated London News* in 1919 that a vessel called *Pathan*, 'in her "dazzle" paint of stripes, angles, and quadrilaterals', was 'suggestive of futurism or cubism'.[36] By that time, Wadsworth had decided to make one of his woodcuts, 'Liverpool Shipping', the basis of an immense canvas he produced for the Canadian War Memorial Fund. The outcome, 'Dazzle-Ships in Drydock at Liverpool' (fig.5), is one of his finest surviving paintings. It celebrates the vitality of the asymmetrical patterns as they turn the vessel's bulk into a battle-ground of crisply orchestrated diagonals and verticals. This painting is the apotheosis of Wadsworth's consistent passion for stripes, which had emerged as a major preoccupation eight years before in the 'Portrait of Mrs Violet Wallis'. Her boldly patterned shawl announces a fascination which runs through his Vorticist pictures, most notably in a major gouache called 'Enclosure', where the boisterous orchestration of stripes can be read as aerial views of cultivated fields or the colliding directional forces of hostile armies.[37] Vorticism rejoiced in abstraction's ability to suggest a multiplicity of references to the modern world. Wadsworth's lost 1915 painting 'Blackpool' deployed a sequence of coloured stripes which prompted Lewis to offer a complex interpretation. According to Lewis, its 'striped ascending blocks' derived from 'the elements of a seaside scene, condensed into the simplest form possible for the retaining of its vivacity'.[38] Although a blurred newspaper reproduction of this important painting makes it look like one of Wadsworth's most non-representational images,[39] Lewis claimed that 'the striped awnings of Cafés and shops, the stripes of bathing tents, the stripes of bathing-machines, of toy trumpets, of dresses, are marshalled into a dense essence of the scene'.[40]

In spite of their continuing infatuation with stripes, the dazzle-camouflage woodcuts are in other respects more traditional than Wadsworth's previous experiments with print-making. 'Liverpool Shipping' was 'legible' enough, on a representational level, to lend itself easily to adaptation as a poster for the Imperial War Museum in 1936. Like so many other innovative artists of his generation, Wadsworth revised his attitude towards mechanistic abstraction after the Armistice. When he made a momentary return to the northern industrial scenes which had inspired so many of his Vorticist pictures, his vision of the Black Country was significantly bleaker and more disturbing than before.[41] 'Blast Furnaces (2) (Netherton Furnaces)' (69), printed in black on orange paper, sees its subject as a vehement fusion of flames and smoke, an inferno more savage by far than the woodcut 'Newcastle' he had made six years earlier. The machine age finally lost its innocence in the Great War and, after 1918, Wadsworth shared the widespread desire to seek out an alternative to the mechanised inventions which had caused such appalling devastation on the battlefields of Europe. His little 1920 woodcut 'Northern Roofscape' bids pictorial farewell to a region he would never again study with such zeal. It also marks the moment when he lost interest in a medium which had fostered so many of his outstanding images during Vorticism's brief yet potent existence.

The woodcuts Wadsworth executed over this period stand

Fig.5 *Dazzle-Ships in Drydock at Liverpool* 1919 (W/A 40), oil on canvas, 302.5 × 243.5, National Gallery of Canada, Ottawa

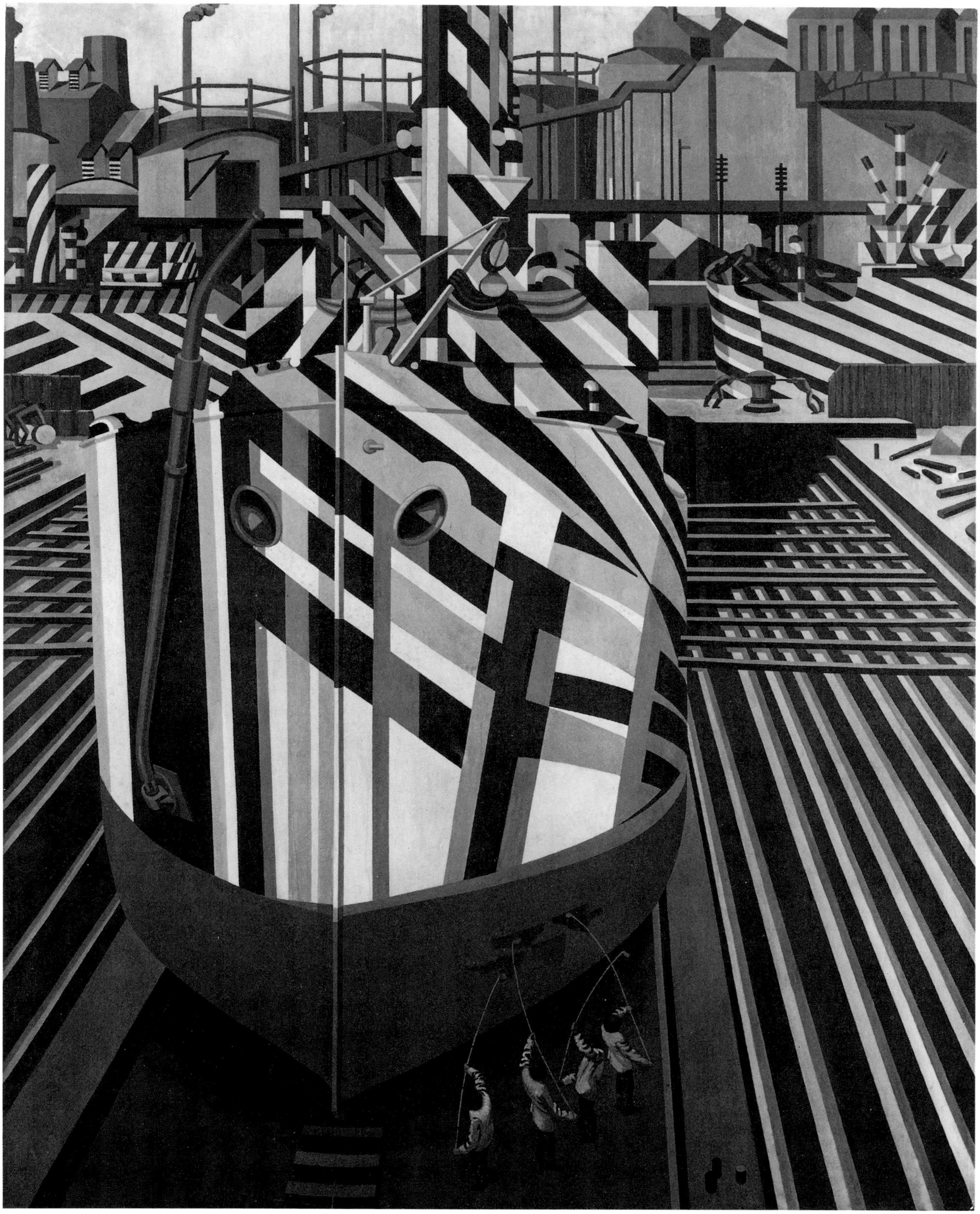

today among the most consistently poised and resourceful works achieved by any of Vorticism's adherents. Since none of the oil paintings he produced between 1913 and 1918 has so far come to light, the woodcuts offer an especially valuable insight into the development of his imagination at a time when he was defining his identity as an artist. At once audacious and serene, these prints establish him as a disciplined, enquiring and quietly confident member of the Vorticist movement. Their peculiar immediacy and resolution give these woodcuts a unique place in Wadsworth's œuvre, as he admitted when responding to a letter from the great New York collector John Quinn, who had purchased a number of his pictures. 'You seem to like the woodcuts best', Wadsworth wrote. 'To a certain extent I agree with you: I think they are probably the best in that they are the most complete – that is to say, the means of expression is in a more complete accordance with the thing expressed *in them* than some of the other things which are perhaps more experimental and less mature.'[42] Intimate in size and yet surprisingly monumental in implication, their appeal prompted Etchells to point out that 'the woodcut is a thing to handle and look at closely. It does not demand wall space and yet can have the seriousness and dignity of a large painting in an accessible form.'[43] Wadsworth's woodcuts present his Vorticist work at its most compressed, and their sustained inventiveness ensures that they occupy a distinguished place in the history of British print-making.

Notes

Woodcuts not reproduced in this publication may be found in Mark Glazebrook, *Edward Wadsworth 1889-1949. Paintings, Drawings and Prints*, exh. cat., P and D Colnaghi and Co Ltd, London 1974. Several of Wadsworth's paintings referred to in the present essay are reproduced in Richard Cork, *Vorticism and Abstract Art in the First Machine Age*, I and II, London 1975 and 1976.

1. In a review of an exhibition at the Bradford Arts Club, published in the *Yorkshire Post* on 10 October 1910, 'the influence of Whistler' was detected in a Wadsworth self-portrait and his portrait of 'Cuthbert Kelly' 1910 was compared with Whistler's 'Carlyle' 1872-3.
2. Marquet's 'Sainte-Adresse', painted in 1906, is surprisingly close to Wadsworth's 'Plage au Havre', in both style and subject-matter.
3. *Times*, 8 January 1913.
4. 'L'Omnibus' was listed as no.66 in the catalogue of Frank Rutter's *Post-Impressionist and Futurist Exhibition*, held at the Doré Galleries, London, October 1913.
5. 'Get Inside the Picture: Futurism as the Artist Sees It by Gino Severini', interview with Severini, *Daily Express*, 11 April 1913.
6. Gino Severini, catalogue of *The Futurist Painter Exhibits His Latest Works*, Marlborough Gallery, London, April 1913. 'The Motor Bus' was listed as no.1 in the catalogue.
7. According to an inscription on the only surviving photograph of this lost painting, 'Harrogate Corporation Brick-Works' was painted at Harrogate in December 1908. It was exhibited in London at the New English Art Club in 1911.
8. Both Lewis and Wadsworth were members of the organising committee for a dinner in Marinetti's honour at the Florence Restaurant, London, on 18 November 1913.
9. Nevinson befriended Severini in Paris after leaving the Slade in 1912.
10. Wyndham Lewis (ed.), *Blast No.1*, London 1914, p.23.
11. Wyndham Lewis, ibid, p.39.
12. The German exhibition included works by Kandinsky, Marc, Pechstein, Bolz and others.
13. Wyndham Lewis, 'Note (on some German Woodcuts at the Twenty-One Gallery)', *Blast No.1*, op cit, p.136.
14. Edward Wadsworth to Wyndham Lewis, 23 July 1915, quoted in Barbara Wadsworth, *Edward Wadsworth: A Painter's Life*, Wilton 1989, p.68.
15. Edward Wadsworth to John Quinn, n.d. [1917], ibid, p.73.
16. Wyndham Lewis, 'Edward Wadsworth: 1889-1949', *Listener*, 30 June 1949.
17. Edward Wadsworth, 'Inner Necessity', *Blast No.1*, op cit, p.122.
18. 'Long Acre' was exhibited at the Friday Club show in February 1912 when Frank Rutter made this observation in the *Sunday Times*.
19. Wyndham Lewis, 'The Vorticists', *Vogue*, September 1956.
20. Ezra Pound, 'Edward Wadsworth, Vorticist', *Egoist*, 15 August 1914.
21. Ezra Pound, 'Vortex, Pound', *Blast No.1*, op cit, p.154.
22. Ezra Pound, 'Edward Wadsworth, Vorticist', op cit.
23. Edward Wadsworth to Frank Rutter, 9 April 1914, unpublished letter owned by Anthony d'Offay, London.
24. Frederick Etchells, 'A Note' in the catalogue of the *Exhibition of Original Woodcuts and Drawings by Edward Wadsworth* held in March 1919 at the Adelphi Gallery, London.
25. 'The Open Window' is not dated on any of its surviving impressions but on stylistic grounds it seems to have been executed in 1914.
26. Edward Wadsworth to Wyndham Lewis, 23 July 1915, quoted in Barbara Wadsworth, op cit, p.68.
27. The quotation, also published in the catalogue of Wadsworth's 1919 exhibition (see footnote 24), misses out a small portion of Conrad's original passage.
28. *Blast No.1*, op cit, p.23. The passage was printed as vertical column in the magazine.
29. Henri Gaudier-Brzeska to Edward Wadsworth, 18 November 1914, quoted in Ezra Pound, *Gaudier-Brzeska. A Memoir*, London 1916, p.81.
30. 'Disruption' used to be known as 'Scene for a Fairy Tale' but Barbara Wadsworth, the artist's daughter, has now found a copy of the print inscribed by Wadsworth with the correct title.
31. Frederick Etchells, 'A Note', op cit.
32. Norman Wilkinson, 'The Dazzle Painting of Ships', paper delivered to the Victory Meeting at Newcastle-upon-Tyne, 10 July 1919, published in abridged form in the catalogue of the *Camouflage* exhibition, Edinburgh 1988.
33. Ibid.
34. Frederick Etchells, 'A Note', op cit.
35. Gertrude Stein, *The Autobiography of Alice B. Toklas*, in Carl Van Vechten (ed.), *Selected Writings of Gertrude Stein*, New York 1972, pp.84-5.
36. 'Sea Camouflage Against U-Boats: The Art of "Dazzle-Painting"', *Illustrated London News*, 4 January 1919.
37. 'Enclosure' was listed as no.46 in the *Vorticist Exhibition* held at the Doré Galleries, London, in June 1915. For a detailed discussion of this important work, see Richard Cork, op cit, II, pp.374-6.
38. Wyndham Lewis, 'The London Group. 1915 (March)', *Blast No.2*, London 1915, p.77.
39. 'Blackpool' was reproduced in the *Daily Mirror*, 11 June 1915, along with another lost Wadsworth painting called 'Combat'.
40. Wyndham Lewis, *Blast No.2*, op cit, p.77.
41. *The Black Country* was the title of Wadsworth's one-man show at the Leicester Galleries, London, in January 1920.
42. Edward Wadsworth to John Quinn, n.d. [1917], quoted in Barbara Wadsworth, op cit, p.73.
43. Frederick Etchells, 'A Note', op cit.

38. *Townscape* 1920
40. *Northern Roofscape/A Black Country Village* 1920
41. *Portrait of Rupert Doone* 1920

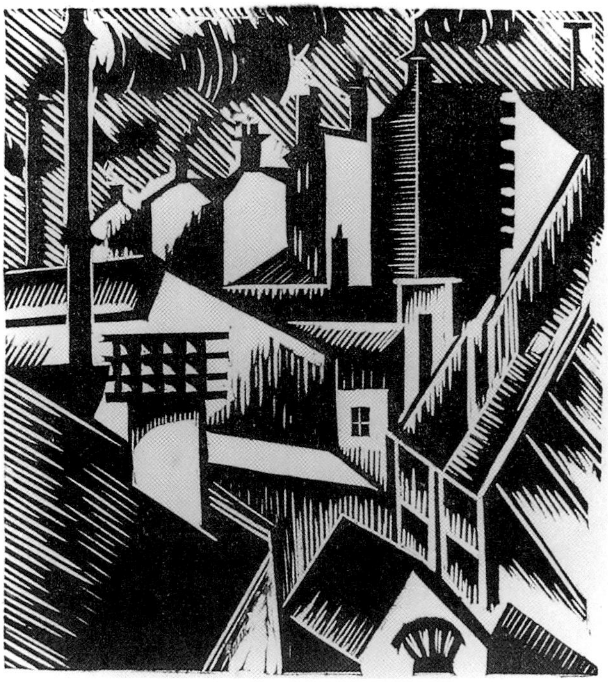

38

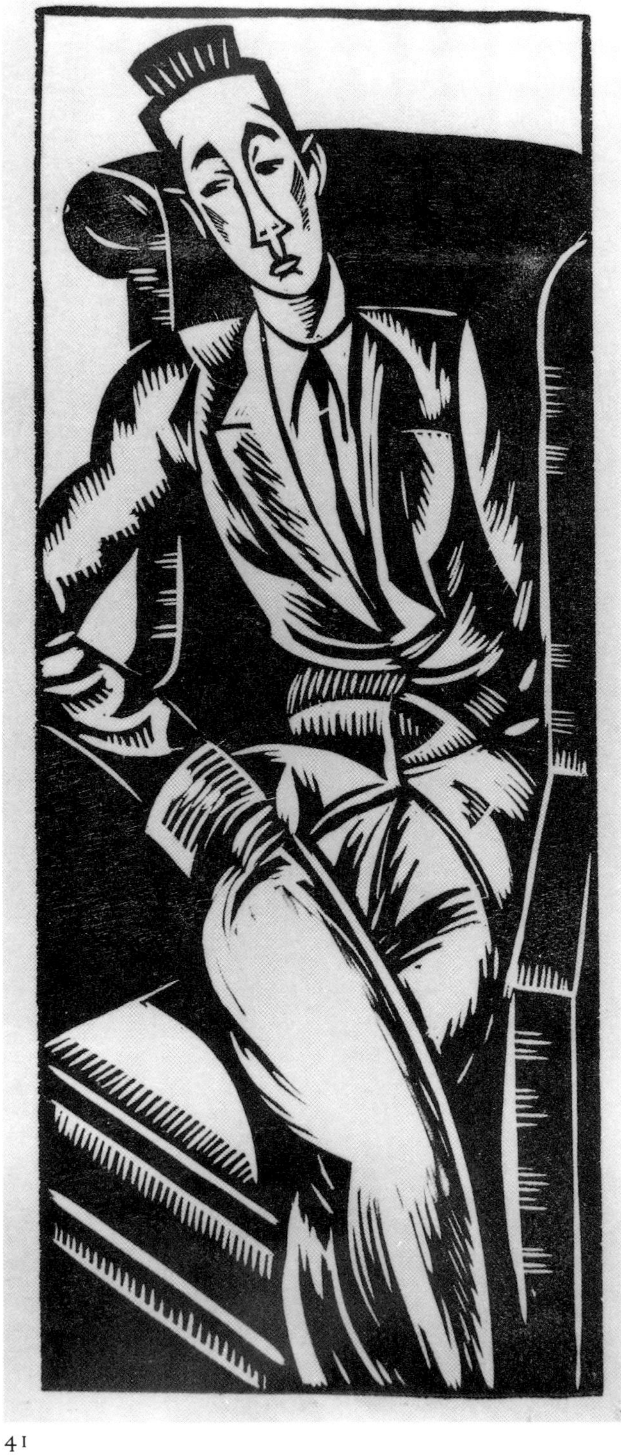

41

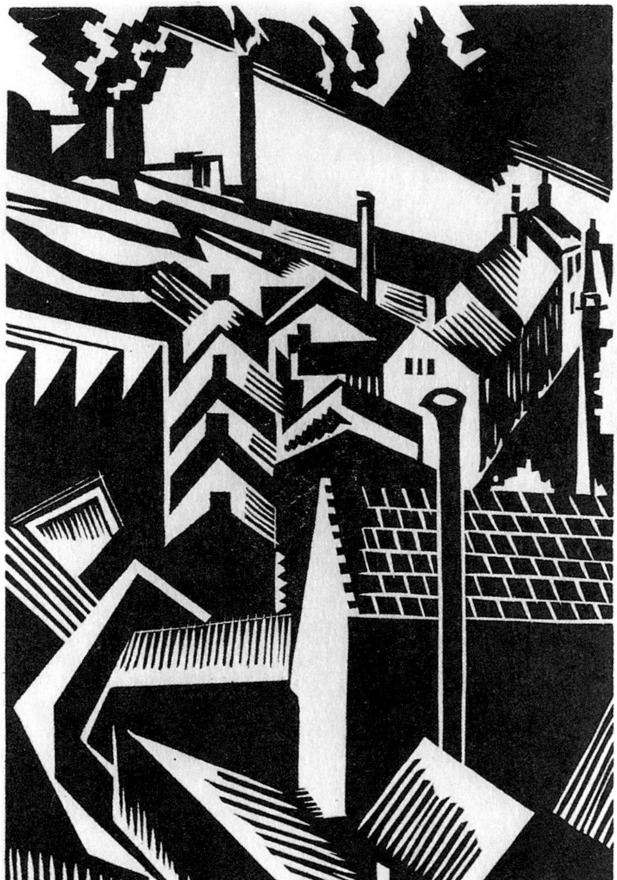

40

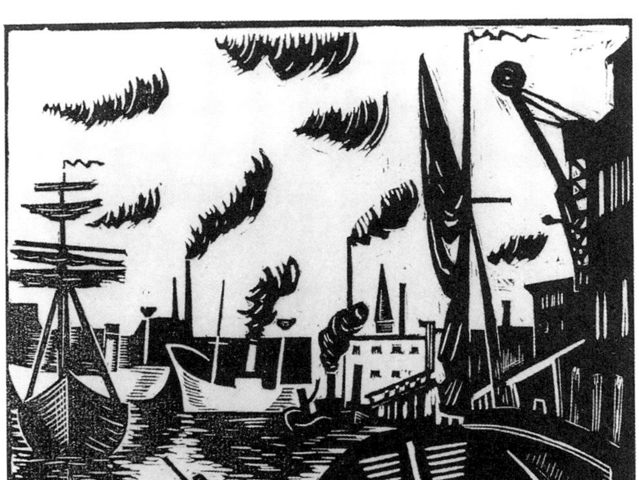

43

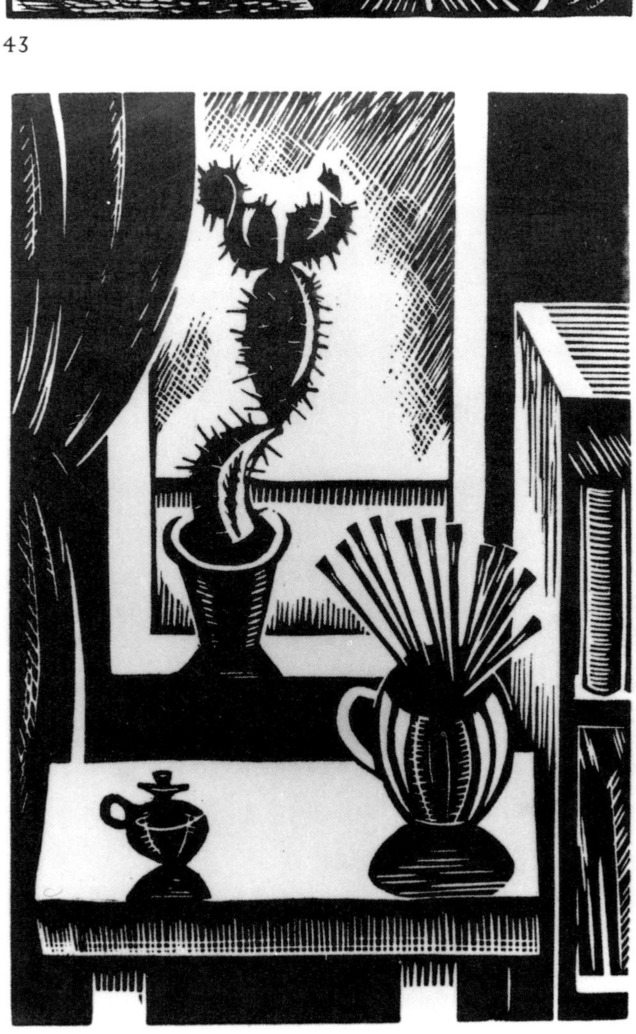

44

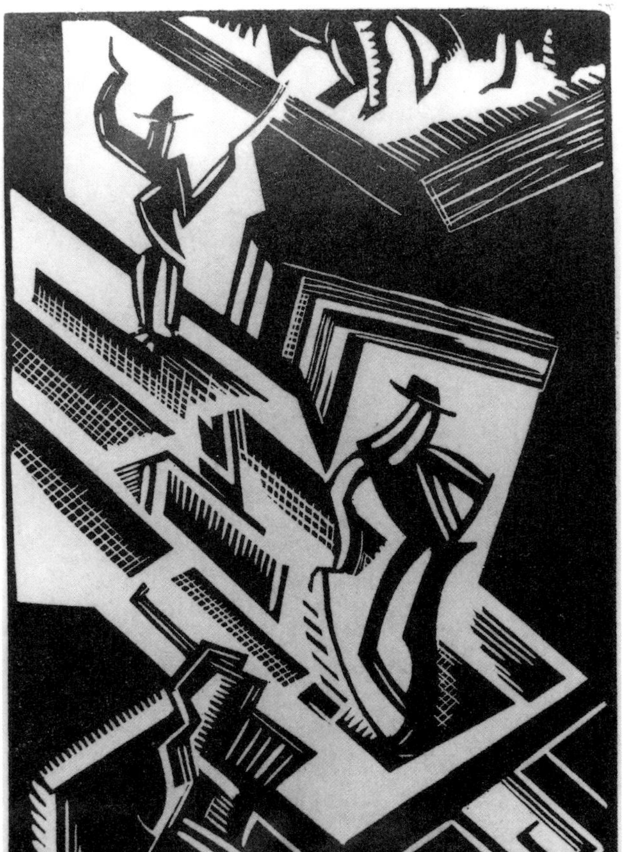

45

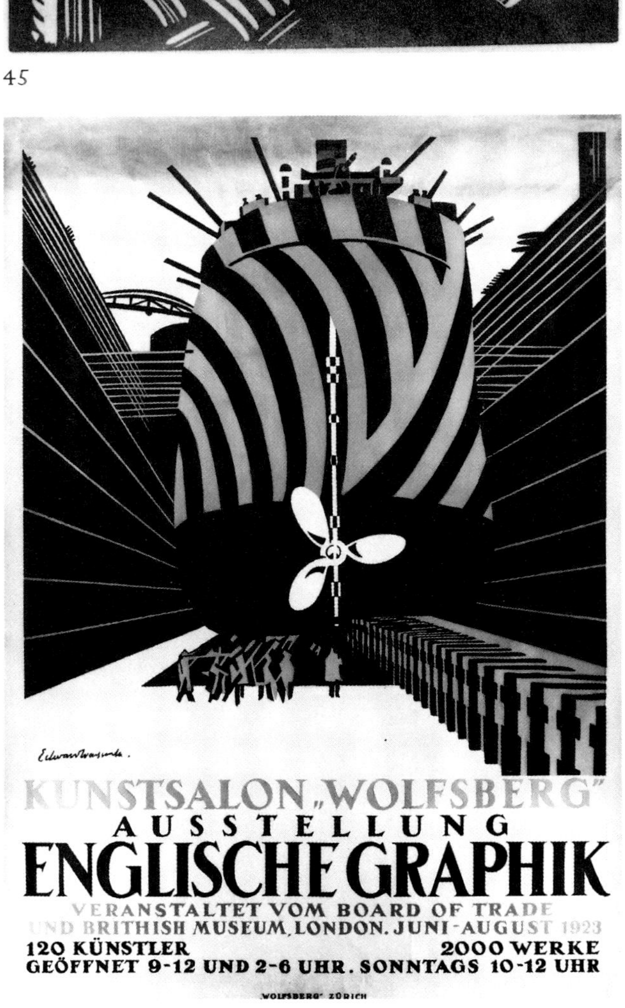
KUNSTSALON „WOLFSBERG"
AUSSTELLUNG
ENGLISCHE GRAPHIK
VERANSTALTET VOM BOARD OF TRADE
UND BRITHISH MUSEUM, LONDON. JUNI-AUGUST 1923
120 KÜNSTLER
2000 WERKE
GEÖFFNET 9-12 UND 2-6 UHR. SONNTAGS 10-12 UHR

52

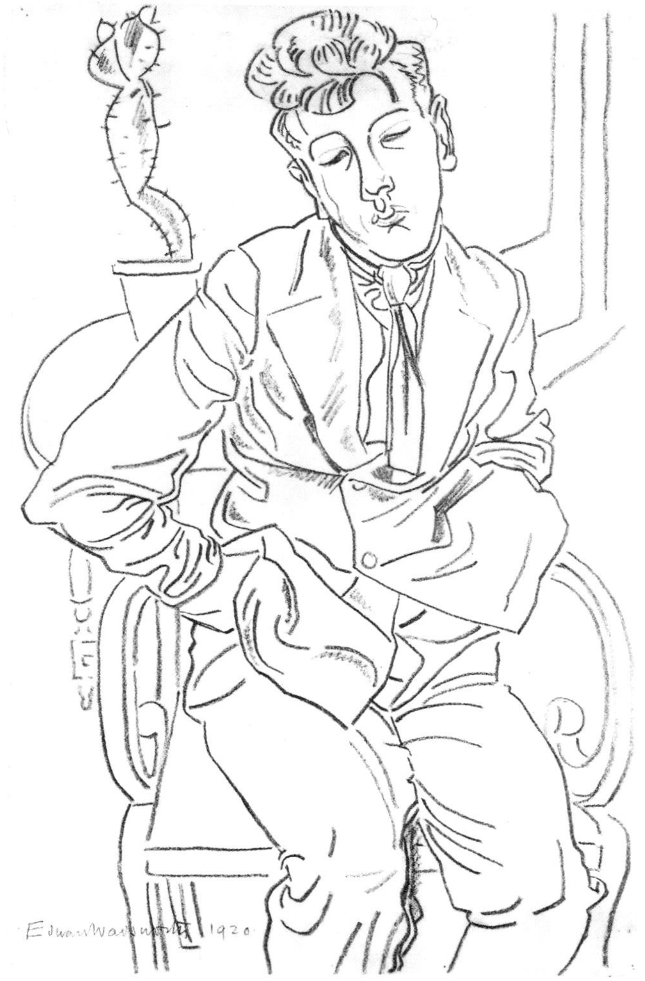

48

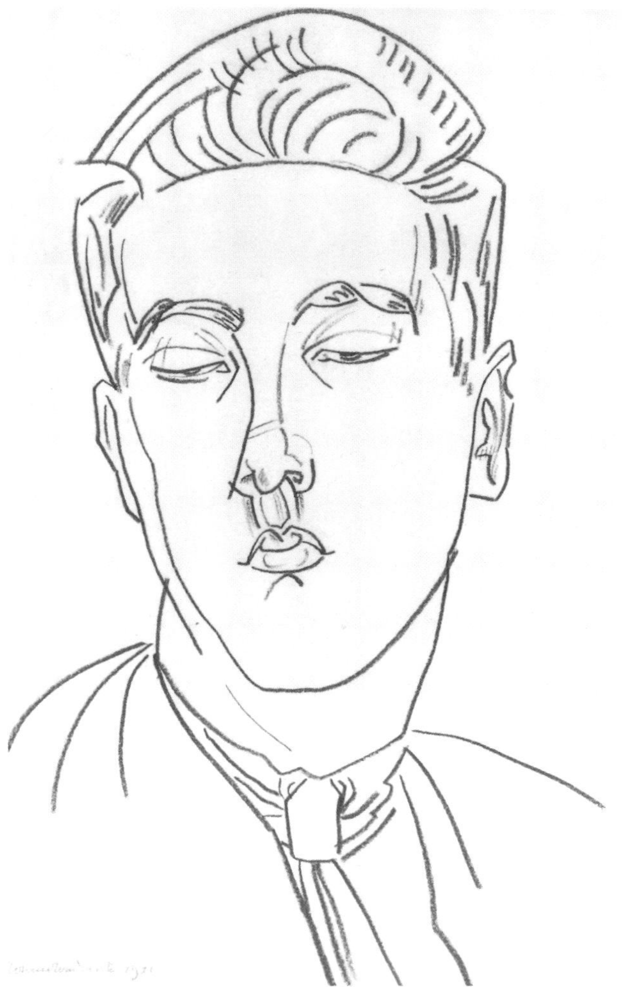

49

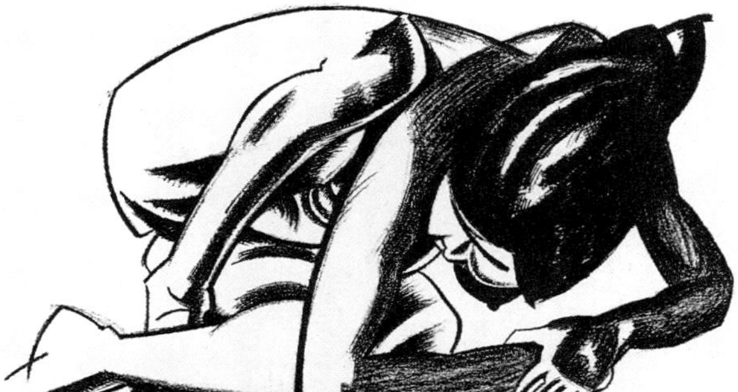

50

43. *Wapping* 1920
44. Still Life 1921
45. Theatre 1920
52. 'Englische Graphik' Exhibition Poster 1923
48. Portrait of Rupert Doone 1920
49. Head of Rupert Doone 1921
50. Crouching Nude 1920

Andrew Causey

Wadsworth in the Early Twenties

'Since I last wrote about painting [in 1922] there has been nothing very much to report.' Wadsworth's Vorticist colleague Wyndham Lewis wrote thus in 1929 about avant-garde art and subsequent opinion has mainly accepted his view.[1] The ten years after the end of the First World War was a period of artistic retrenchment, valuing detachment, objectivity and tradition. Wadsworth's landscapes and harbour scenes of the early twenties possess all these characteristics and have been seen to show him marking time between the high points of Vorticism and the metaphysical and abstract paintings of the end of the decade and after. However, although sparks did not fly after 1918 as they had in the Vorticist period, the decade has been misjudged through being assessed by standards of radicalism to which it did not aspire. Exhibitions such as *Tendenzen der Zwanziger Jahre* (Berlin 1977) and especially *Les Réalismes* (Paris 1981) have started to revise critical opinion but England was not well represented in them, with the result that no clear picture of English art in the twenties has emerged, let alone of Wadsworth's contribution to it.

The postwar years were difficult for artists. Patronage was scarce after the imaginative ventures initiated by the British and Canadian war records had dried up and few commercial galleries were willing to take risks. New exhibiting societies were less forward-looking than the London Group had been at its inception in 1914 or Unit One was to be in 1933. Few significant artistic reputations were made and an increasingly stale group of critics did little to stimulate artists. English taste was conservative, landscape satisfied a feeling for security people required after the war and the celebratory urban art Wadsworth had been involved with was no longer wanted. As in other countries there was a reassessment of national tradition, although what this implied, and what the word 'modern' meant in England in the twenties, has not been thoroughly examined. The eighteenth century was held in high esteem and picturesque taste was popular, although neither Ruskin nor the Pre-Raphaelites were as completely forgotten as has been thought. With a cautious approach to radical ideas reinforced by renewed respect for the old masters, the traditional English love of Italy took on a new lease of life. These were the conditions confronting Wadsworth as he returned to civilian life after completing war service and war art commissions. The nature of his commitment to modernism changed as he found his way between the contemporary demand for a traditional approach and a personal need to innovate.

Wadsworth had his first one-man show, of woodcuts, at Frank Rutter's Adelphi Gallery in March 1919, followed by an exhibition of watercolour drawings of the Black Country at the prestigious Leicester Galleries in January 1920. He was still close to Lewis and showed some of the Black Country drawings at the Group X exhibition organised by Lewis at Heal's Mansard Gallery in April 1920. Wadsworth had been a force in avant-garde art before 1914 but he was never as independent of Lewis as other avant-garde artists like Epstein and Bomberg who had one-man shows before the war. The critics now responded very positively, especially to the Black Country drawings, which received further publicity when they were published in book form in the autumn of 1920. Wadsworth found himself at the forefront of artistic debate.

He had first recognised the artistic potential of the bleak but powerful industrial landscape between Birmingham and Wolverhampton on regular train journeys to Liverpool, when he was working on the wartime camouflage of ships. The iron and steel furnaces with smoking chimneys are shown, if at all, in the background, while attention is concentrated on slag, the impurities left from the process of steel-making, which was taken from the furnace by railway wagons or tipping trucks on overhead gantries and dumped on nearby heaps. Wadsworth's interest was not in industrial production itself but almost exclusively in the waste.

The Black Country drawings say nothing *directly* about people: they are essentially landscapes, records of the way industry destroys nature and creates urban wildernesses. They are like the drawings Paul Nash had created to evoke the devastation of Passchendaele; Nash's exhibition, *Void of War*, at the Leicester Galleries in November 1918 had caused a considerable stir and, although his drawings (see fig.6) were reactions to the horror of a particular moment, they stayed in people's minds as symbols of postwar disillusion. The circumstances of Wadsworth's drawings were different from Nash's. Although the Black Country was a part of industrial England where iron- and steel-making were in relative decline, Wadsworth worked there at the moment of the sensational if short-lived industrial boom that coincided with postwar reconstruction. The barren deserts of slag should not, therefore, be read only as the artist's reflections on a dying industry, even if it had been Wadsworth's habit

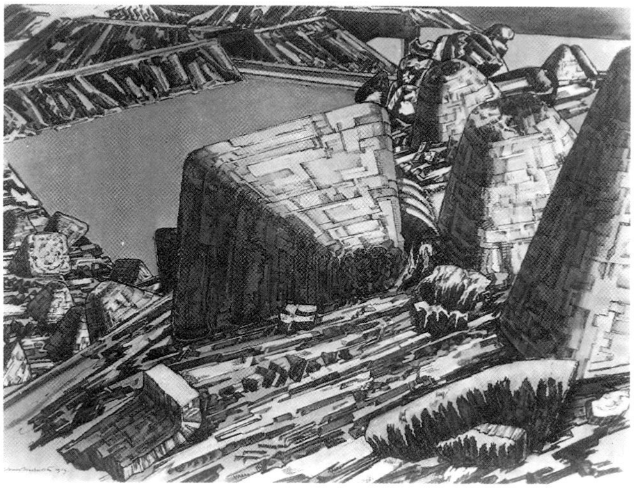
53

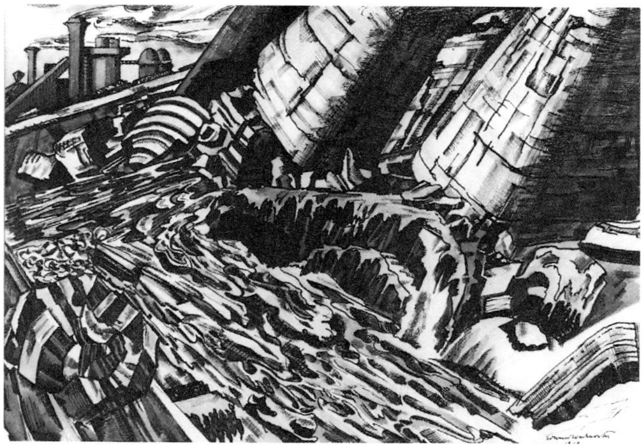
57

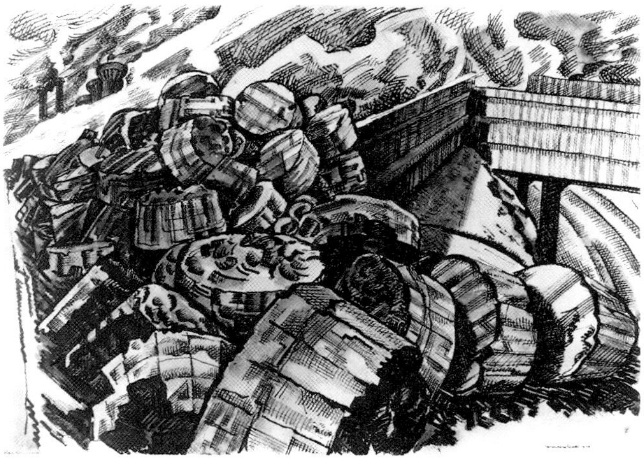
54

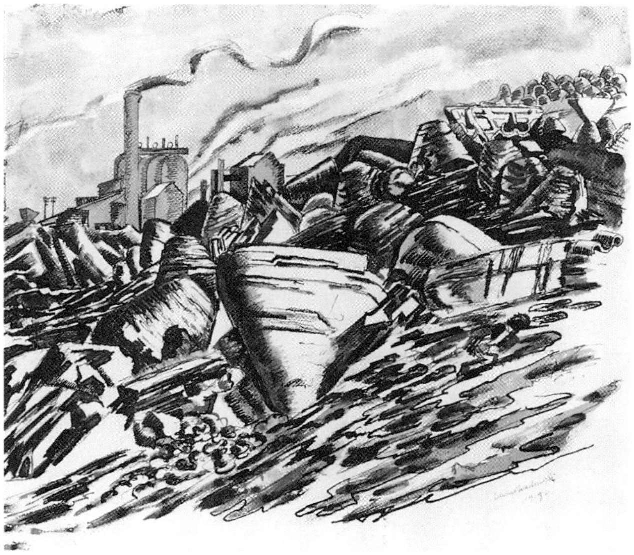
58

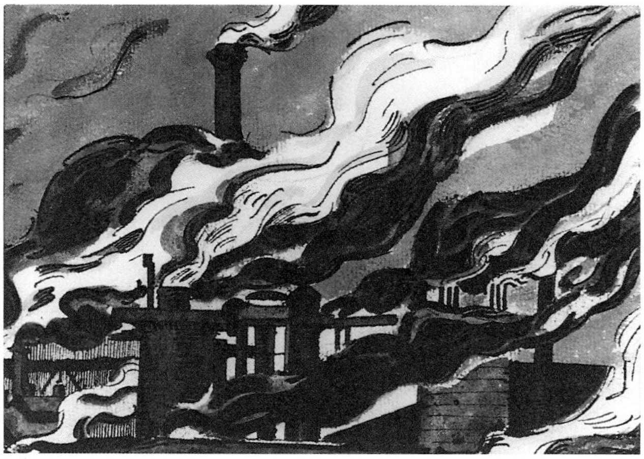
56

53. *Ladle Slag* 1919
54. *Slag Heaps at Leeds Steelworks* 1920
56. *Netherton Furnaces* 1919
57. *Blast Furnaces* 1919
58. *Tipton* 1919

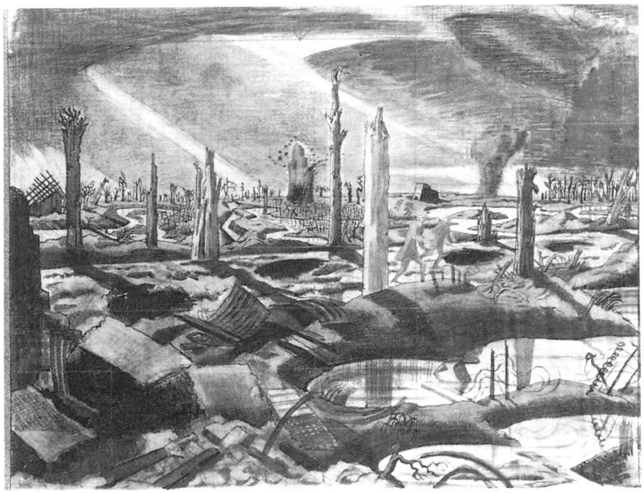

Fig.6 Paul Nash, *The Menin Road* 1917, ink, pencil, chalk and watercolour, 40.6 × 57.8, The Trustees of the Imperial War Museum

to approach his subjects in this way. They are better seen as a reaction, not necessarily conscious, to the decline and disillusion that inspired Eliot to invent the title *The Waste Land* in 1922.

The Black Country designs were received with approval by critics such as Alan Clutton Brock of the *Times*, Frank Rutter of the *Sunday Times* and P G Konody of the *Observer*,[2] writers active before the war who had seen the need for artistic renewal but mistrusted modernism in its most radical forms. Wadsworth's drawings represented a compromise between representation and abstraction of which they approved. Clutton Brock's review, 'Mr Wadsworth's Realism', speaks for these critics' common position:

> The different and, to many, unintelligible forms of abstract art, Cubism, Vorticism and the like, are beginning to be justified, not in themselves, but in their children. Modern painting had so much lost the sense of design and of three dimensions that it needed perhaps a severe and even repellent discipline if it was to recover these. The Cubists and the Vorticists, having gone as far as they could in the way of abstraction, now seem to be returning to the visible world, but with a richer sense of design.

The stress on design and the feeling that the modern movement had saved English painting from the excess of detail in Pre-Raphaelitism was a constant refrain of critics in the twenties. Wadsworth's reviewers repeatedly stressed the advantage gained from his having been a Vorticist while expressing relief that he had returned to representation.

When the Black Country drawings were published as a book, a more closely argued review appeared in the *Times Literary Supplement*. The writer rejected the 'heresy of pure abstraction' on the grounds that if the rhythms of the design were not based on reality they would be empty of meaning. Wadsworth, according to the critic, was using the despoiled landscapes as a source for rhythmic designs but had also expressed in the drawings an energy equivalent to the human energy that had made the landscape what it was.[3] The critic was allowing the expressionist character of art, which had been a feature of Vorticism, while insisting on the importance of representation.

The relation of the two elements of expressiveness and representation was a matter of contemporary debate. Vorticism had based its claim to modernity on the idea that the machine as symbol of the twentieth century should be regarded not picturesquely, from the outside, but in terms of its essential character, its energy and efficiency. On the other hand the war had produced a felt need to illustrate heavy industry's contribution to the war effort in a directly comprehensible way for popular consumption. O R Drey, reviewing the Black Country drawings, instanced Joseph Pennell, American-born protégé of Whistler, as an artist who achieved this.[4] Pennell had capitalised on a prewar reputation as an etcher of city and industrial scenes to acquire a semi-official wartime role, recording industrial operations in several countries, and published two books of lithographs showing munitions factories and other heavy industrial plant in England and America.[5] Drey argued that Pennell, like the prewar Italian Futurists, treated his material picturesquely, giving it an external glamour that did not reflect the real vitality of the industrial processes. However Wadsworth, he asserted, captured the authentic feel of the subject and his direct, unidealised presentation bore witness to his integrity; there was no false evocation of interest in theatricality. The comparison of Wadsworth with Pennell seemed valid even though Wadsworth's landscapes were not visually at all like Pennell's compositions of furnaces and hearths. Drey seems to have been observing that Pennell, serving the role of war propagandist, was impelled to glamourise, while Wadsworth was a free agent, distancing himself as far as possible from picturesque approaches.

In a similar vein the *Times* critic quoted Whistler's view that the ugliness of London was transformed by night and mist, pointing out that by contrast to this picturesque standpoint Wadsworth was a realist who 'extenuates nothing nor sets down anything in malice. What he gives us is the terrific energy of the whole industrial process represented, as energy can only be represented, with rhythmical and orderly forms.' It is interesting how much the discussion revolved round the issue of picturesqueness and how, implicitly at least, it was Wadsworth's Vorticist background that protected him, in the critics' eyes, from the false romanticism surrounding other representations of industry.

Apart from his very early work Wadsworth had not painted human figures and he seems – like Nash in his

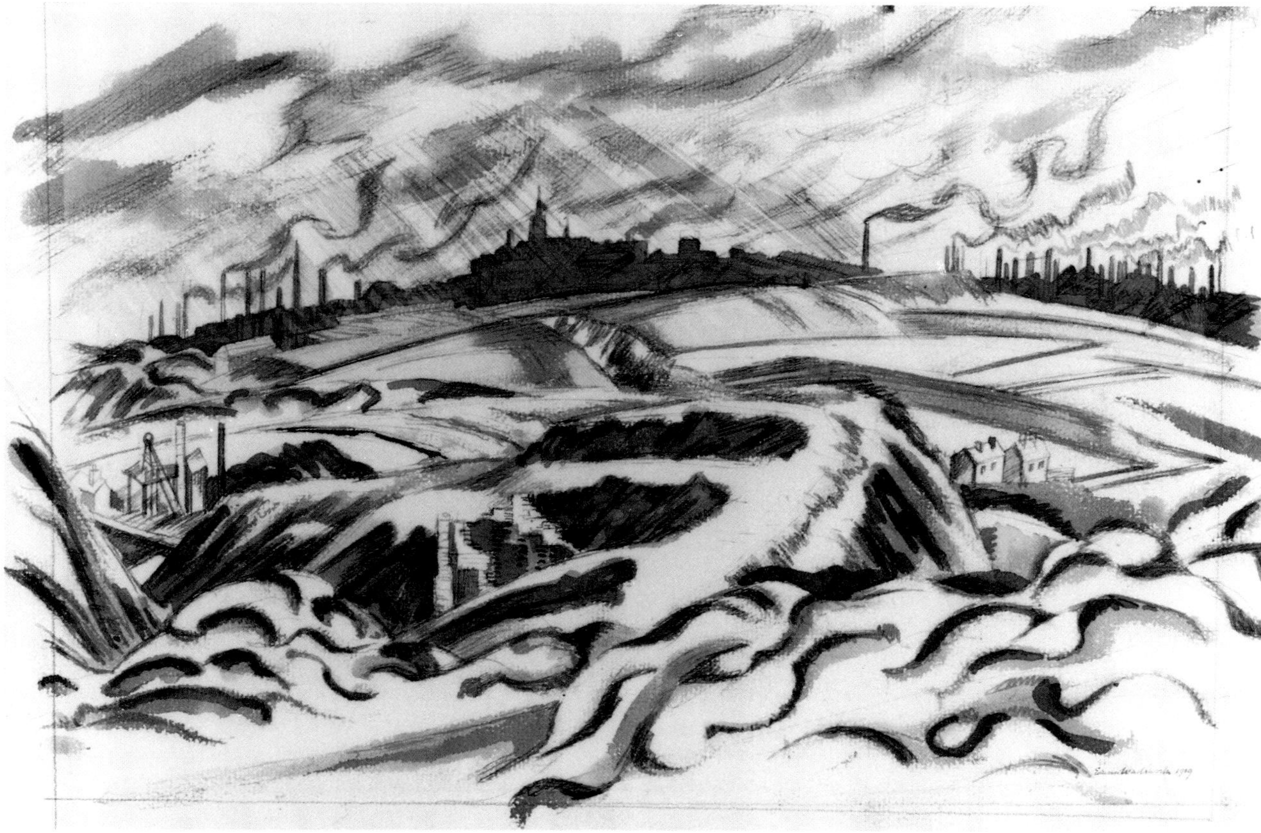

60

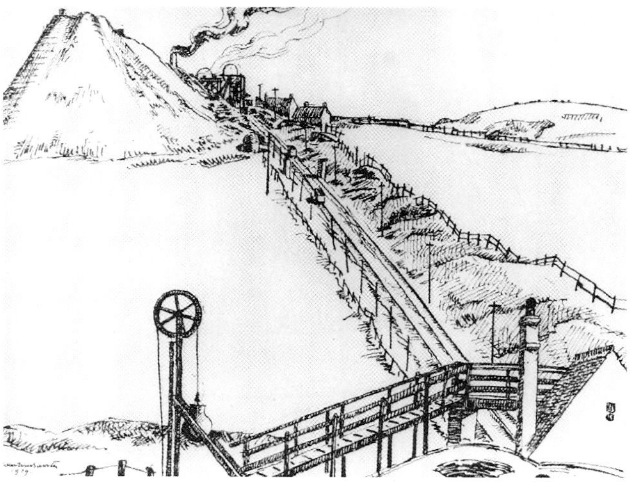

61

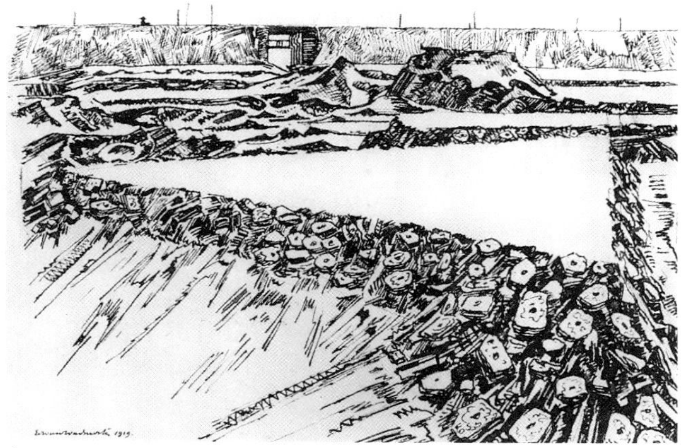

62

60. *Factories/View of Wednesbury* (1) 1919
61. *Windmill End* 1919
62. *Railway Embankment, Ockenhall, Gospel Oak/Slag Heap at Bilston* 1919

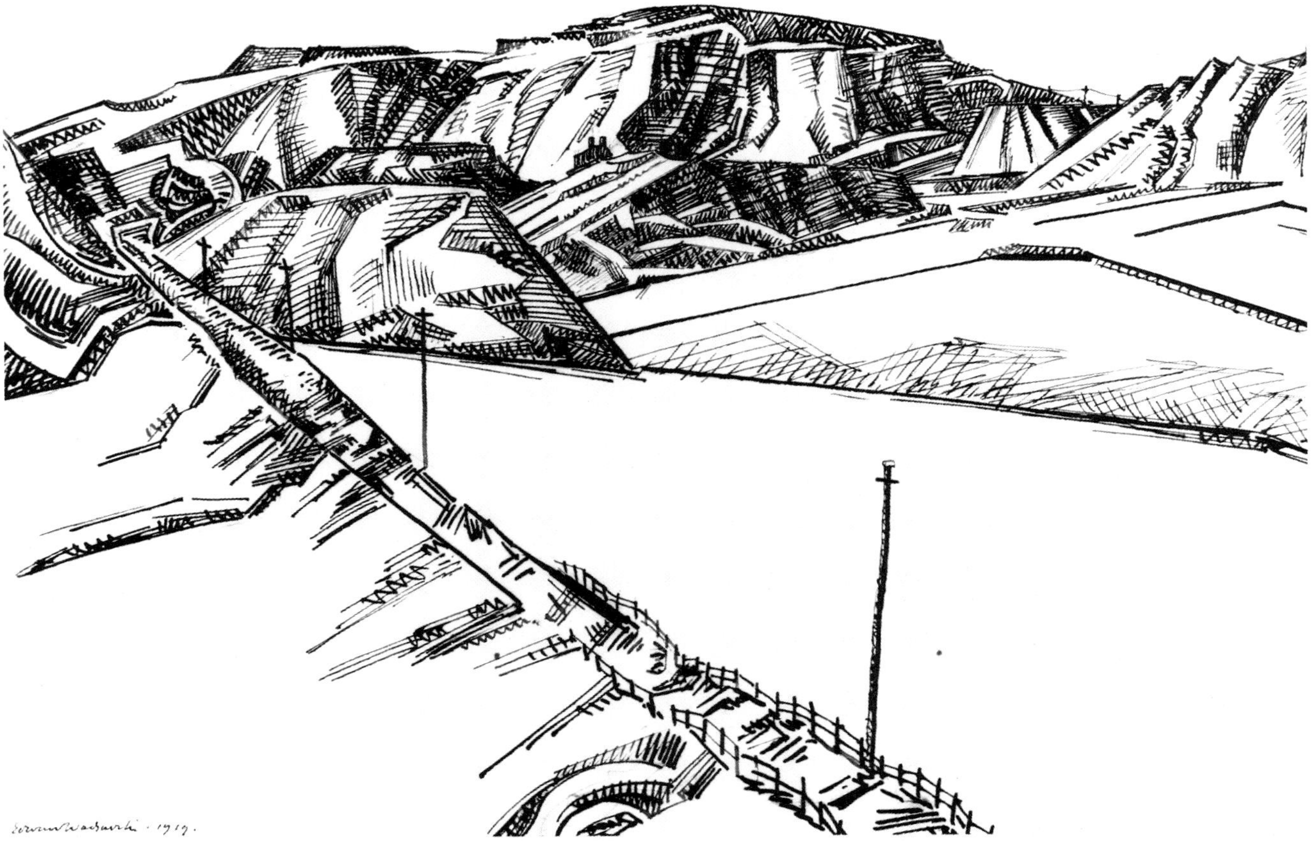

63

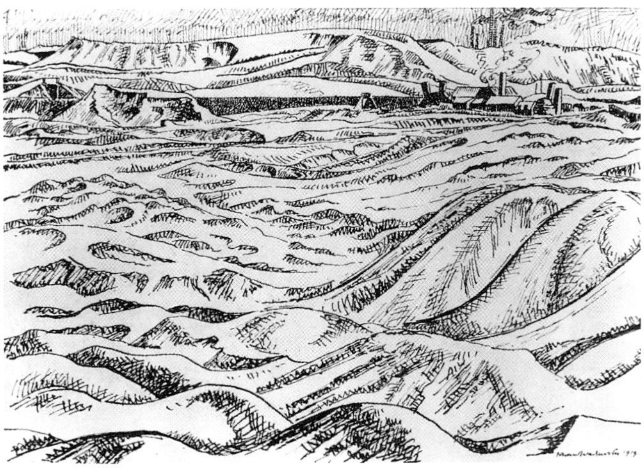

65

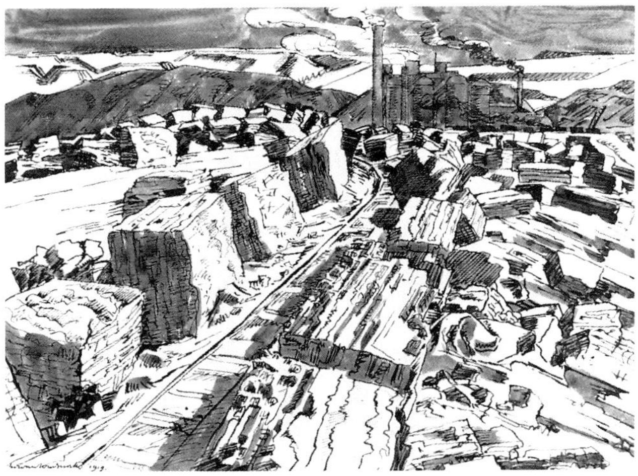

66

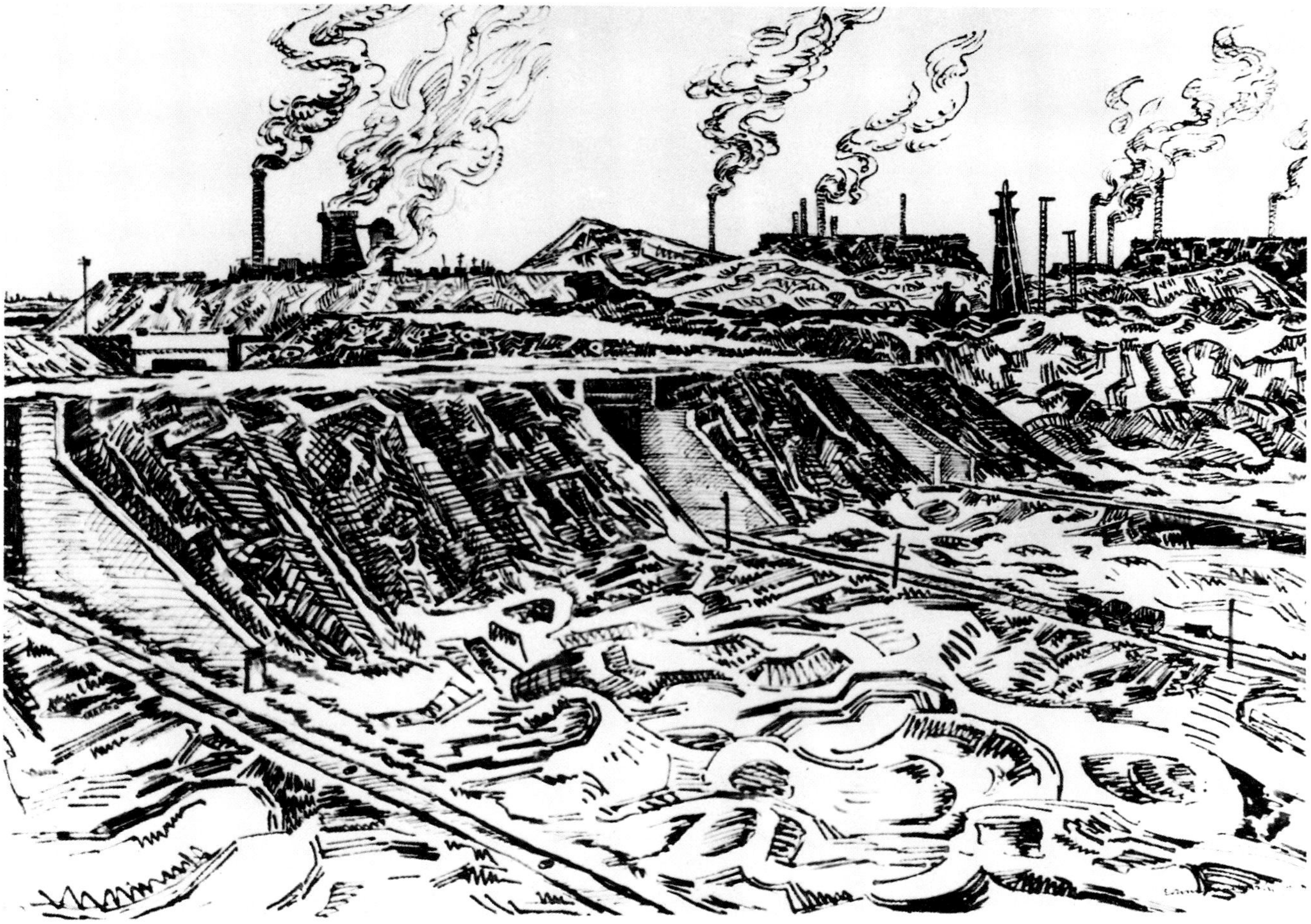

64

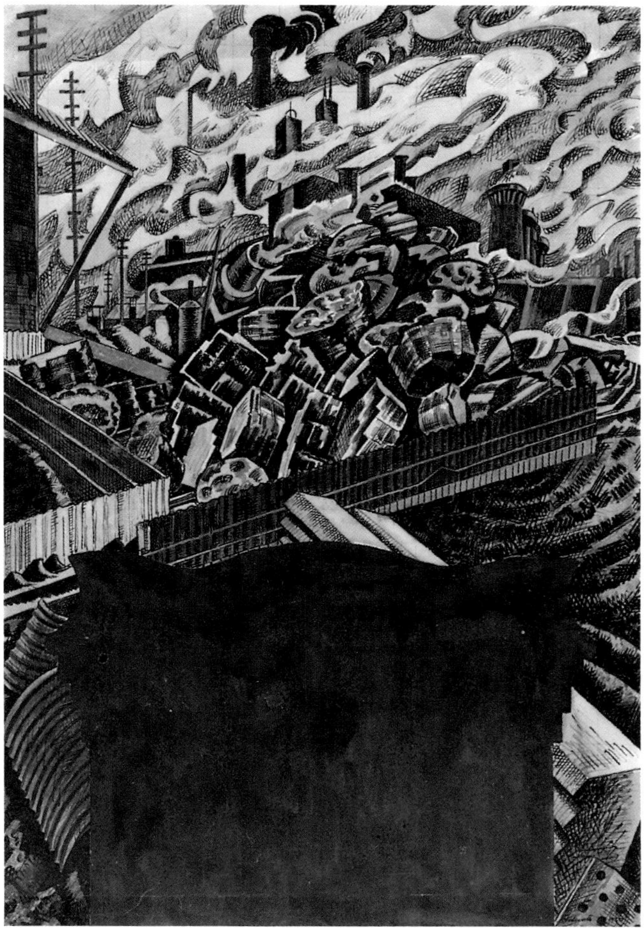

67

63. *Granite Quarries, Darby Hill, Oldbury* 1919
65. *View near Tipton, Staffs.* 1919
66. *Ladle Slag, Hingley's Furnaces, Old Hill* 1919
64. *View near Bilston* 1919
67. *Mural Design for Leeds City Hall* 1920

Passchendaele landscapes – to have found that the impact of man's effect on landscape is better conveyed without physical presences. This area of the debate was taken up in the *New Statesman* which used the Black Country drawings as the focus for an article on 'Art and Industrialism'.[6] Starting with artists' flight from industrial subjects in Pre-Raphaelitism, the writer went on to the work of Millet, Meunier and, in England, Brangwyn, whose approach through the dignity of labour served a 'nervous bourgeoisie' as a 'weapon of protective politeness'. This, the writer felt, was a compromise that could not hold and Wadsworth's realism was seen as a resolve to replace overblown sentiment (Brangwyn?) with the direct expression of truth. In these terms the critic regarded Wadsworth's Black Country drawings as 'without question the most convincing and satisfactory phenomenon which has yet emerged from the English contribution to modern aesthetic research'.

The only popular paper to review the Black Country drawings was the *Daily Herald*, whose critic remarked that there had been 'much talk lately of democratising art, bringing it to the people' and that Wadsworth's drawings 'can be understood by all classes of workers'.[7] The vision and force of the drawings' expression, according to the reviewer, gave them something in common with the labour movement itself. It was an adventurous argument, even if it seems naive from the standpoint of more sceptical times. In the flux of immediate postwar Europe remarkable visions of the social role of the artist were thrown up, although not notably in England. Some war commissions had taken painters into the world of the people at work and a few artists after the war, such as Bomberg, Roberts and Ginner, seemed briefly to be moving in the direction of social realism. Wadsworth, however, had a different field of vision from Roberts, the only significant artist to follow up urban social realism in the twenties, and never had the makings of a social realist himself. As a native of urban industrial west Yorkshire, Wadsworth could share the excitement of industry at work but clearly sensed its destructive power as well. There is a strong inner dynamic in the Black Country drawings, especially the close-ups of massive boulders of slag, which emphasise the detritus of civilisation rather than its possible positive social implications. For all its modernity Vorticism was steeped in *fin-de-siècle* pessimism and, in this respect, the Black Country drawings are little different.

In the spring of 1920 Wadsworth was one of six artists invited to submit designs for murals for Leeds town hall.[8] The idea was the brainchild of Michael Sadler, Vice-Chancellor of Leeds University, who was inspired by the commissions for huge war paintings for the projected Imperial War Museum and felt that Leeds needed an equivalent to the Ford Madox Brown murals in Manchester. After consulting William Rothenstein, who agreed to select the artists and vet their designs, Sadler approached the city council and won acceptance for a scheme by which he would pay the artists for their designs and, subject to Rothenstein's approval, submit them to the council. If the council agreed, the designs would then be offered to wealthy local people who would be asked to sponsor them. Rothenstein nominated Wadsworth, although as Sadler had already bought Black Country drawings for himself, Wadsworth's participation can never have been in doubt. Apart from Rothenstein's rejection of Stanley Spencer's project, the scheme at first went ahead uneventfully, with Sadler seeing the first designs in July and telling Rothenstein that he thought the city council would accept them. But in October Sadler suddenly wrote to Rothenstein that he had decided not to submit them to the city. Rothenstein replied on 17 November with surprise, saying that he had not realised Sadler was going to judge them himself. Sadler was described in the *Yorkshire Post* as saying the designs were 'too discordant in character to be suitable for juxtaposition on the walls of the town hall'.[9] The artists were angry and Wadsworth and Albert Rutherston protested, in a letter to the *Yorkshire Observer*, that the five artists whose designs had been accepted by Rothenstein should have been allowed to come together to bring their designs into accord.[10] The affair petered out after Wadsworth sued a local paper, which reproduced a design of his without permission, for breach of copyright and won £11. The designs, which Sadler tried unsuccessfully to present to the British Museum and then the Tate Gallery, ended up after his death in the collection of Leeds City Art Gallery.

The Leeds affair is worth recounting in detail because it occurred at a crucial moment for Wadsworth and had implications for British art as a whole. The clue to Sadler's curious retraction lies in his correspondence with Rothenstein in October. Sadler told him: 'We could not have fallen on worse days. I am afraid there is not the slightest chance at present of getting people to subscribe for the execution of these works.' Rothenstein agreed, adding, 'No one can expect any decision until things have changed.' The postwar industrial boom peaked in May 1920, the month after the artists had held a successful collective meeting to view the town hall and gone away to prepare their designs. The ensuing slump was so rapid that within twelve months near full employment in iron and steel was replaced by 23 per cent out of work nationally. Sadler was surely right in fearing he would not get sponsorship for the scheme. Business, which had not been particularly enthusiastic in the first place, would not have paid and the celebration of industry in any case looked less appropriate now. It was not until the Second World War, when Sutherland and others again painted industry at work and Moore painted miners at the coalface – the subject of

68. *Blast Furnaces* (1) (Netherton Furnaces) 1919
70. *Black Country* 1919 (state c)

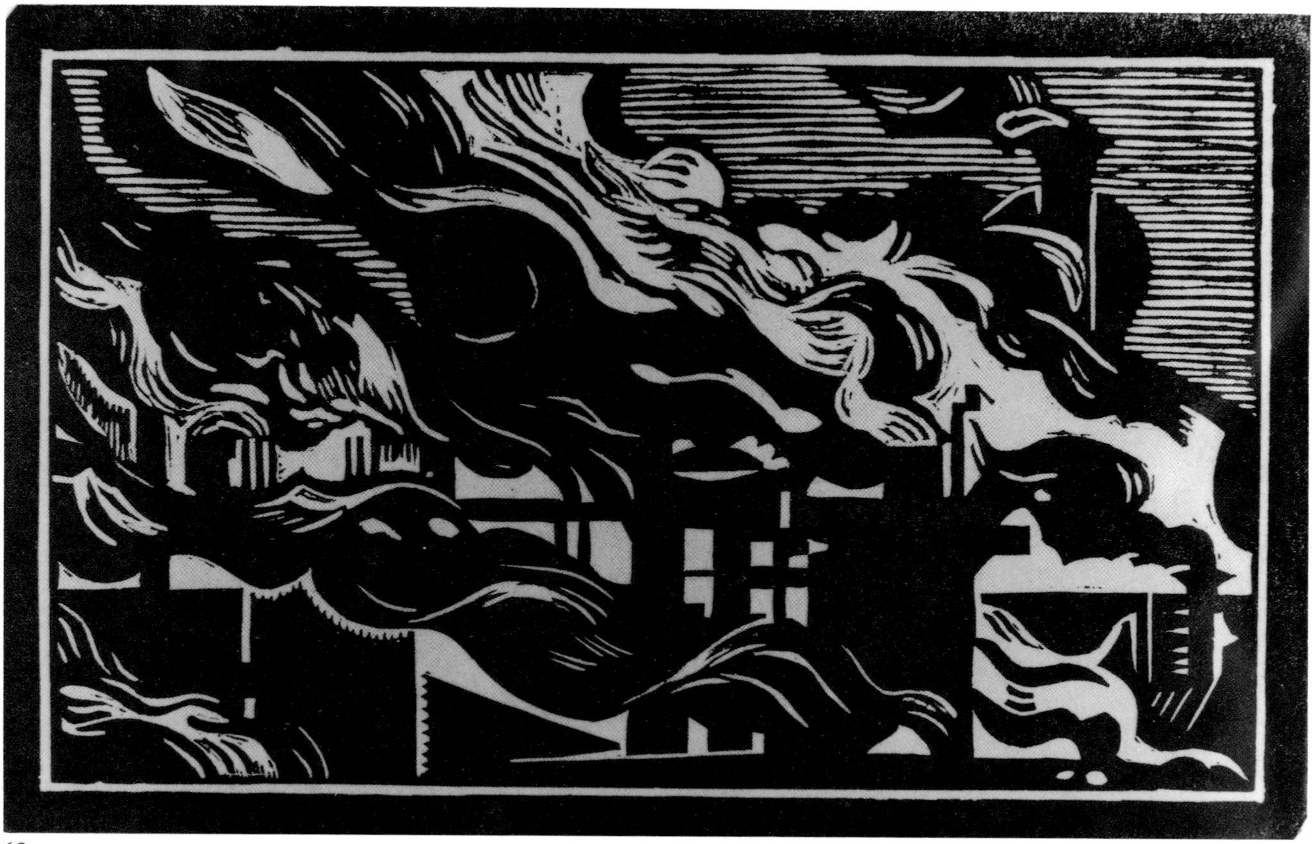

68

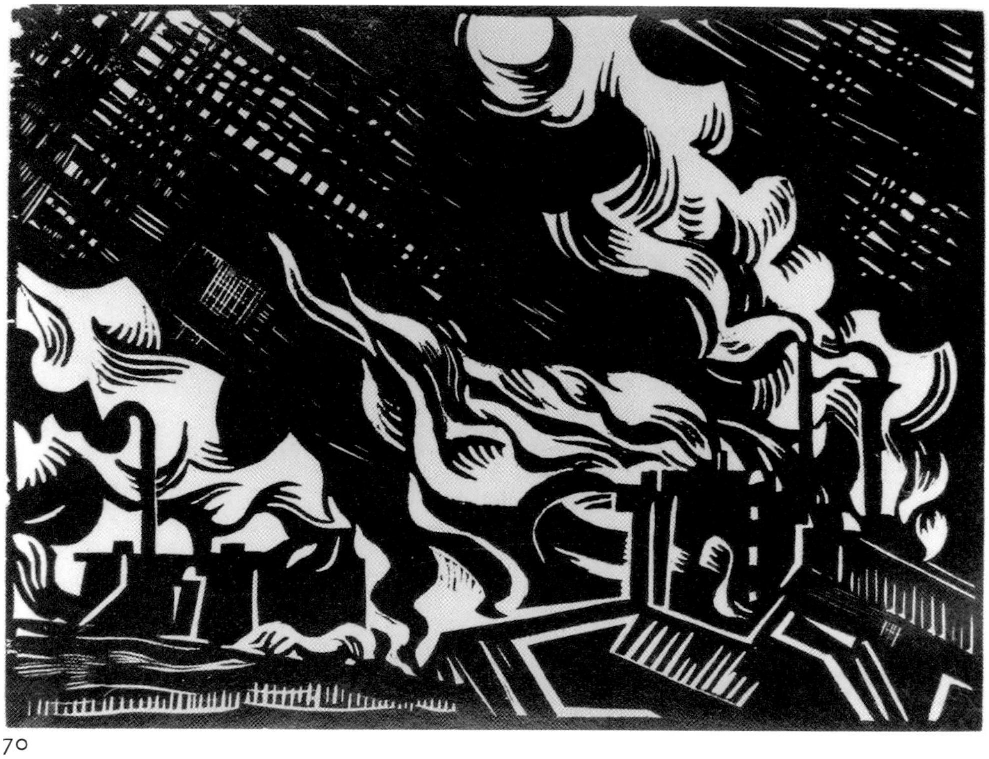

70

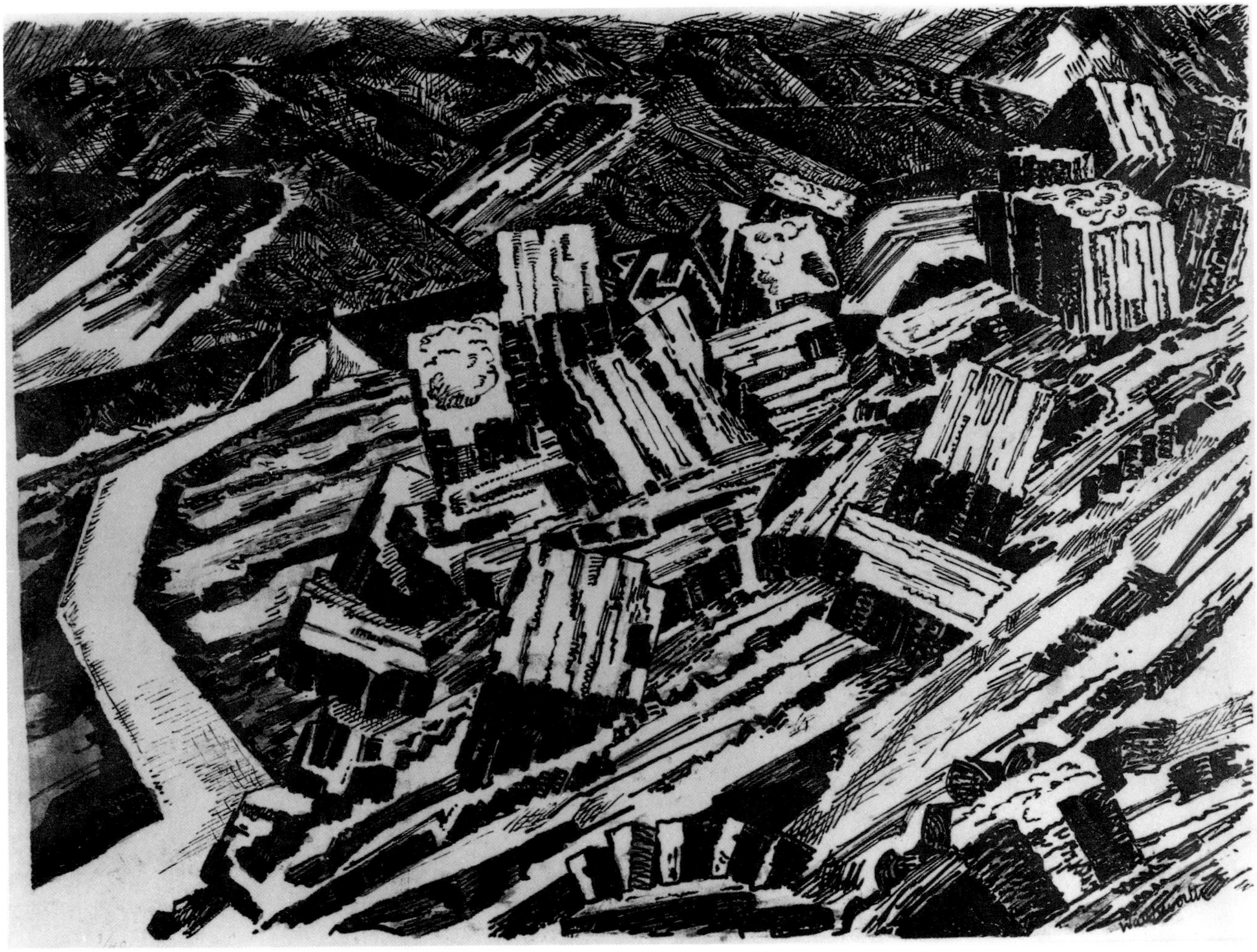

72

72. Ladle Slag, Old Hill(1) 1919-20
73. Ladle Slag, Old Hill (2) 1919-20
74. Devon Clay Pits 1920

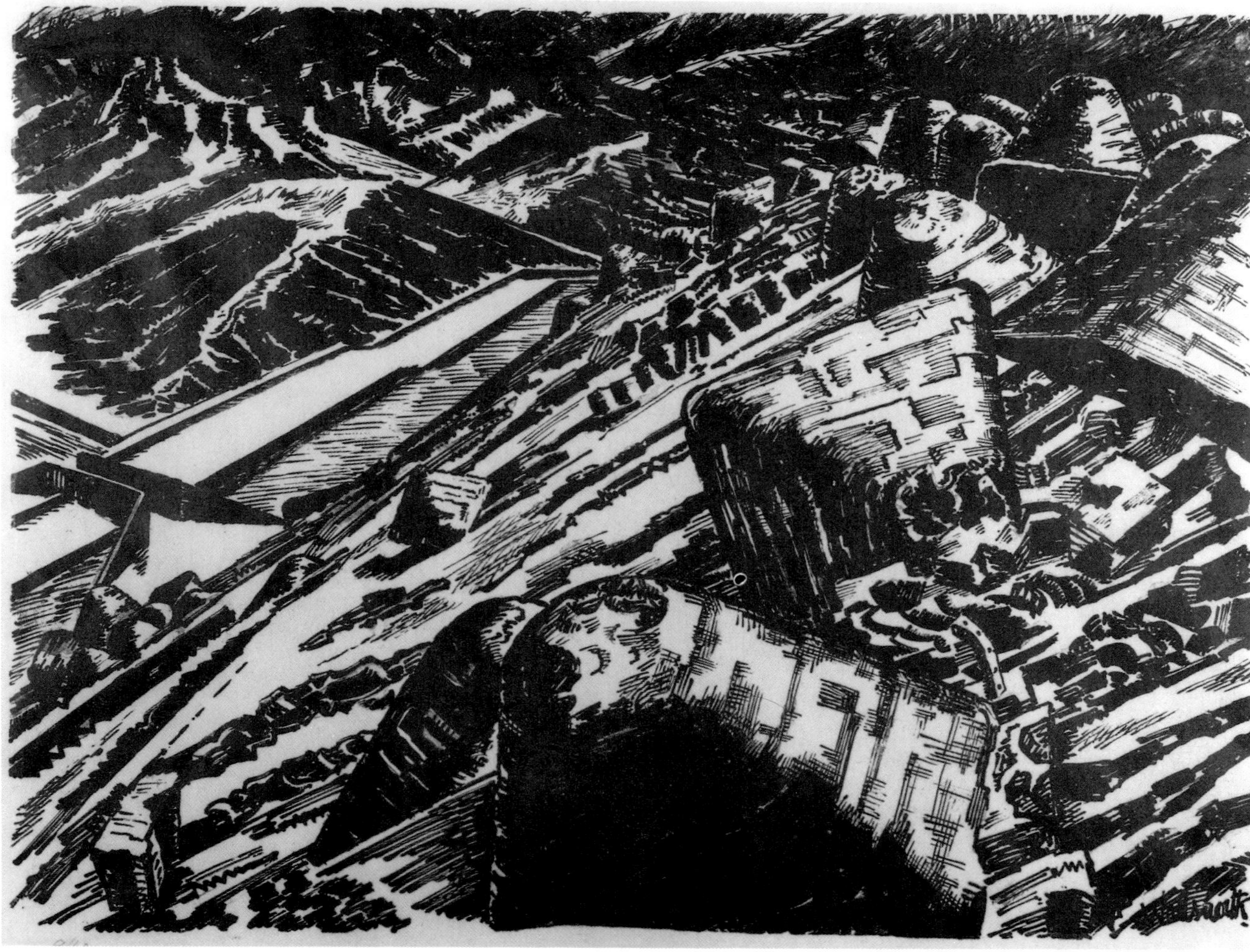

73

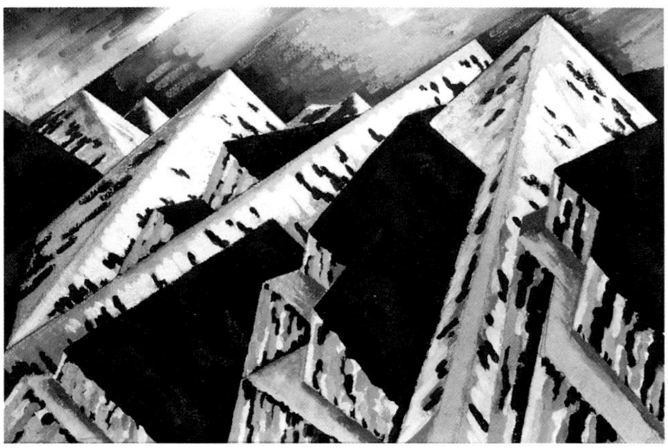

74

Jacob Kramer's contribution to the Leeds project – that the opportunity lost in 1920 recurred. Wadsworth's industrial drawings belong as a group to a brief period when the iron and steel industry, already much talked about because of its key role in the war, was seen as a marker for Britain's post-war recovery. The slump found its reflection in Wadsworth's switch from industrial to rural landscape.

Frank Rutter's article 'Extremes of Modern Painting', in the *Edinburgh Review* in April 1921, was probably the last contemporary notice of the Black Country drawings to appear and forms an interesting postscript to this phase of Wadsworth's work. Rutter complimented Wadsworth, as he had done before, but this time there was a new twist to the argument: Cubism was justified for industrial subjects, as it had been for war art, because both caused men to behave like machines and Cubism was a machine-type art. The wise artist now, according to Rutter, was one like John Nash who applied the new principles of design to nature. This was not a radically different approach, because even landscape painting was to take account of modernism, but it implied that Rutter saw the immediate future of British painting in landscape, underpinned by good orderly design, but not necessarily by anything as radical as Cubism.

After the successful reception of the Black Country drawings and the submission of his Leeds designs, Wadsworth took a house at Newlyn in Cornwall for a family holiday. The sculptor Frank Dobson, a colleague in Group X, was there, as were the painter Cedric Morris and R H Wilenski, an artist by training who was then at the start of a career as an influential art critic. At the end of August, instead of returning to London by train, the Wadsworths decided to walk. In the event Fanny, Edward's wife, caught the train at Plymouth, but Edward covered the whole distance to London on foot and, as he did so, began to evolve a plan for a set of designs of the ports of England. He told a journalist in 1923 that he was inspired by Ruskin's *The Harbours of England* with engravings by Turner,[11] an unusual choice for a convinced modernist at a time when Ruskin was out of fashion. Wilenski, a Ruskin enthusiast and the future author of a book on him, published in 1933, may have introduced the idea. Wadsworth was not in a hurry with the plan, exploring only two ports on this trip, Plymouth and Portland, and explaining in 1923 that the project would take many years.

There were apparent precedents for Wadsworth's long walk from Cornwall: for example, Hilaire Belloc's walk from France to Rome in 1901, Gwen and Dorelia John's hike across France in 1903 and the gipsyish wanderings of the whole John family. However, Wadsworth was a practical person, not intellectual by nature and untouched by the romantic, poetic attitudes of these earlier figures. There is little real connection between Wadsworth and these pre-war expressions of delight in the open road. Comparison has been made between Wadsworth's images of industrial wastelands and Paul Nash's paintings of war but when Wadsworth turned to rural landscapes, the fundamental differences between the two become clear. While Nash was interested in the meaning for him, personally, of familiar nearby scenes, Wadsworth was more objective and did not in the twenties paint the places, London and Sussex, where he lived. The firm cubistic forms of Wadsworth's new paintings do not bear any resemblance to the mysterious shadowy presences in Nash's early watercolours. Wadsworth's most recent landscape paintings, done in 1913, had been of trees over water and already had the crystal clarity of form that became the hallmark of his paintings in the twenties.

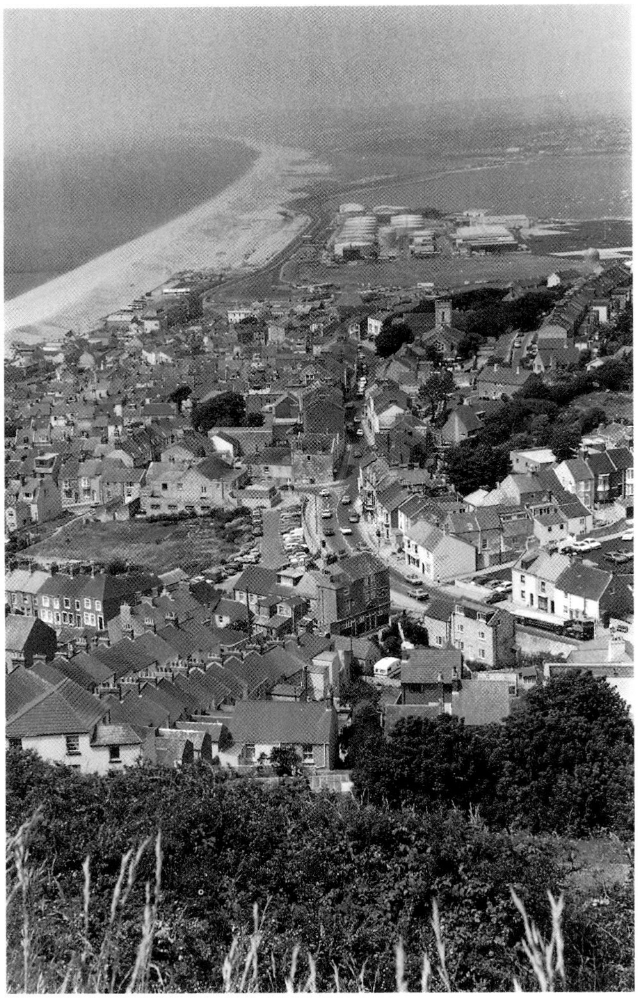

Fig.7 Fortune's Well, Isle of Portland (photo. Andrew Causey)

An enthusiastic motorist, Wadsworth painted subjects geographically far apart and the simplified, graphic style he now developed has affinities with posters. The twenties marked the beginning of the age of popular travel and posters of landscapes, beauty spots and historic places were beginning to be published by petrol and railway companies and tourist organisations. With an upsurge in the sale of guidebooks and the popularity of charabanc tours, visiting the country became a pastime. While Nash remained even in the twenties something of the romantic wanderer in nature, Wadsworth created tourists' landscapes. Although he first drew Portland when visiting it on foot, he chose for his vantage point the island's principal beauty spot looking over Chesil Bank and Dorset from above Fortune's Well (75), where even then there was a car park (fig.7). Wadsworth's villages generally have prominent motor roads and although they are not conventionally picturesque, they have the visual balance of buildings and trees to satisfy the idea of a village. As paintings these are among Wadsworth's most successful; as images of British towns and countryside, they have an initial seductive charm, but both the simplification of form and the absence of people give them a hollow ring and the emphasis on surface perfection is in the end curiously oppressive.

Colour p.50

Wadsworth had unconsciously achieved a new kind of landscape painting appropriate to the era of the car, landscapes of alienation expressing the restlessness of the age of tourism. His preference for hill towns, from Fortune's Well to the Peak District, picks up an interest already evident in his woodcuts. It recalls, too, a particular strain of modern French work from Cézanne's paintings of Gardanne (1886) through Picasso's of Horta de Ebro (1909) to Derain's of Cadaqués (1910) (fig.8). Derain was at the height of his reputation in England after the war. He was regarded by Clive Bell and other leading critics as the outstanding figure in the reaction against Cubism and as responsible for bringing modern French art back into touch with the great traditions of the Italian Renaissance and French classicism. Wadsworth was not supported by the Bloomsbury critics, although at first sight he seems to represent the dispassionate classicism they were looking for better than the artists like Duncan Grant, whom they championed. Ultimately, however, Wadsworth's work is unlike the French art the Bloomsbury critics admired, even Derain at his most austere. Wadsworth's graphic and linear tendencies, and the lack of flow and richness in his paint, distinguish him from the French but made tempera a congenial medium. Tempera had a distinct following in England in the twenties precisely because it has an even, unmodulated overall character that appealed to artists with graphic tendencies.

Wadsworth's second one-man show at the Leicester Galleries in March 1923 was well received by much the same group of critics as had praised the Black Country drawings two years before. They observed the sure control he exercised

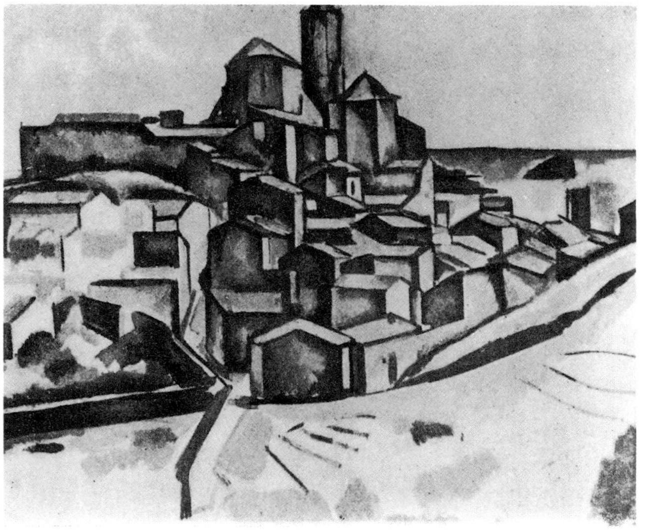

Fig.8 André Derain, *Cadaqués* 1910, oil on canvas, 60 × 73, Nàrodni Galerie, Prague

over his new medium and liked the grace, order and geometry of his work. The artistic ferment that stimulated much of the discussion in 1921 had disappeared and it was not altogether the critics' fault if disappointingly little was said that was new. A certain complacency exists in their writing, a lack of curiosity about what lay behind Wadsworth's choice of subjects and what caused the air of unease that the silent, non-expressive surfaces of his unpeopled compositions communicate. It was a critical problem that became acute by the time of the next exhibition in 1926.

The Wadsworths had made one continental tour since the war, the trip to the Mediterranean in 1921 that had produced 'Near Marseilles' 1922 (79). Now, after the exhibition, they left on their first journey to Italy, with Fanny Wadsworth keeping a diary of the visit in which she noted her husband's reactions to art. They entered Italy by way of Genoa, visiting Pisa, where they admired the Benozzo Gozzolis in the Campo Santo. In Florence Edward was again excited by the Gozzolis in the chapel of the Medici-Riccardi Palace and, of the art they saw later in the city, only the Fra Angelicos in San Marco impressed them more. In the diary there are comments on many Quattrocento artists in the Uffizi, including praise for Gentile da Fabriano, Uccello, Pollaiuolo and, with some reserve, Botticelli. The Ghirlandaio frescoes in Santa Maria Novella were found disappointing and Michelangelo's 'David' aroused no interest. In Siena Gozzoli again caught their attention as did the early Sienese painting in the art gallery, the Lorenzetti fresco of 'Good Government' in the town hall, which impressed Wadsworth very much, and the Pintoricchio frescoes in the Piccolomini library of the cathedral . From Siena they went to San Gimignano, where

Colour p.51

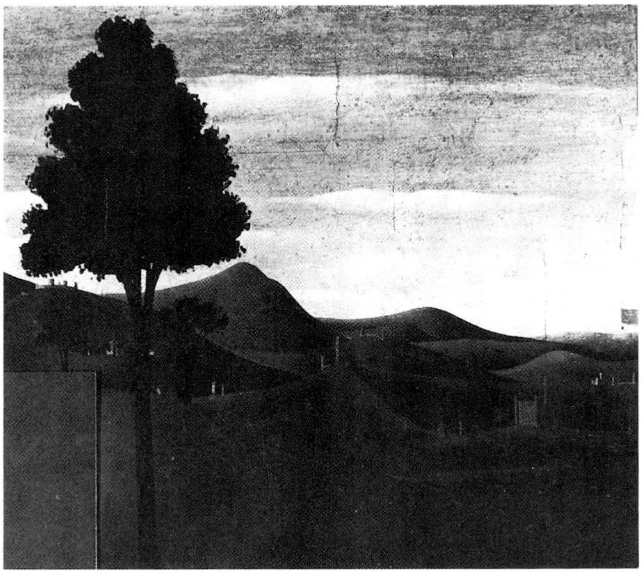

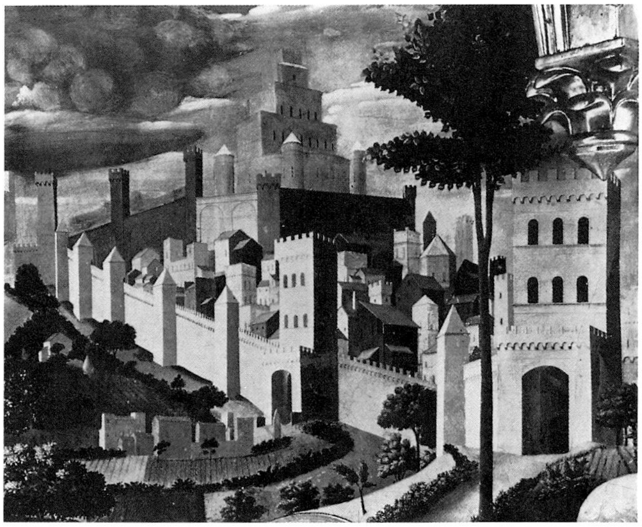

Fig.9 TOP Fra Angelico (c.1400–55), *The Lamentation over the Dead Christ* (detail), Museo di San Marco, Florence

Fig.10 BOTTOM Fra Angelico (c.1400–55), *The Descent from the Cross* (detail), Museo di San Marco, Florence

Gozzoli, Ghirlandaio and earlier artists were praised, and from there via Ravenna and Ferrara to Venice, which for the most part they did not enjoy. They liked the earlier paintings of the thirteenth and fourteenth centuries and looked at Carpaccio, whom they found disappointing.

Interest in Italian art was important for English modernism. Wadsworth's 'Near Marseilles', finished in 1922, looks modern with its cubical white houses in a simplified, rhythmical landscape but comparison with a Fra Angelico landscape (fig.9), which Wadsworth was to see for the first time in 1923, suggests that being modern and admiring Italian Renaissance painting could be compatible. Comparing Wadsworth's hill towns with Angelico's (fig.10) confirms the argument. At the Slade Wadsworth would have had a chance to hear the lectures Roger Fry gave at University College, at the time when Fry was evolving his theory that the modern movement was essentially a reassertion, via Cézanne, of the primacy of stucture exemplified in the old masters. Of more immediate significance, however, was the fact that the last friend the Wadsworths saw before arriving in Italy was R H Wilenski, who was working for the League of Nations in Geneva. Wilenski shared Fry's concern with the 'architectural' in art and believed, as he said in a review of Wadsworth's 1926 exhibition, that a study visit to Italy at the right moment in a modern painter's development was essential. In 1930 Wilenski was to be co-author with P G Konody of a book on Italian Renaissance painting which, like almost all writing on the Renaissance at that time, only valued the period from Giotto to about 1520. Within that period Wilenski and Konody tended to follow Ruskin in preferring the decorative artists of the Quattrocento like Ghirlandaio, Gozzoli and Pintoricchio while more modern writers like Berenson and Fry stressed the contribution of a rigorously architectural painter like Piero della Francesca. Piero is not singled out in the Wadsworth diary and there is no suggestion that they visited his major works as they could have from Florence in their car. Contemporary guides, Murray's and Baedeker, were still following Ruskin and reserving their accolades for the later Florentine Quattrocento as against Piero. Wadsworth reached his conclusions personally on the basis of what he saw but the places he visited, and the art he looked at, followed closely the precepts of Ruskin and Wilenski. Wadsworth was not alone here. Nash's journey to Italy in 1925 followed much the same pattern and Stanley Spencer's tastes, although never supported by a visit to the country, lay in the same areas. Nicholson, visiting Italian Switzerland in the early twenties, was oriented towards the earlier, more primitive art, in keeping with his abstract, conceptualising and less decorative approach.

Having had the initial idea for a series of harbour scenes in the summer of 1920, Wadsworth worked on it slowly, as he was engaged with other kinds of outdoor scenes at the same time. 'The Cattewater, Plymouth Sound' (80), the subject he had come to first, was finished only in 1923 in time for his exhibition at the Leicester Galleries in March and, although it was not the first painting completed, it marked the beginning of Wadsworth's period of most intense involvement with this subject. The idea of travelling round the coast to make a set of views for publication is a picturesque one and there are picturesque elements in the variety of incident and the sense of artifice that arises from

Colour p.53

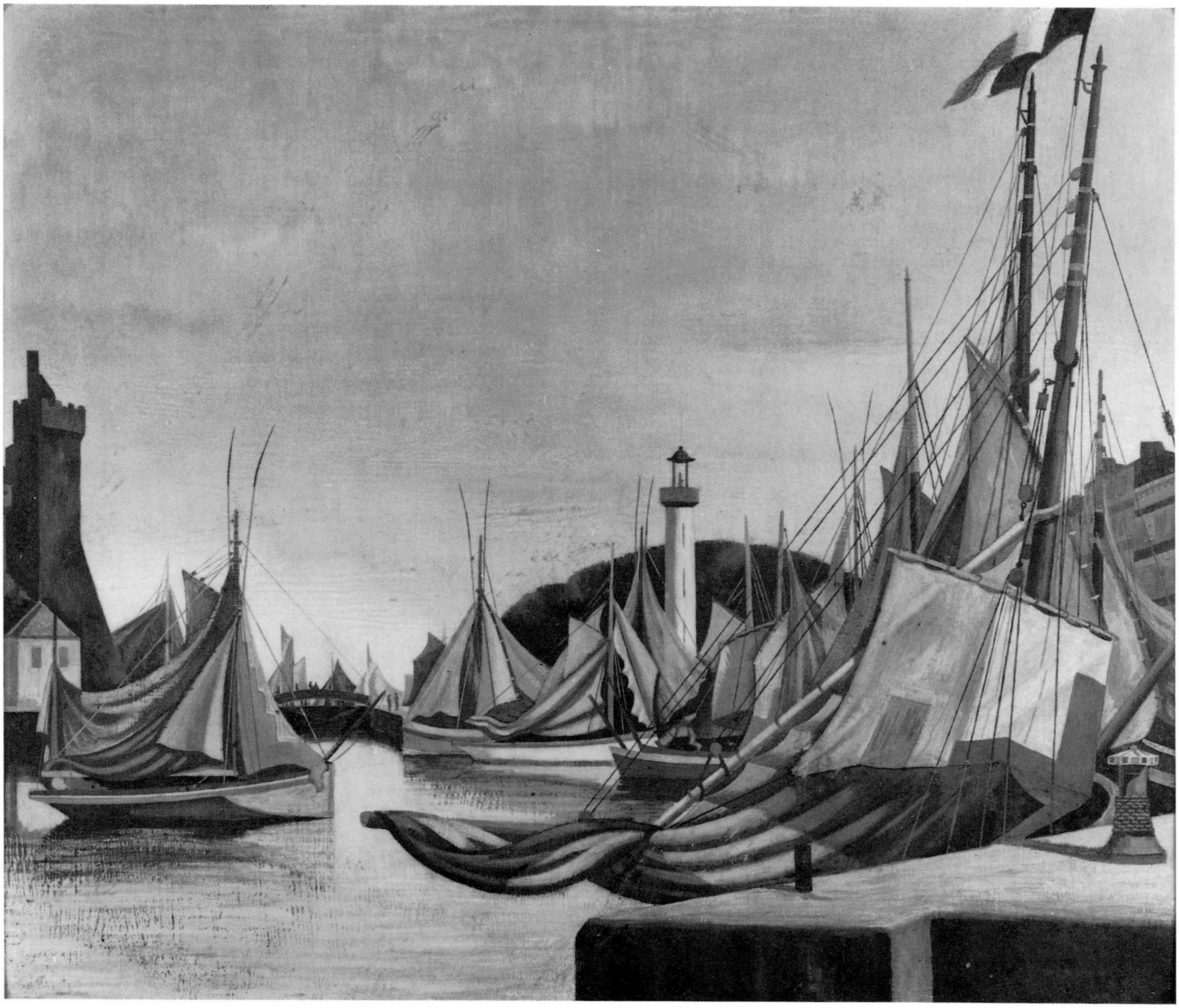

82. La Rochelle (2) 1923-4

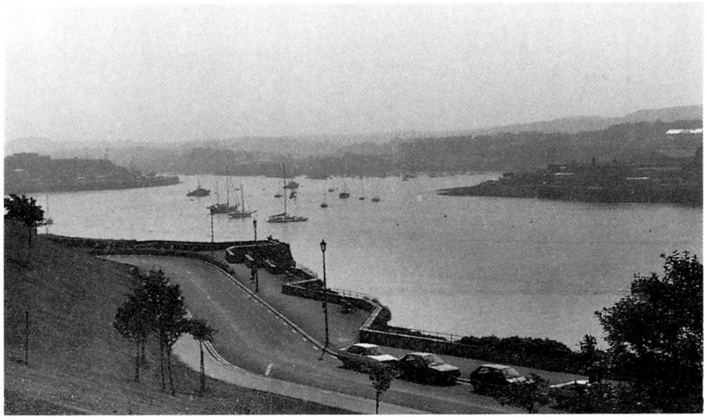

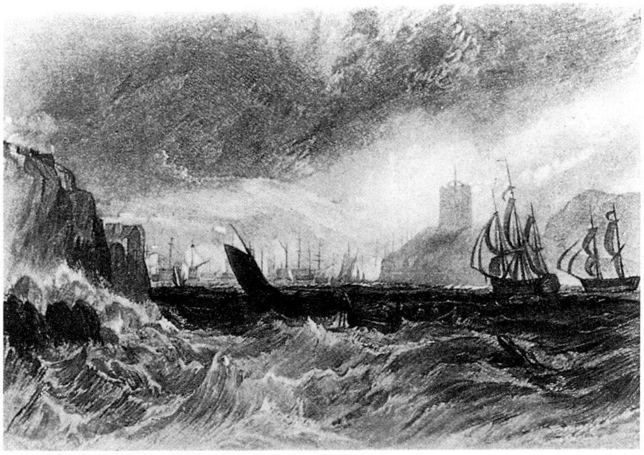

Fig. 11 TOP The Cattewater, Plymouth Sound (photo. Andrew Causey)

Fig. 12 BOTTOM J M W Turner, *The Catwater*, engraving from John Ruskin, *The Harbours of England*, London 1856

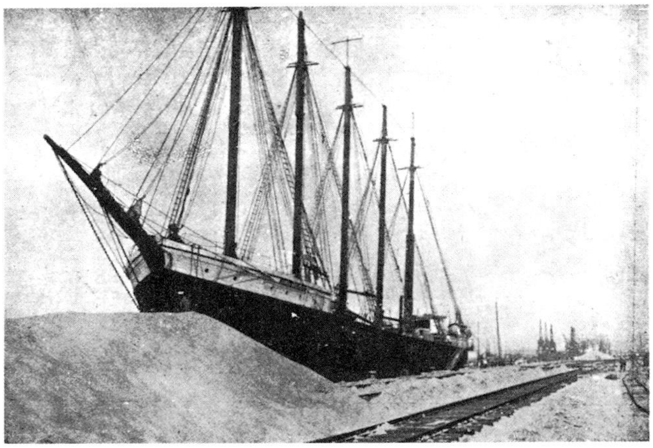

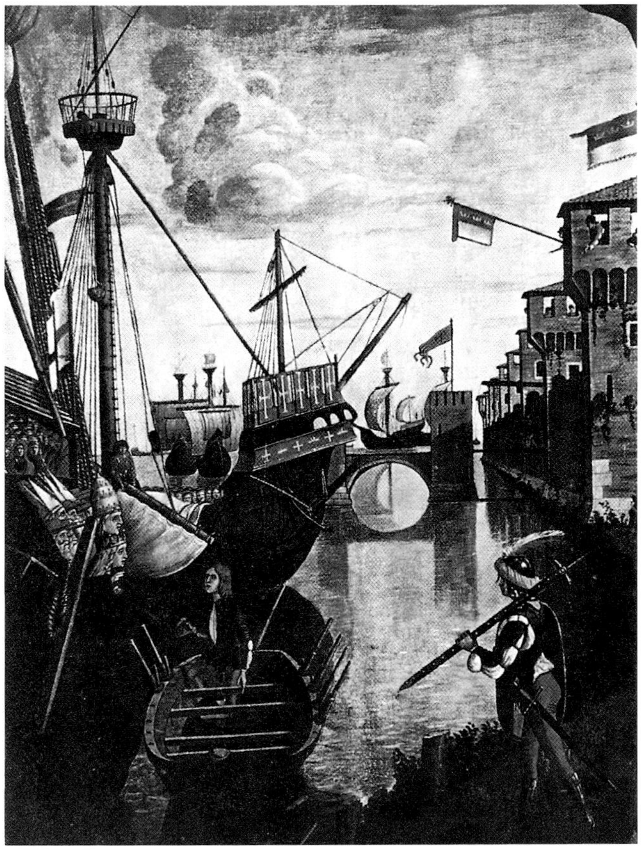

Fig. 13 TOP Port d'Anvers : vieux voilier en bois à cinq mâts, from *Varietés*

Fig. 14 BOTTOM Vittore Carpaccio (*c.* 1465 - 1526), *Arrival of the Pilgrims in Cologne* (detail), Gallerie dell'Accademia, Venice

the technique, creating the feeling of a theatrical backdrop. However, the severe objectivity of Wadsworth's design establishes, in contrast, a sense of the modern. It is an extremely skilful compromise between old and new and very much in keeping with the aesthetic demands of the moment. The view (fig. 11) is the same as in Turner's engraving (fig. 12) though Turner has allowed himself poetic licence in romanticising the scene, and by Wadsworth's time a sea wall had been created with some artful 'Vorticist' zig-zags where in Turner's day there had been spiky rocks. The picturesque had been brought up to date. While Turner had made two engravings of Plymouth, the other being of the naval base, Wadsworth was interested only in the Cattewater which serves the fishing port and the recreational end of the city.

Wadsworth's obsession with the subject of sailing vessels is not easy to account for. He did not sail, indeed was not particularly interested in sport at all, and his own recent experience was with warships which he omitted from most of his port scenes, sometimes even from Portland, which was a naval base. Ports had been 'blessed' in *Blast No. 1*, perhaps because Lewis felt them to be special nodal points with an energy and excitement of their own but Wadsworth's port scenes, with their soft colours and smooth, unmodulated surfaces, convey a curious feeling of solitude, existence outside and beyond time. They are a mixture of fact, often presented with documentary precision and dreamlike recreation of a lost past. As such they have little connection with the *Blast* period. Wadsworth seems to be turning his back both on Vorticism and his naval experience.

The boats Wadsworth painted existed in reality. Photographs appeared in journals such as the illustration of 1927 from the Belgian Surrealist-oriented *Variétés* with which Wadsworth was familiar (fig. 13). In 1926 Wadsworth himself made a set of copper plate engravings for a book about existing, if in some cases rare, sailing vessels, *Sailing Ships and Barges of the Western Mediterranean and Adriatic Seas*. Nonetheless Wadsworth was archaising. Several of the Quattrocento fresco cycles he saw, such as the Pintoricchios in Siena and Carpaccio's illustrations for the St Ursula legend in Venice (fig. 14) included boats with distant similarities to those Wadsworth painted now. Wadsworth exhibited some of his seaports in 1923, just before he went to Italy, and his existing interests must have drawn him to the frescoes, as much as the frescoes influenced his own painting. The narrative cycles of the Quattrocento had been part of English taste since Ruskin's day and there are Pre-Raphaelite paintings in which the sailing vessel is used as an image of escape from an unhappy present. There were contemporary artists, also, notably Joseph Southall, who had taken up tempera long before Wadsworth and also painted harbour scenes in which people, if present at all, seem like intruders in a naturally empty and silent scene (fig. 15).

Wadsworth's harbours have a lazy, immobile, 'Sunday afternoon' character that recalls Seurat's Normandy port scenes from the later 1880s (fig. 16), which are also unpeopled, non-functioning, apparently abandoned. Like Wadsworth's they have atmosphere, not in the sense of air that can be breathed, but in the sense that their stillness creates tension. In the classicising mood of the twenties Seurat was much dicussed, typically by Roger Fry in an essay in 1926, which stressed the formal design and geometry of the pictures, rather than linking them with the Symbolist movement that was at its peak at the end of the 1880s.[12] Although Wadsworth's even, tempera surfaces are not visually like Seurat's Neo-Impressionist dots, they are similarly artificial and discourage naturalistic readings. Seurat's harbours reject the naturalism of Impressionist boating scenes in the same way that in the twentieth century Wadsworth's are different from Derain's Fauvist views of the Pool of London. The distinction is between a form of naturalism, where people and environment operate in unison, and an art of alienation where the scene confronts the observer as a separate object. Wadsworth is less extreme than Seurat,

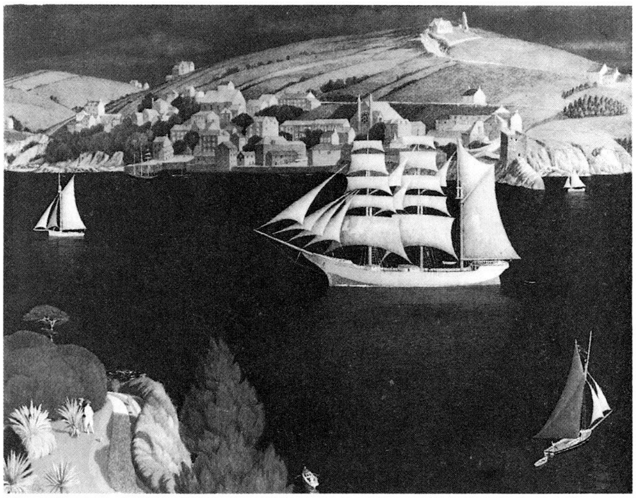

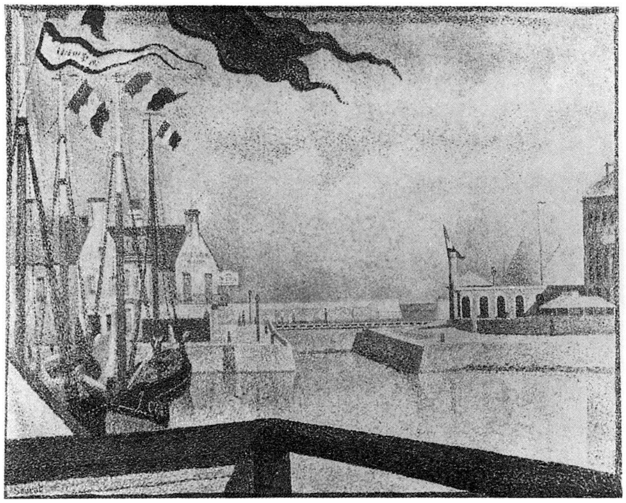

Fig. 15 TOP Joseph Southall, *The Old Seaport (Forrey Bay, Cornwall)* 1919, tempera on canvas, 48.9 × 62.7, Manchester City Art Galleries (Rutherston Gift)

Fig. 16 BOTTOM Georges Seurat, *Sunday, Port-en-Bessin*, oil on canvas, 66 × 82, Rijksmuseum Kröller-Müller, Otterlo

always treading a careful line between realism and invention, constantly retreating from excessive artifice. He allows the spectator to suppose that perhaps the port happened to be empty when he was there and will soon spring to life.

It is commonplace to view the twenties in Britain as a decade of social retrenchment and security that was followed by a period of economic and political disasters. It was actually a time of high employment, serious strikes and skilful outmanoeuvring of the Left. Conservative forces successfully concealed most of the cracks in the political and social fabric but the sense that one is witnessing the Indian summer of a passing order is strong. Once Wadsworth's urban realist phase was passed, his art presents an ostensibly patrician world of well structured towns, villages and harbours but the silent, airless, unpeopled places warn that it is a faked world, not a going concern but an empty relic.

By 1924 some of Wadsworth's designs, especially ones like 'Dunkerque (1)' (83) that show elaborate rigging, had become extremely complex. Although the effects of Cubism still showed in the clarity of structure, the compositions were becoming traditionally illustrative in their detail. Wadsworth had travelled a long way from the austere landscapes of 1921 and it is hard to see that he could have taken the port scenes further in that direction. A new line of research suggested itself when the Wadsworths went with their painter friend Dick Wyndham to the south of France and Italy in the summer of 1924. The ports they visited included Toulon and Saint-Tropez but they spent most of their time in and around Marseilles, whose narrow streets by the old harbour, like the rue Fontaine de Caylus (fig.17) and rue de la Reynarde (92), had become legendary on account of the dense and shifting population of smugglers and petty criminal elements. An exotic glamour was added by the prostitutes who gathered on the corners or sat at the brothel entrances, their names elaborately painted on the buildings' handsome signboards. Suspended from the upper floors of the houses were elaborate pulley systems for hanging out washing, of a kind that Stanley Spencer had noticed in Leeds and pointed out to Wadsworth when Spencer showed him round the city in April 1920.

Colour p.52

Marseilles, and even more the adjacent naval base at Toulon, had become the focus of an avant-garde sub-culture with the mercurial figure of Cocteau, in Toulon to recover from opium addiction, at its head. It was a dandyish disrespectful coterie searching for freedom of expression and personal conduct at a time when the bohemia of prewar Paris was tending to ally itself with the establishment. By the mid twenties the ambience of the Mediterranean ports had international appeal, Toulon having entered the repertoire of George Grosz. Wadsworth and Wyndham were among the first English artists to go there, together with Christopher Wood and Cedric Morris, soon to be followed by Edward Burra, Tristram Hillier and, in 1930, Paul Nash. English writers, like Anthony Powell and Evelyn Waugh, located scenes there and it was to a brothel in the rue de la Reynarde that the hapless Paul Pennyfeather in *Decline and Fall* (1928) was sent to arrange the forward passage of Margot Beste-Chetwynd's girls to South America.

Wadsworth's visit to Marseilles coincided with his final break with Lewis, after a period of deteriorating relations caused by Lewis's ungracious response to the initiatives of Wadsworth and others to help him financially. Lewis's novel *The Apes of God*, a characteristically ebullient onslaught against

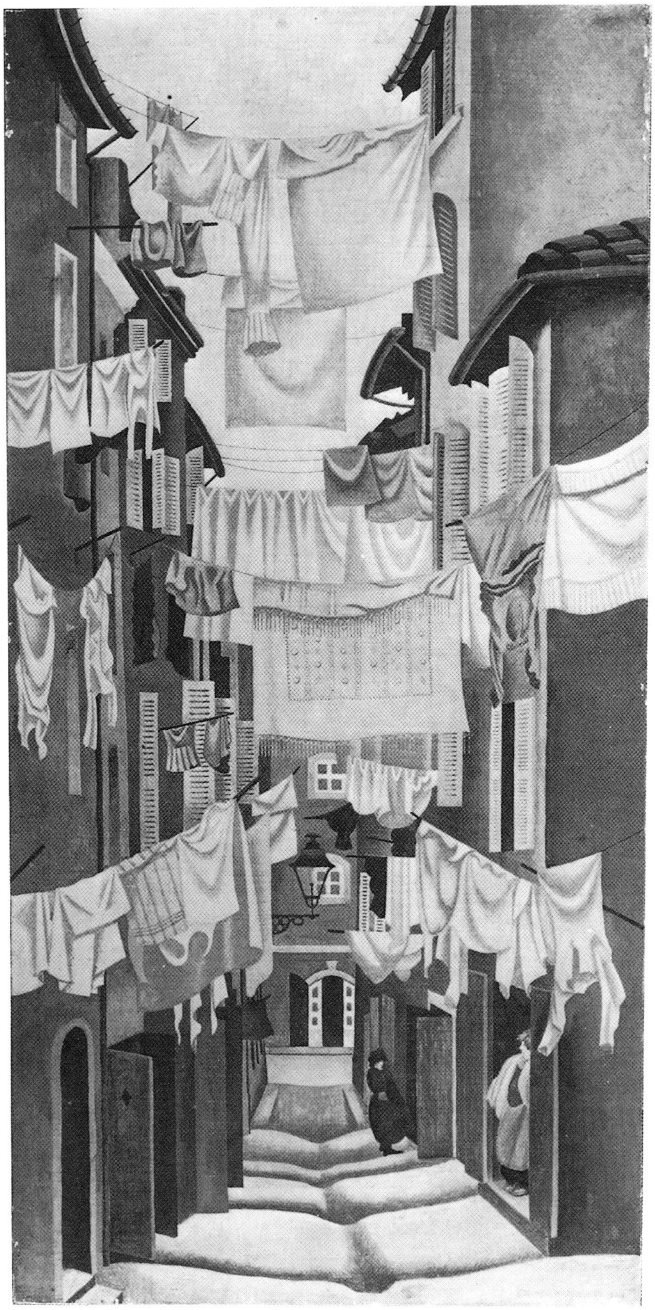

Fig.17 *Rue Fontaine de Caylus, Marseilles* 1924 (W/A 62), tempera, 94 × 45.7, Leicestershire Museums and Art Galleries

'champagne bohemia', the rich amateur who stole the true artist's living, was being serialised in 1924 in Eliot's periodicial the *Criterion*. Wadsworth had a minor part but prominent among Lewis's apes were his friend Dick Wyndham and the Sitwells, one of whom, Osbert, wrote the catalogue introduction for Wadsworth's 1926 exhibition.

A shift was taking place in Wadsworth's art that drew him

temporarily away from classical severity towards a more elaborate and mannered form of expression, objectionable to Lewis's puritanical aesthetic, but offering an important imaginative release from Wadsworth. The new port scenes of 1925 and 1926 are intensely theatrical. Space is no longer measured and open but telescoped and boats are seen through huge curtains which must, in reality, have been sides of marquee-type stores but which, in the paintings, resemble stage curtains and give the impression that the boats are seen through a theatre proscenium. Play is made with the elaborate fall of curtains, bric à brac is piled in front of the spectator and curiosities like strange, carved figureheads on sailing vessels, fancy lettering on shops and bars and eccentric street furniture call for attention.

Wadsworth's third exhibition at the Leicester Galleries in November 1926 was unusually varied, including older harbour scenes, the new more theatrical ones and the first of the metaphysical still lifes. The critics did not, for the most part, respond imaginatively. Older writers, like Rutter and Konody, although respectful, obviously found the new art less congenial and, in spite of the evident ambitiousness of the show, no longer reviewed Wadsworth first in their weekly columns, as they had in 1923.[13] This was an important exhibition, one that started to reset the aesthetic agenda by allowing freer play to the imagination, and must have been an inspiration to painters like Burra, especially, but also to Nash, who were to rebel against the overbearing authority of art as good design.

More daring critics introduced the word 'baroque' among their comments.[14] Although 'rococo' might better describe some of Wadsworth's new intense and highly wrought forms, it is interesting that a new word was entering contemporary critical language to explain the tensions and uncertainties that the new harbour scenes present. Mannerist and Baroque painting were still held in low regard almost everywhere. In England the Magnasco Society to promote later Italian art was founded in the twenties, with Sickert as a sponsor and the Sitwells in prominent support, but it did not become widely known. Sacheverell Sitwell had a unique reputation as a writer on Baroque architecture but this, again, was only a minority taste.

The only critic of the 1926 exhibition who recognised that Wadsworth was doing something new was Anthony Bertram, writing in the *New Statesman*.[15] Bertram who was a friend of Nash and who had not reviewed Wadsworth before, wrote:

> In the Saint-Tropez set he has used the artificial form of a raised curtain to frame his work. Surely the symbolism of yearning for escape can be carried no further: the curtain lifted for a moment that we may glimpse the ships and all they signify. Nonetheless, technically Mr Wadsworth is the least romantic of painters. Every shape is clearly defined and there is no accident of mood.

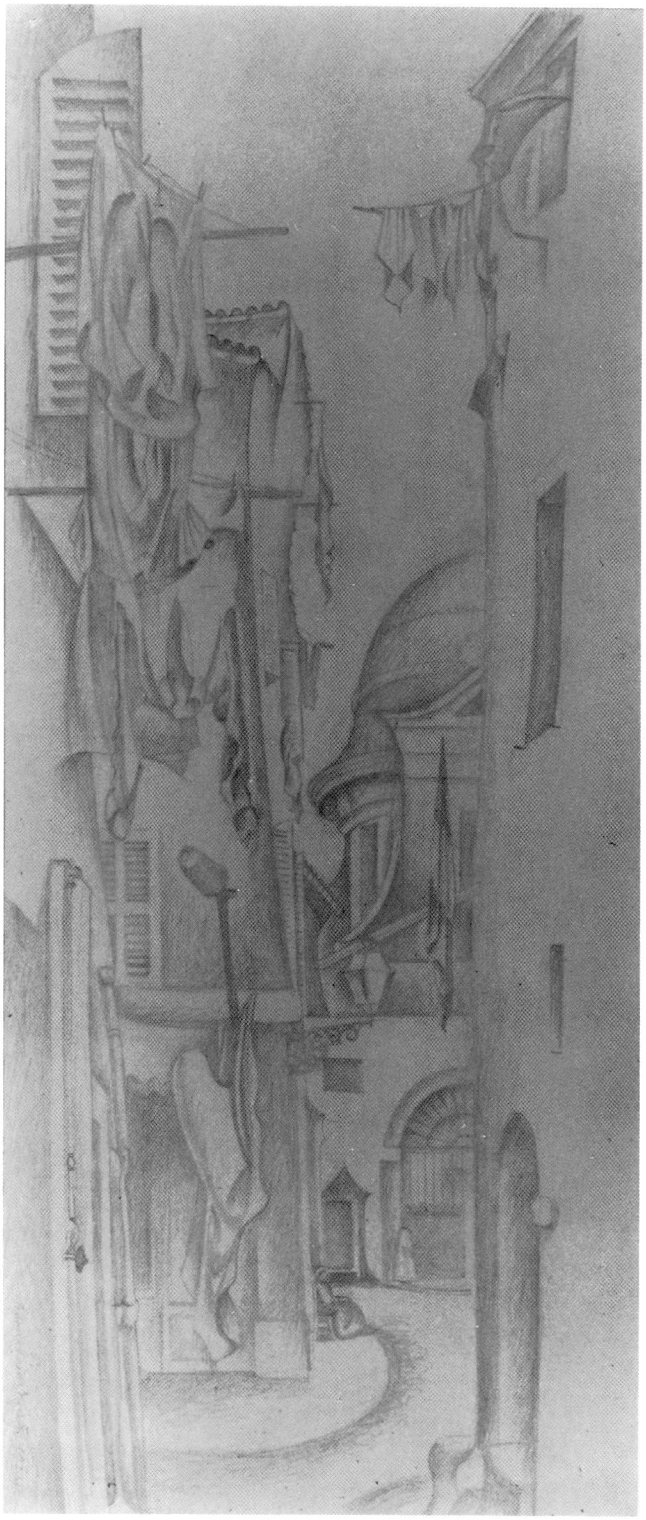

86. *Hospice de la Charité, Marseilles* 1924

Bertram's correct insistence that technically Wadworth was not a romantic was necessary, because he knew that the interpretation he was putting on Wadsworth's subject matter was indeed romantic. The allusion to the idea of the present constriction and possible escape derives historically from a picture like Caspar David Friedrich's 'Woman at the Window' 1822, in which a figure is seen gazing through the closed window of a room at the mast and rigging of a boat floating by on the river that must exist below the wall of the house. The theme of enclosure and longing for release underlines several Pre-Raphaelite paintings and was a particular preoccupation of the Italian Metaphysical painter Giorgio de Chirico whose designs of lonely shrouded figures in shadowed piazzas sometimes have boats sailing across the back. De Chirico, it has always been agreed, was an important influence on Wadsworth's painting later, in 1928-9, as he was on that of Nash and several other English artists. The harbour scenes of Wadsworth, almost certainly made before he was familiar with de Chirico's painting, help explain what it was about de Chirico that English artists were to find so interesting.

Wadsworth's connection with the Quattrocento has been insisted on but the mood of his painting is post-Romantic. The fresco cycles he admired in Italy were didactic narratives in which precise definition of space through accurate perspective helped to give an even tenor to the telling of the story. In post-Romantic art, whether it is Pre-Raphaelitism or Wadsworth's, space is liable to become dislocated, disrupting the spectator's normal perception of an object with the result that an object or part of a picture can acquire an independence from the viewer, a life of its own. This is what had been happening gradually in Wadsworth's painting in the course of the twenties and the process became acute in the 'metaphysical' phase in 1928-9, when still life objects diverged so far from normal proportions and relationships that they became independent events with only tenuous links to the spectator's normal frame of reference.

Notes

1. 'A World Art and Tradition', *Drawing and Design*, February 1929.
2. *Times*, 10 January 1920, *Sunday Times*, 11 January 1920, *Observer*, 18 January 1920.
3. *Times Literary Supplement*, 30 September 1930.
4. *Westminster Gazette*, 27 January 1920.
5. *Joseph Pennell's Pictures of War Work in England ...*, London and Philadelphia, 1917. *Joseph Pennell's Pictures of War Work in America ...*, Philadelphia 1918.
6. *New Statesman*, 9 October 1920.
7. *Daily Herald*, 15 January 1920. Unsigned, but possibly R H Wilenski who sometimes reviewed there.
8. For the project in general see especially, Michael Sadler, *Michael Ernest Sadler: a Memoir by his Son*, London 1949 pp.319-27; also William Rothenstein, *Men and Memories. Recollections of William Rothenstein 1900-1920*, London 1932, p.348.
9. Reported in the *Yorkshire Post*, 12 November 1920.
10. Letter from Wadsworth and Albert Rutherston, *Yorkshire Observer*, 25 November 1920.
11. John Ruskin, *The Harbours of England, with Thirteen Illustrations by J. M. W. Turner, RA*, George Allen, 1856. Report in the *Pall Mall Gazette*, April 1923.
12. Fry's article was first published in New York in the *Dial* and republished the same year in *Transformations*, London 1926.
13. *Sunday Times* and *Observer*, both 7 November 1926.
14. *Times*, 1 November 1926, *Referee*, 7 November 1926, *London Mercury*, December 1926, *Apollo*, December 1926.
15. New Statesman, 1 November 1926.

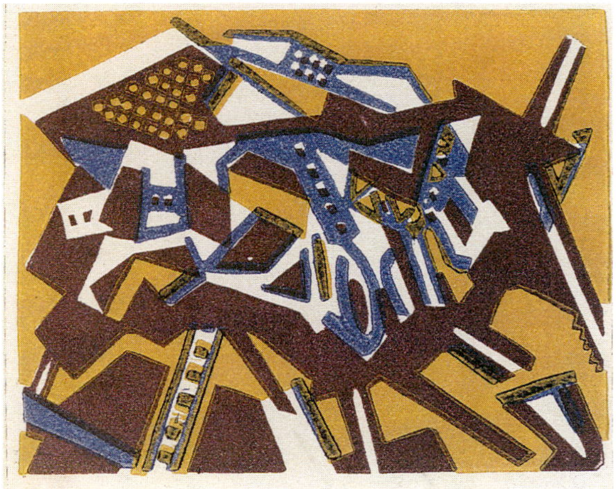

18

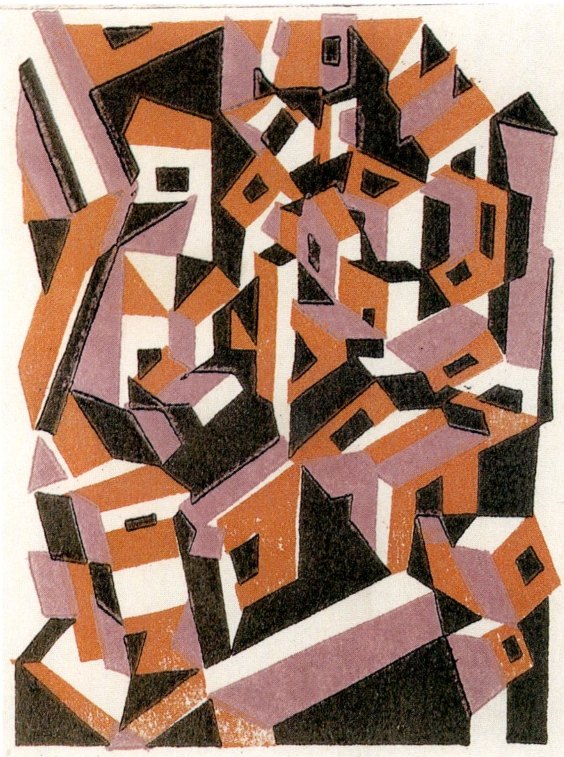

29

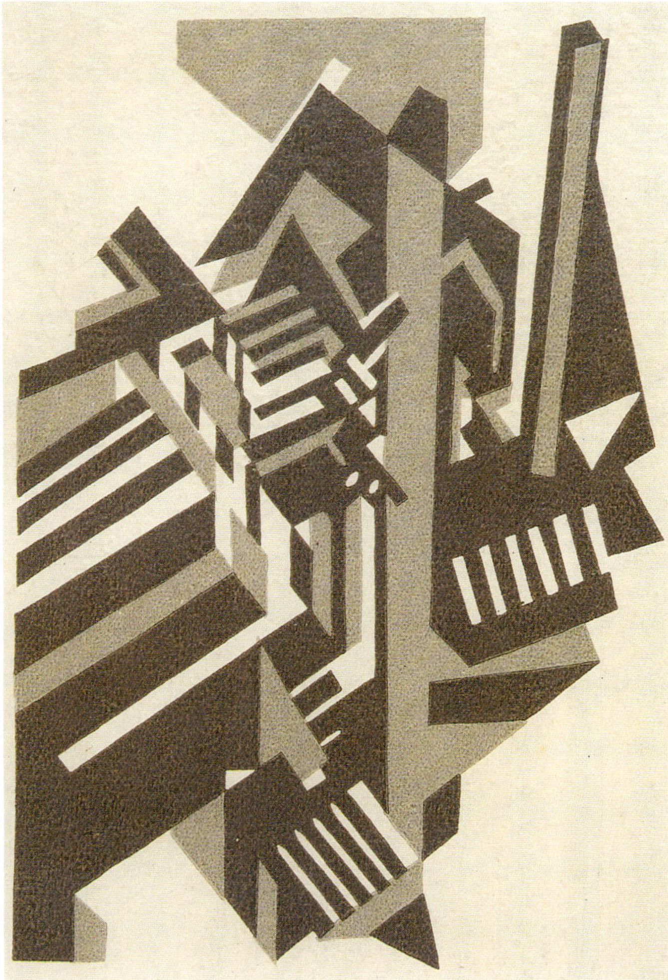

15

18. Landscape 1914-15
29. Riponelli: *A Village in Lemnos* (state f) 1917
15. Bradford: *View of a Town* 1914 (state a)

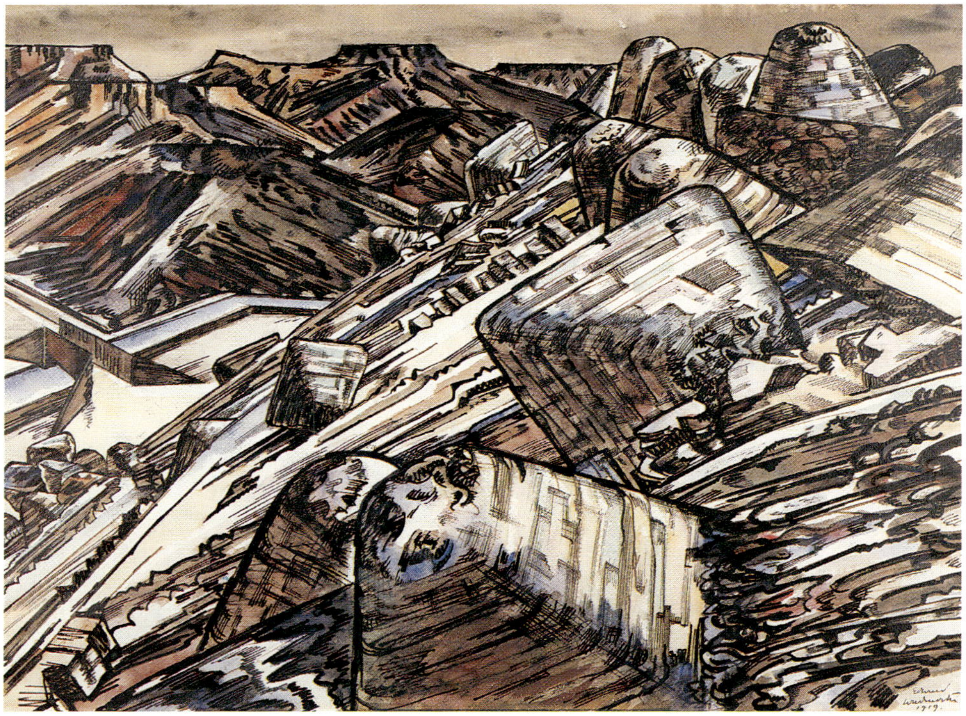

55

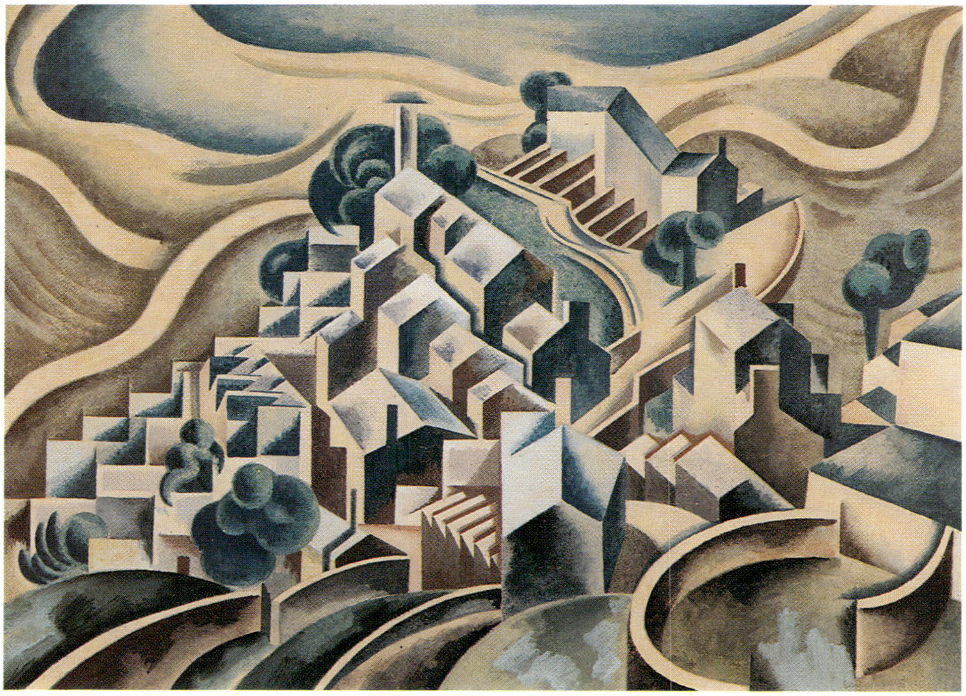

75

55. Ladle Slag, Old Hill 2 1919
75. Fortune's Well, Portland 1921
78. Broadbottom, near Glossop 1922
79. Near Marseilles 1922

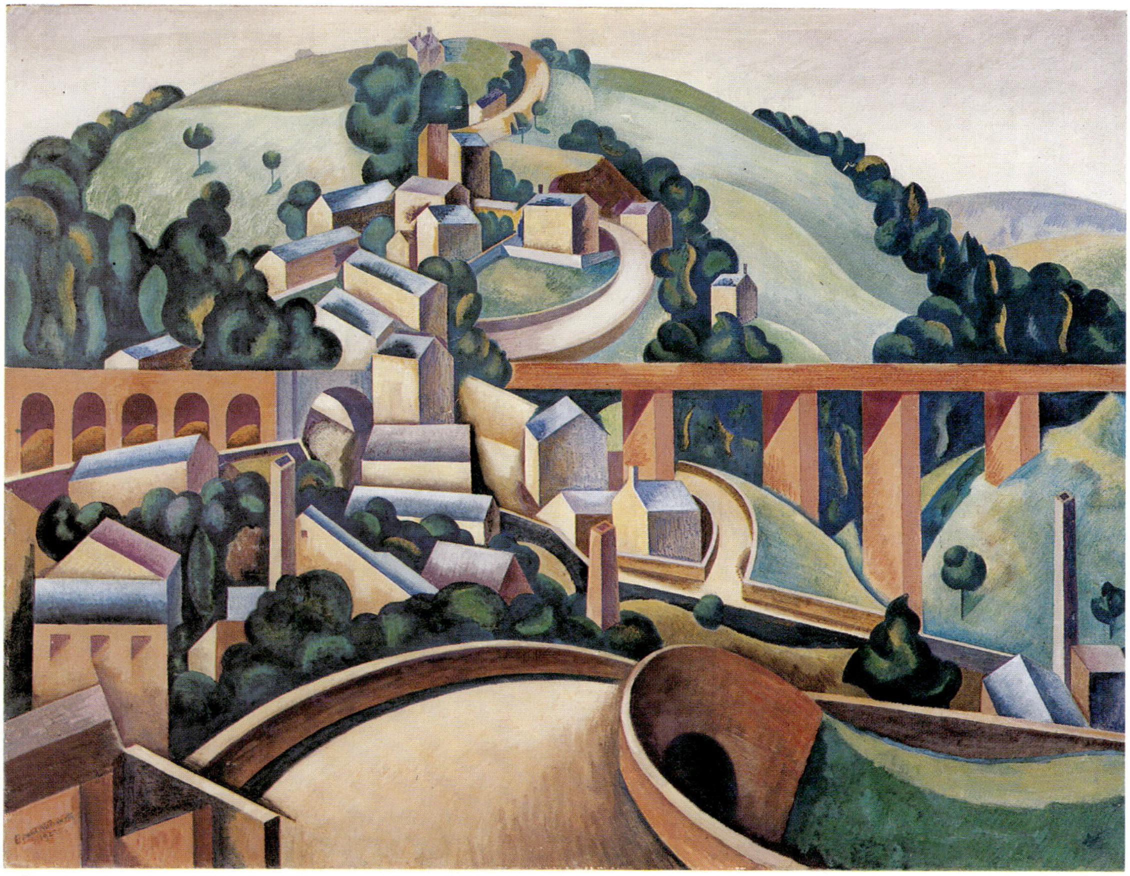
78

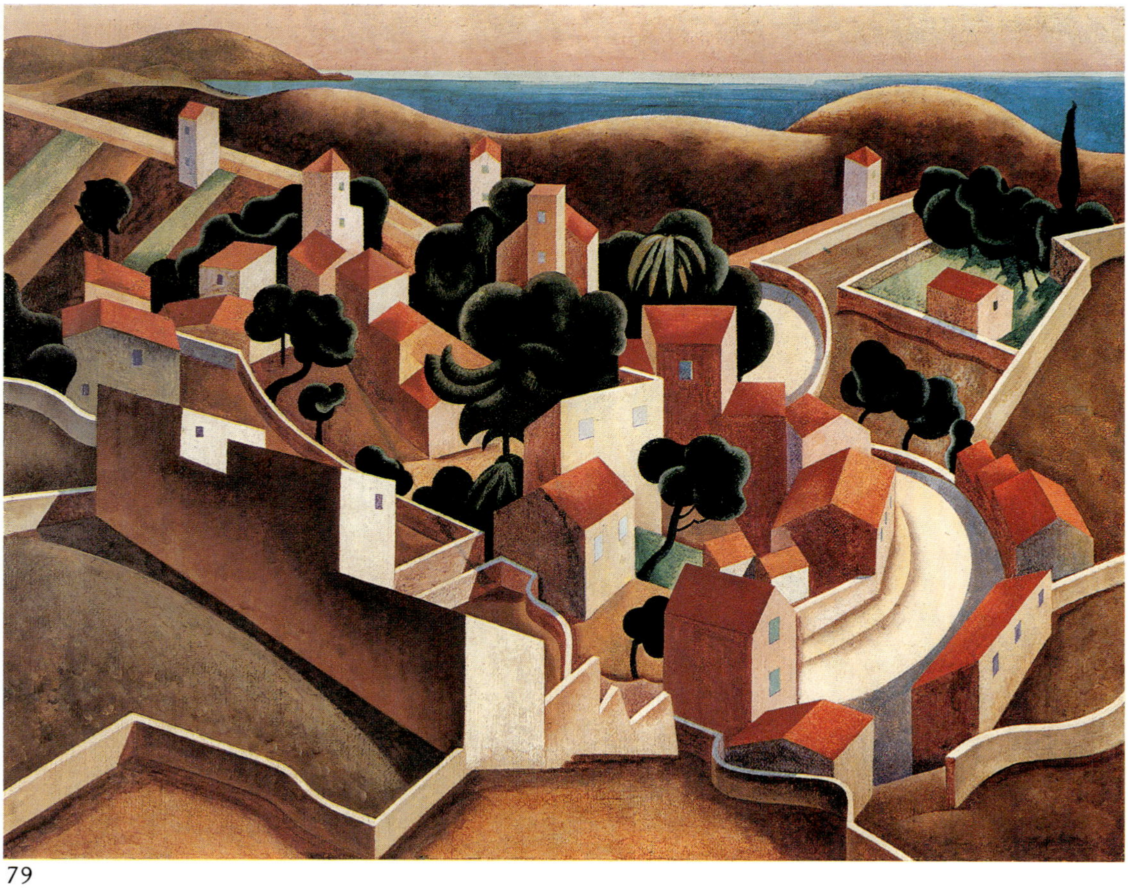
79

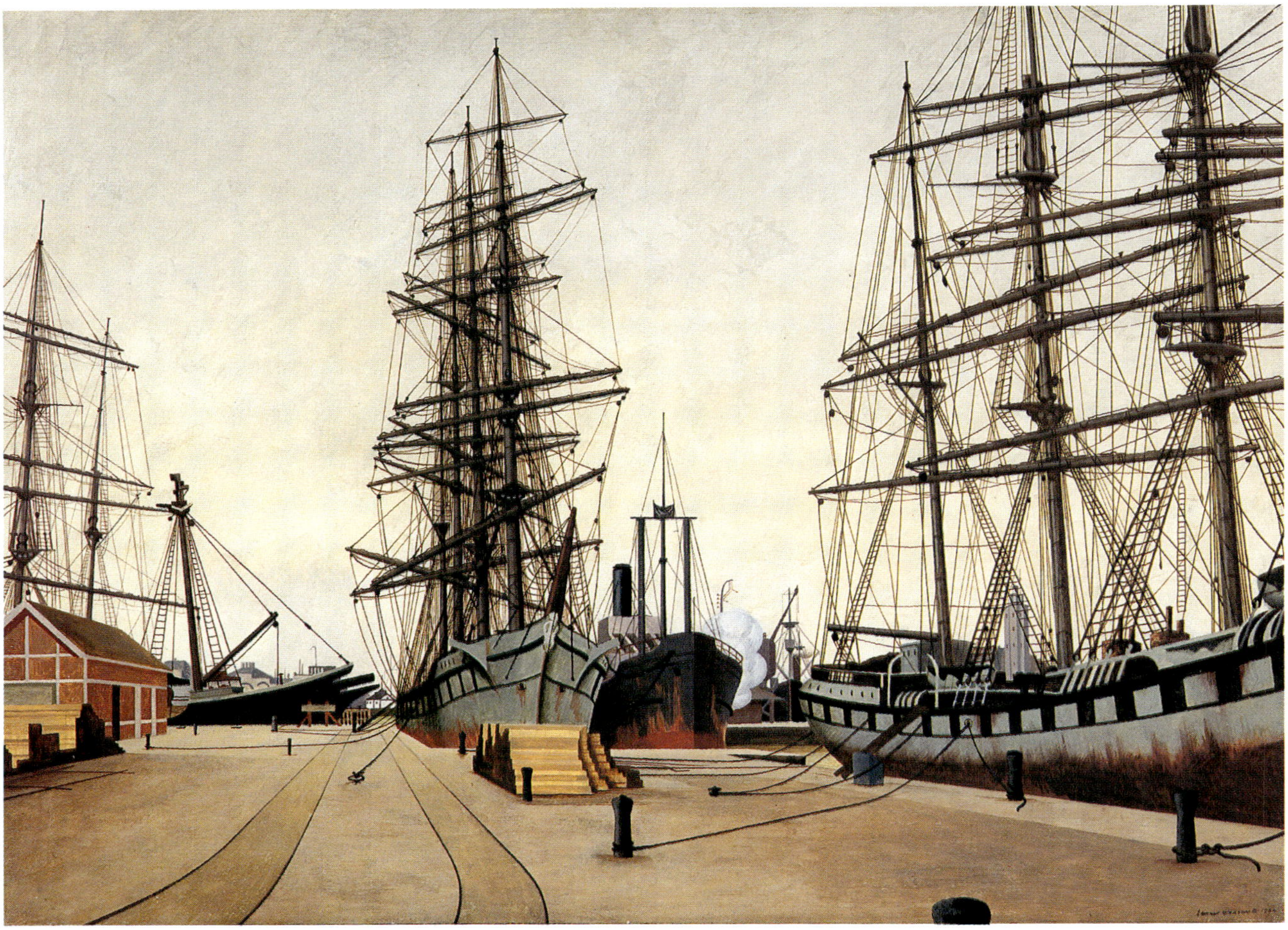

83

83. Dunkerque (1) 1924
80. The Cattewater, Plymouth Sound 1923
81. La Rochelle (1) 1923

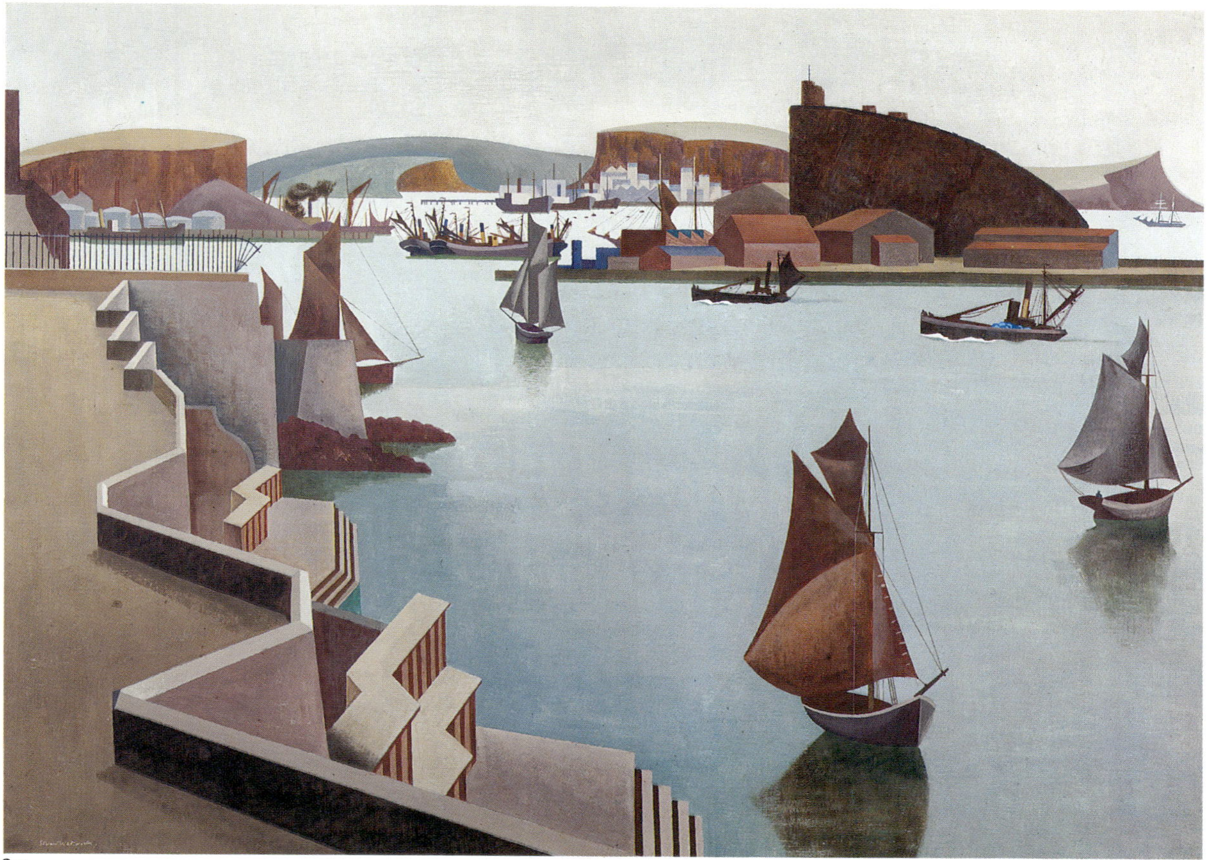

80

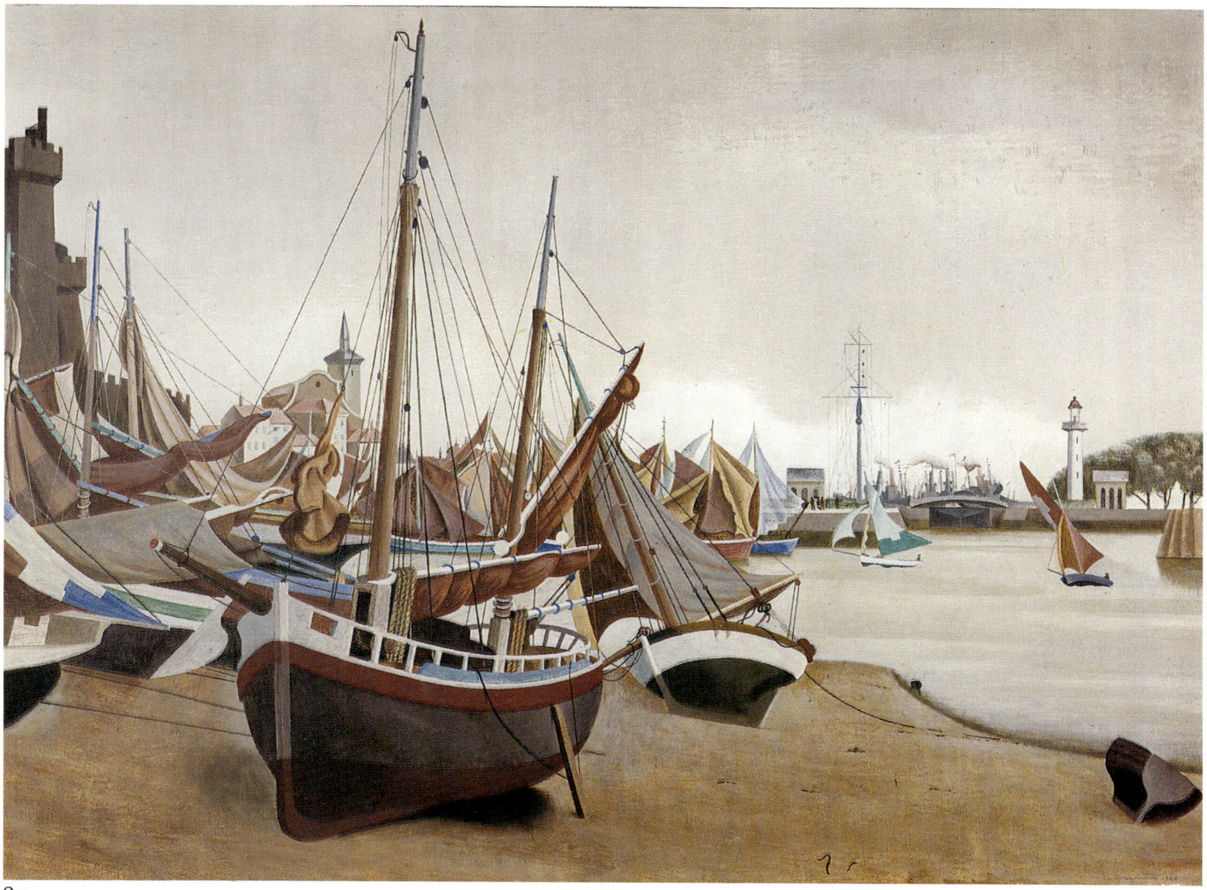

81

93. Coquillages 1926
94a. North Sea 1928

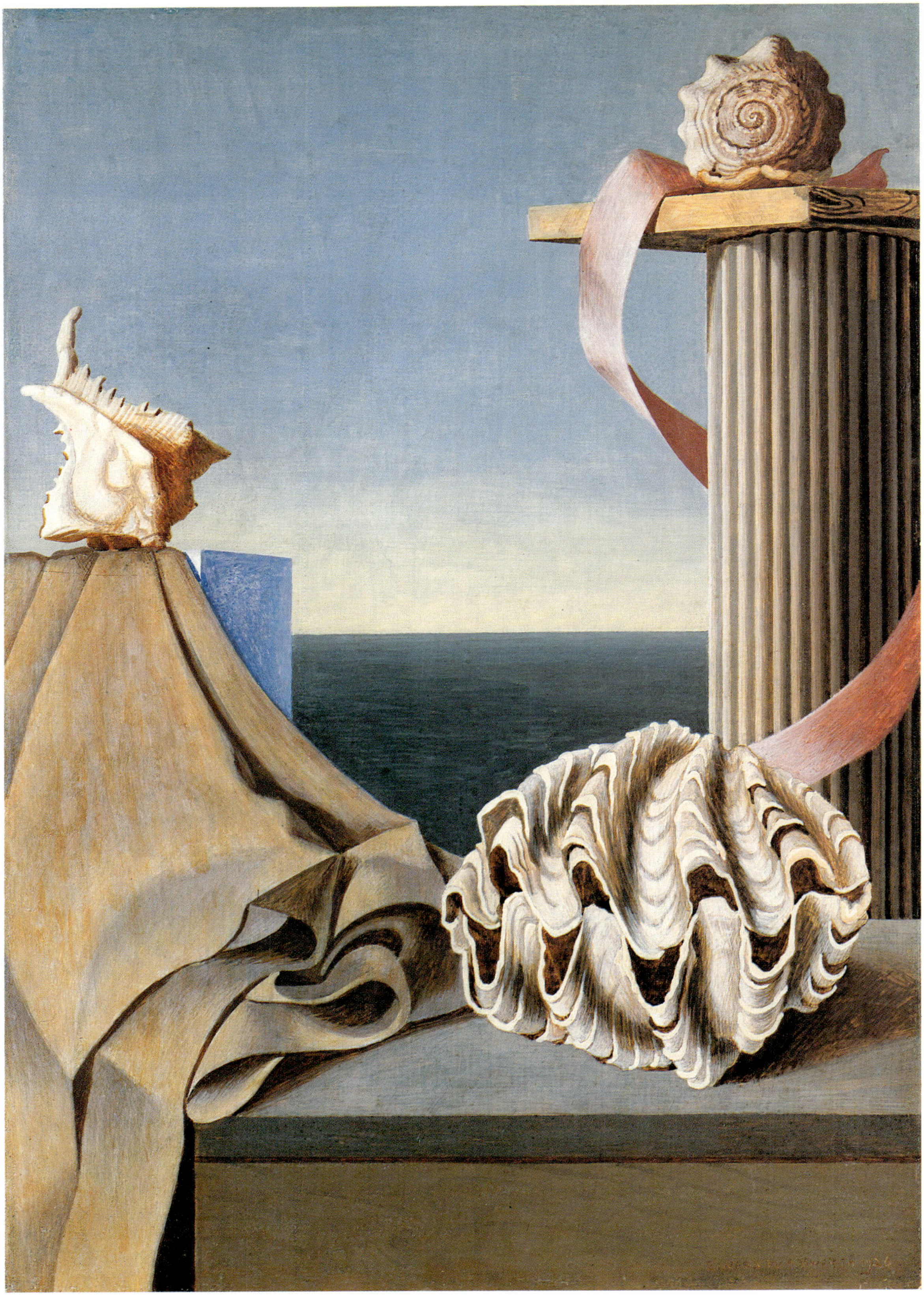

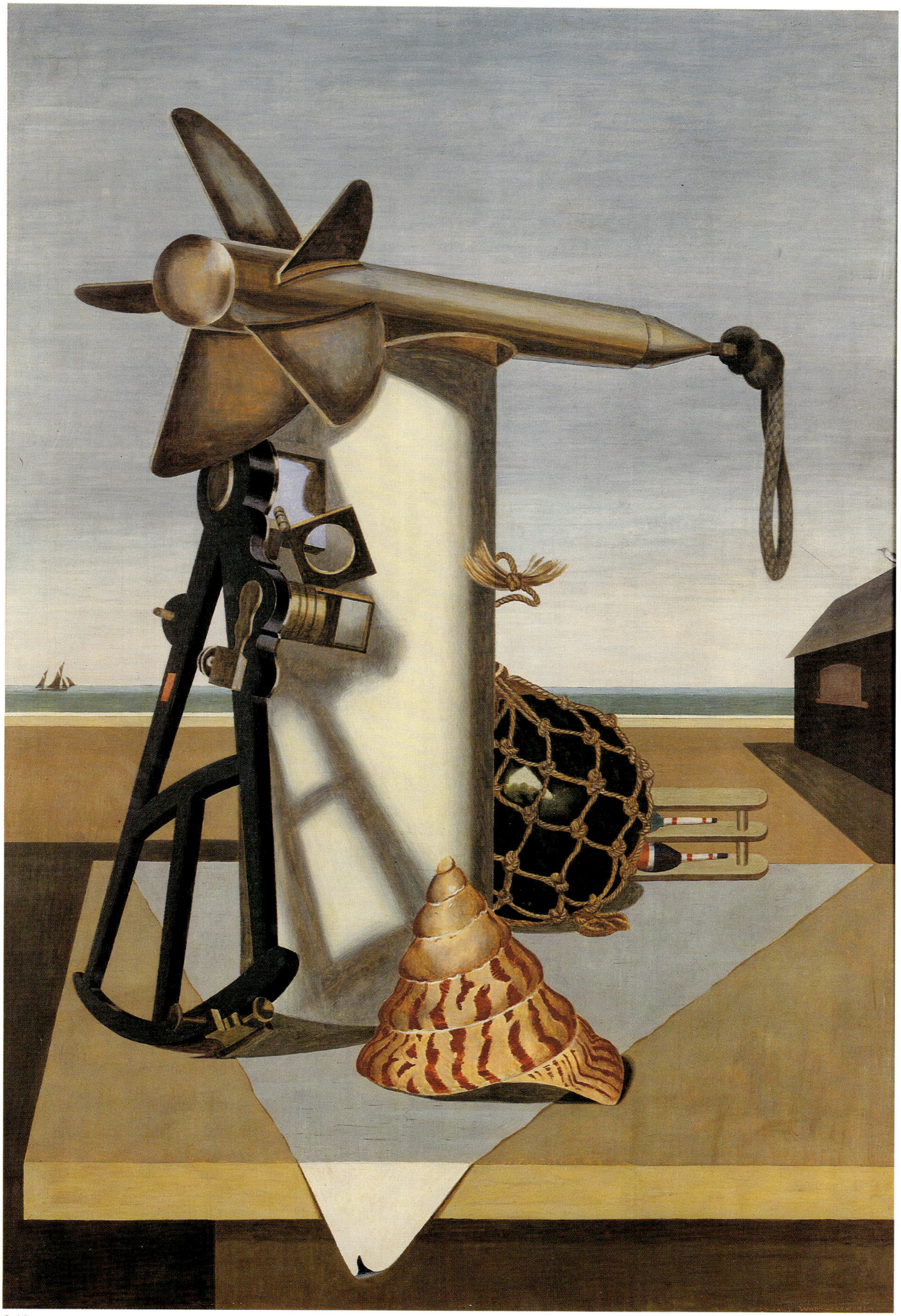

94a

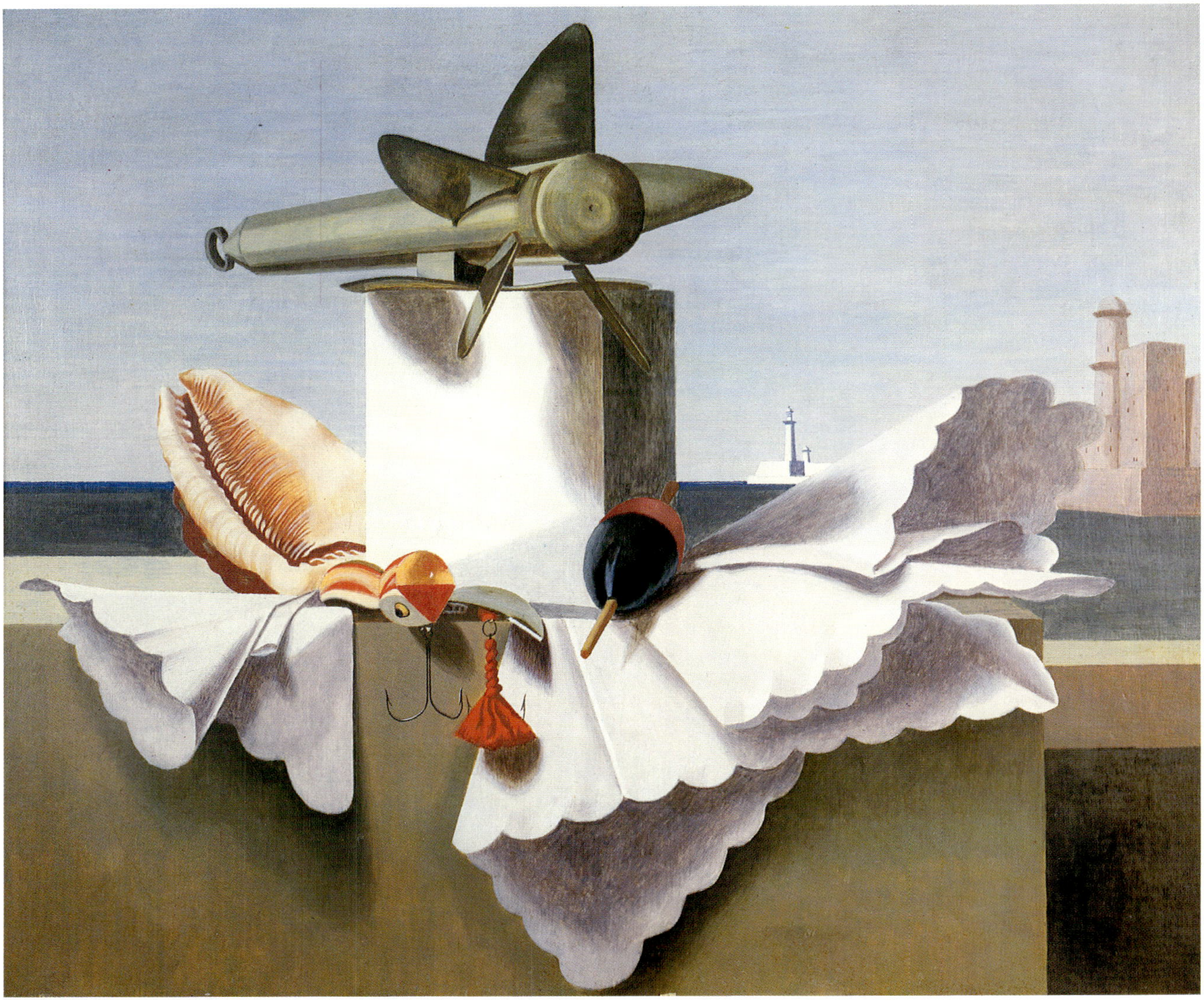

98

98. *Wings of the Morning* 1928–9
96. *Regalia* 1928
97. *Bright Intervals/Song of the Sea* 1928

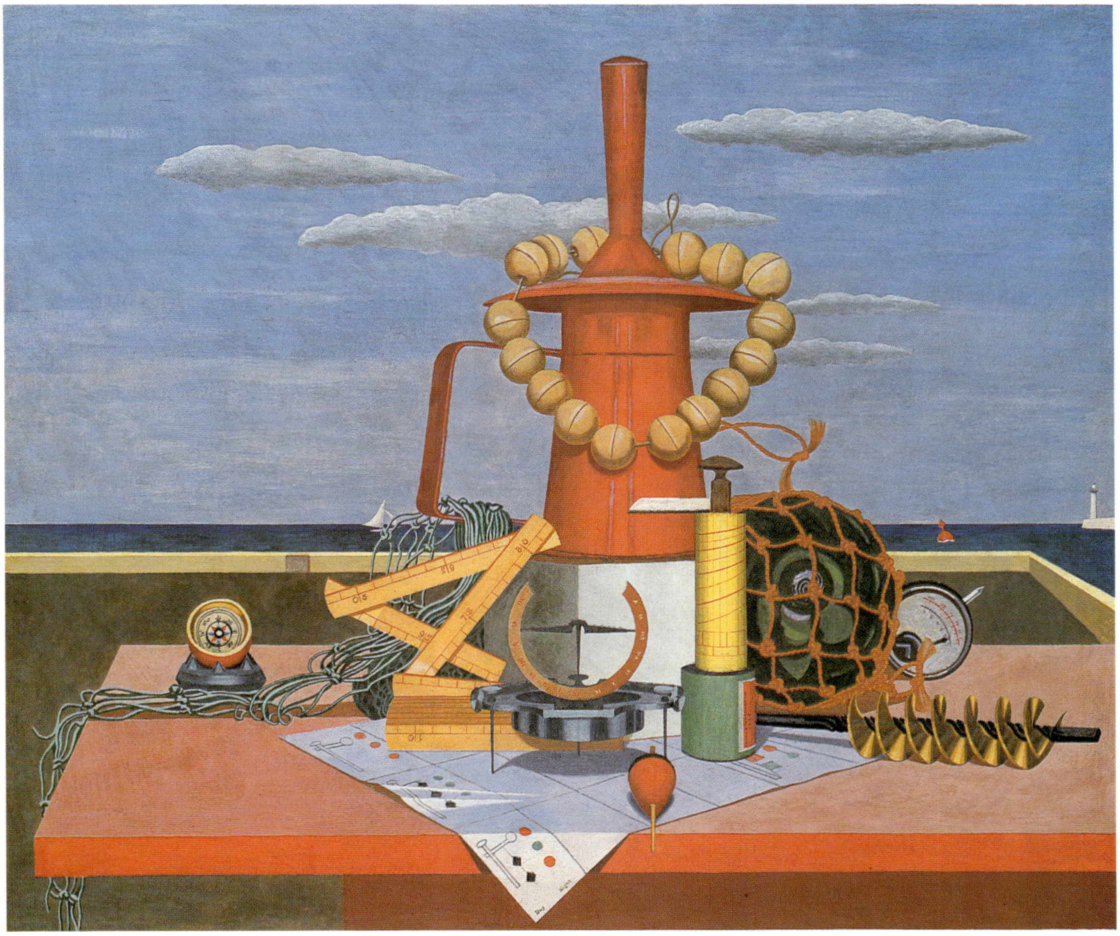

96

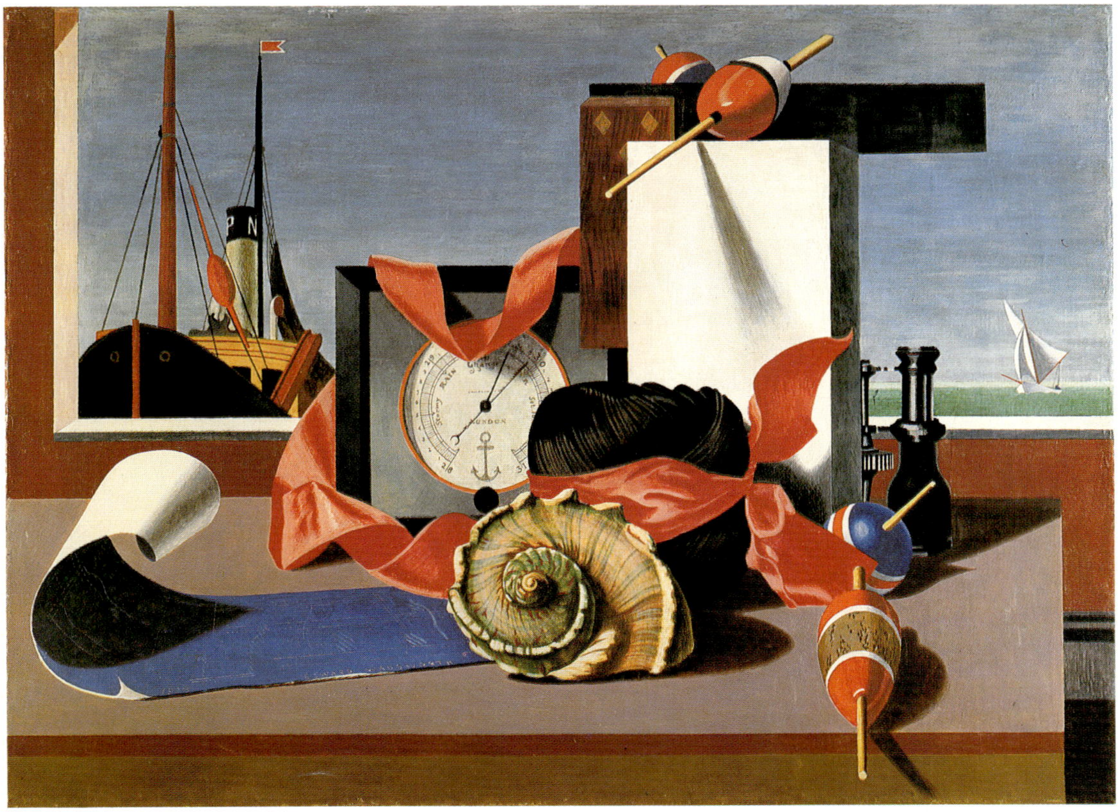

97

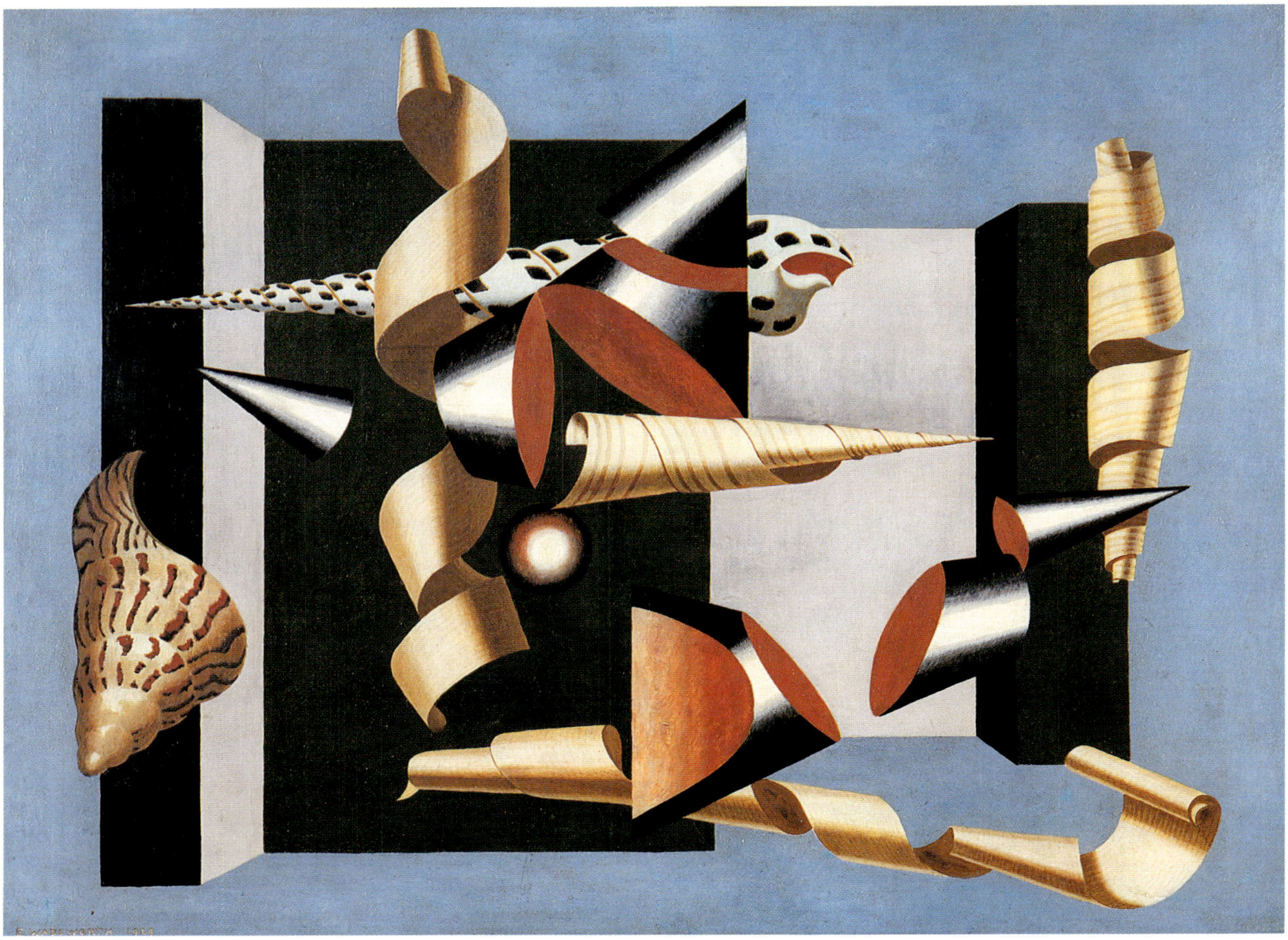

101

101. *Composition, Cones and Spirals* 1929

103. *Composition, Screwhead, Gauges and Bevel Protractor* 1930

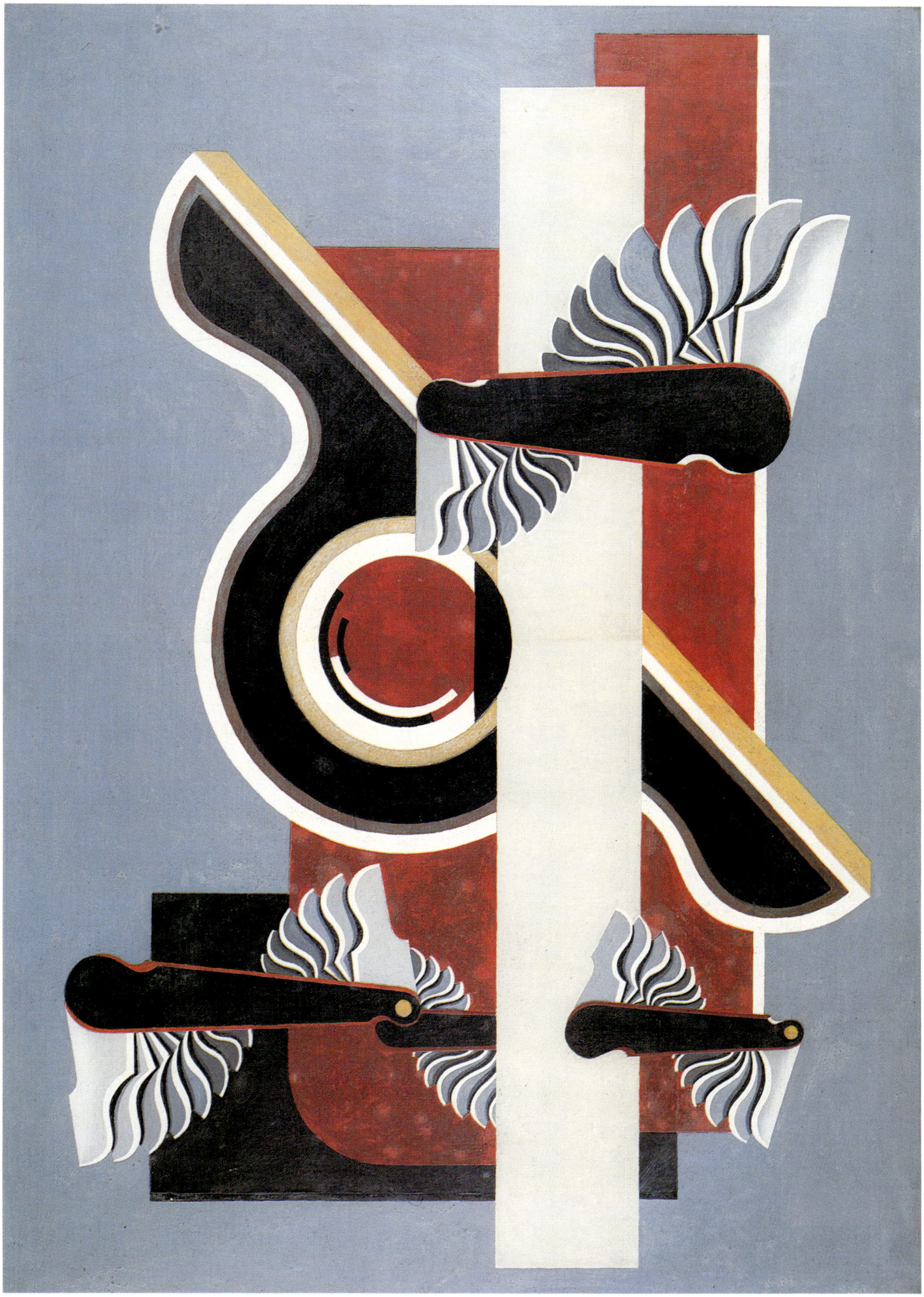

103

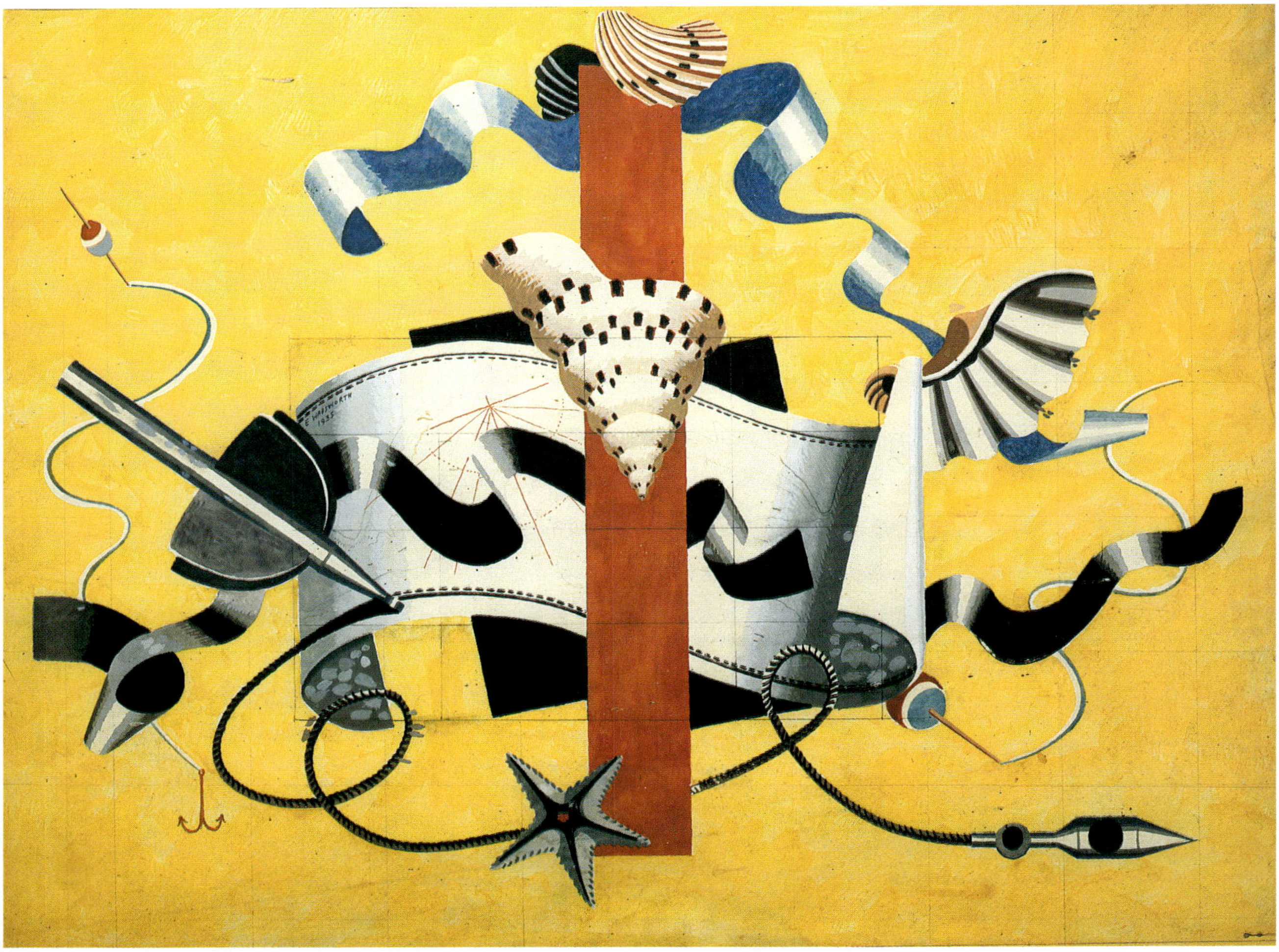

117

117. Study. Sketch for Proposed Design for Bexhill Pavilion 1935

112. The English Channel 1934

120. The Beached Margin 1937

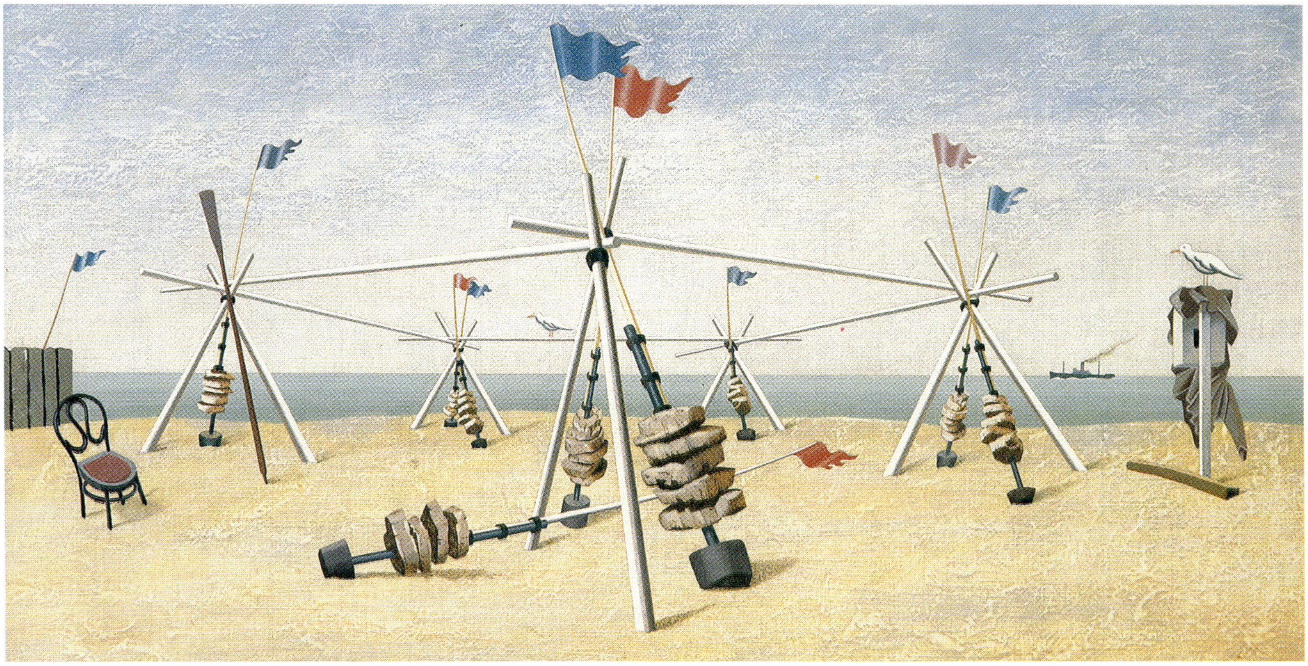

112

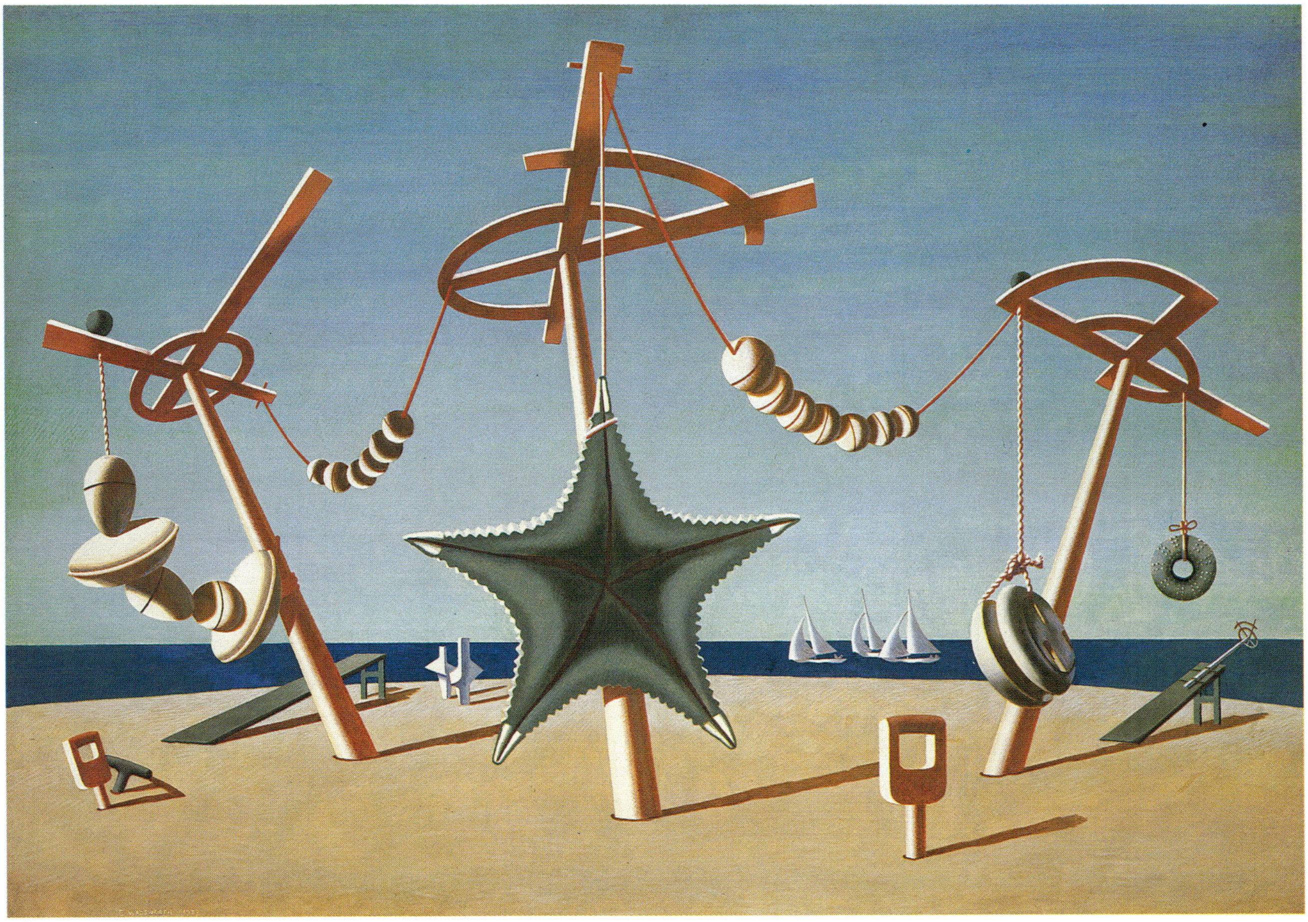

120

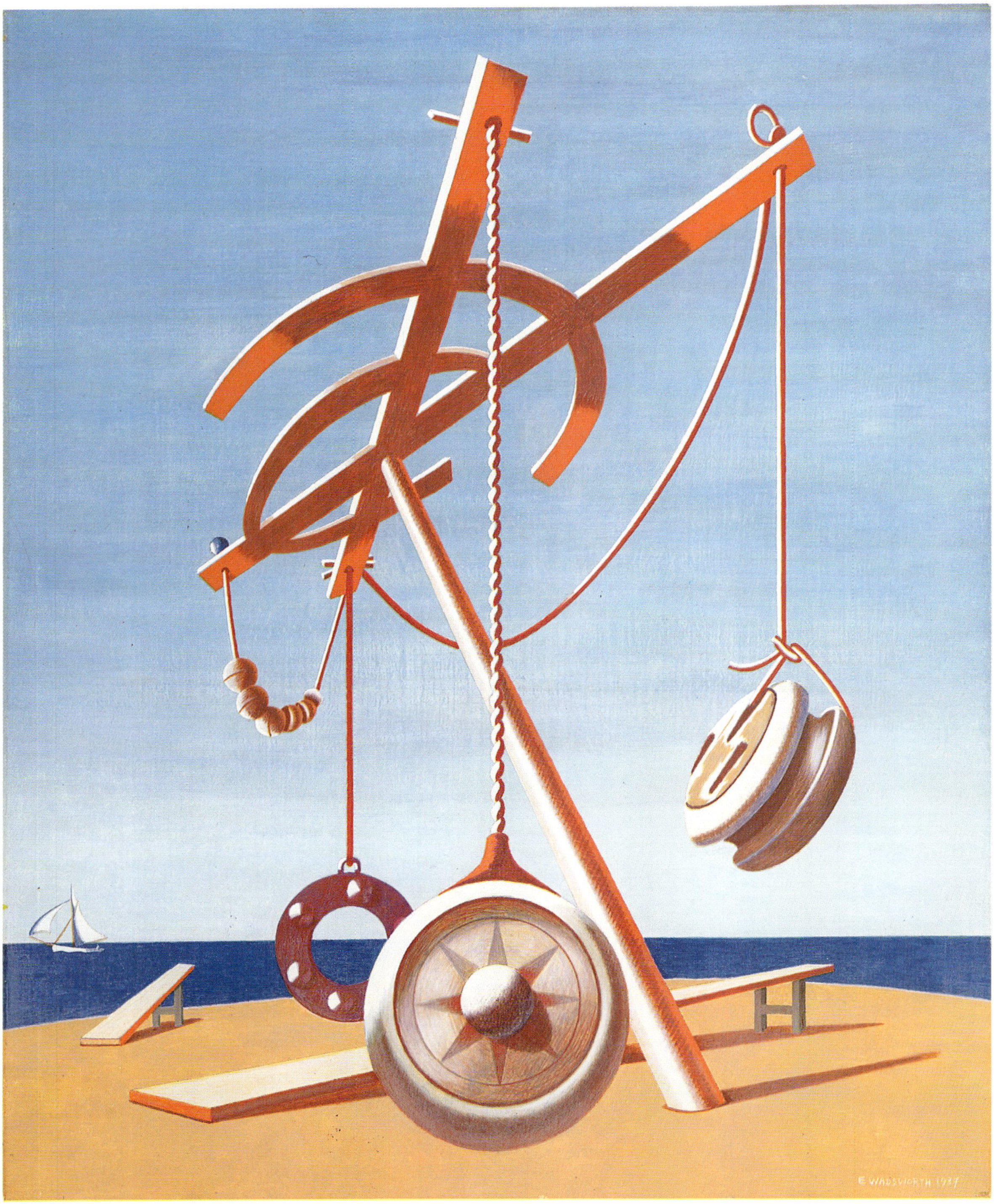

121

121. Souvenir of Fiumicino 1937
122. The First of the Ebb 1938

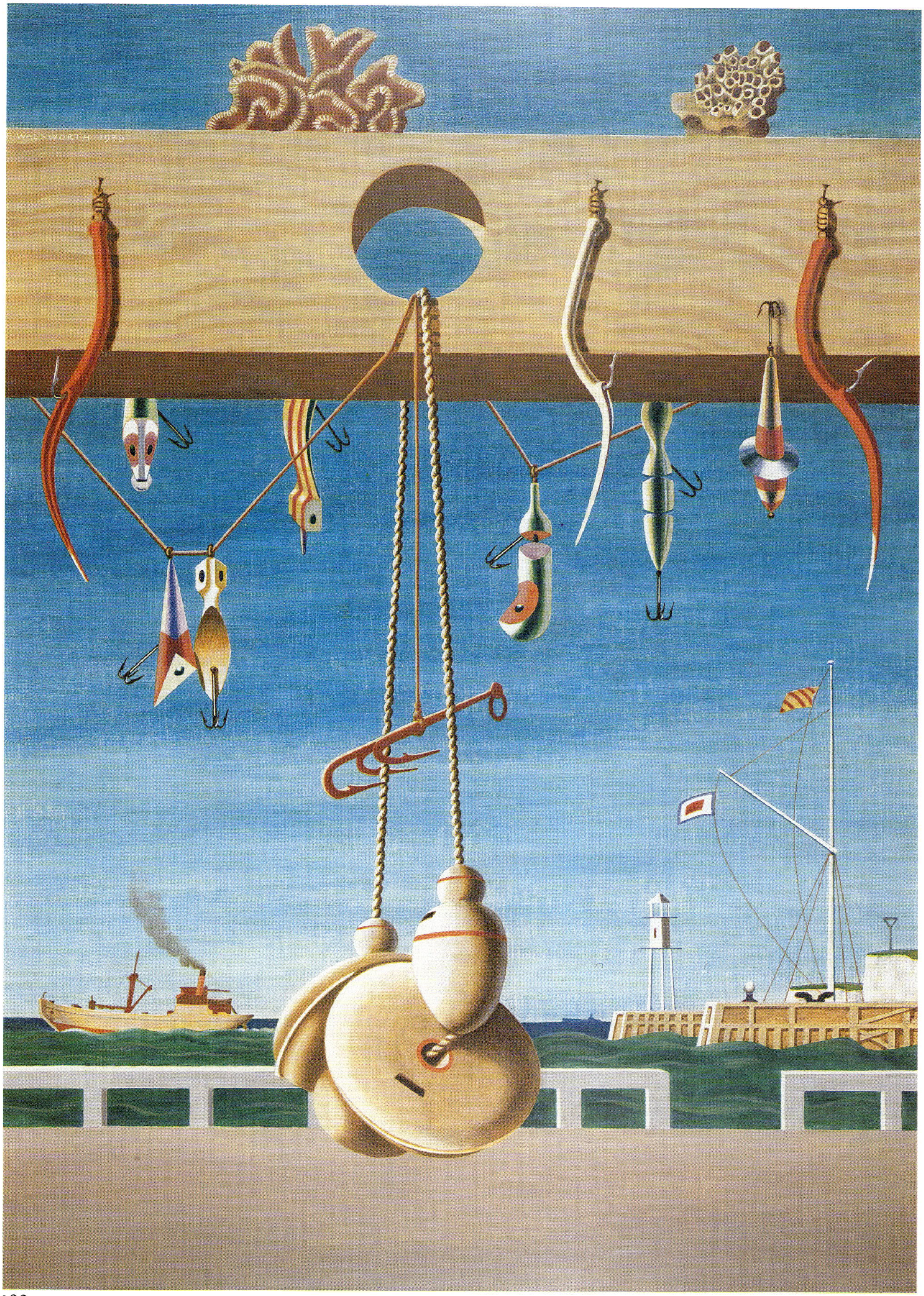
E. WADSWORTH 1938

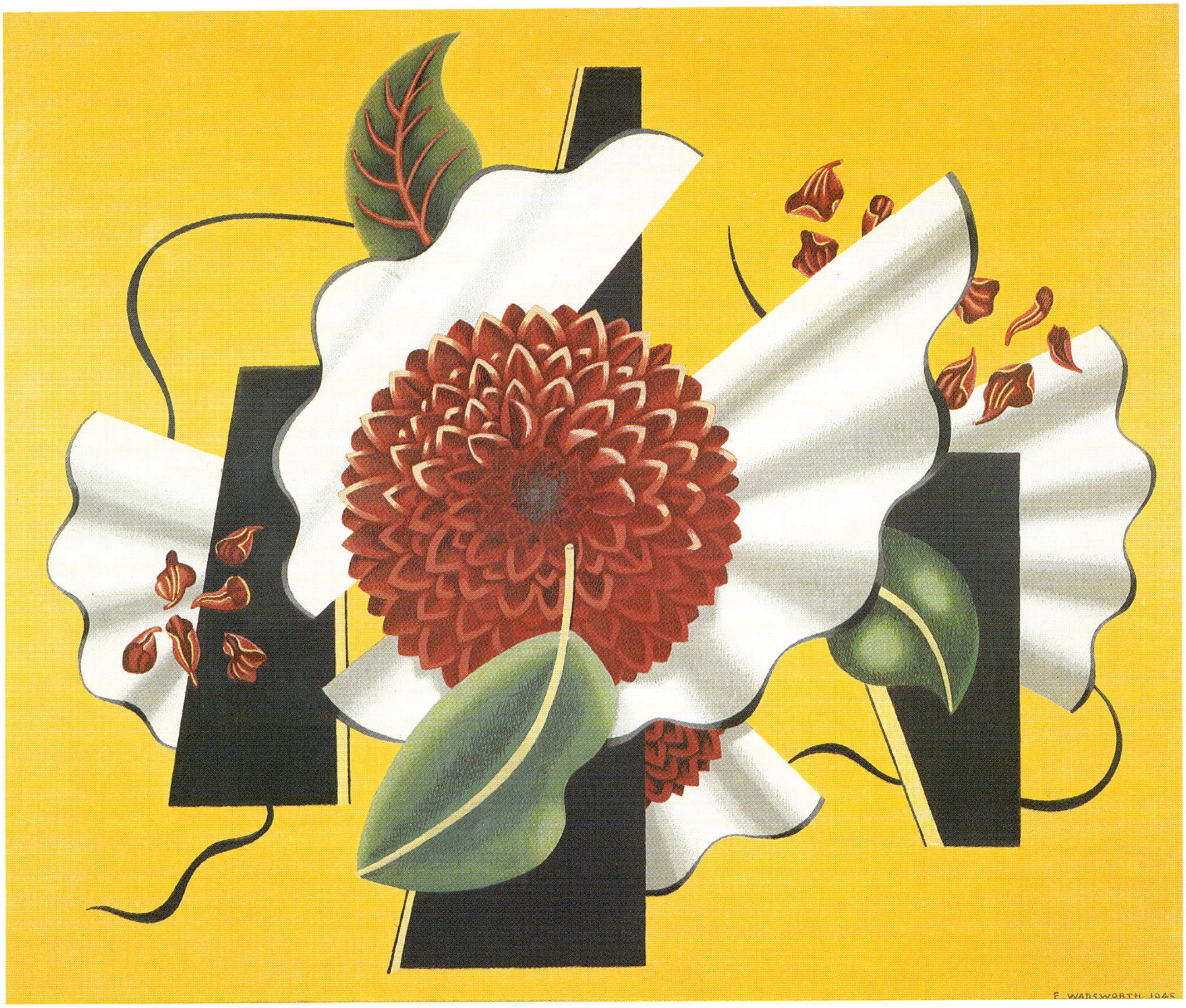

138. Button Dahlia/Flowerpiece 1945

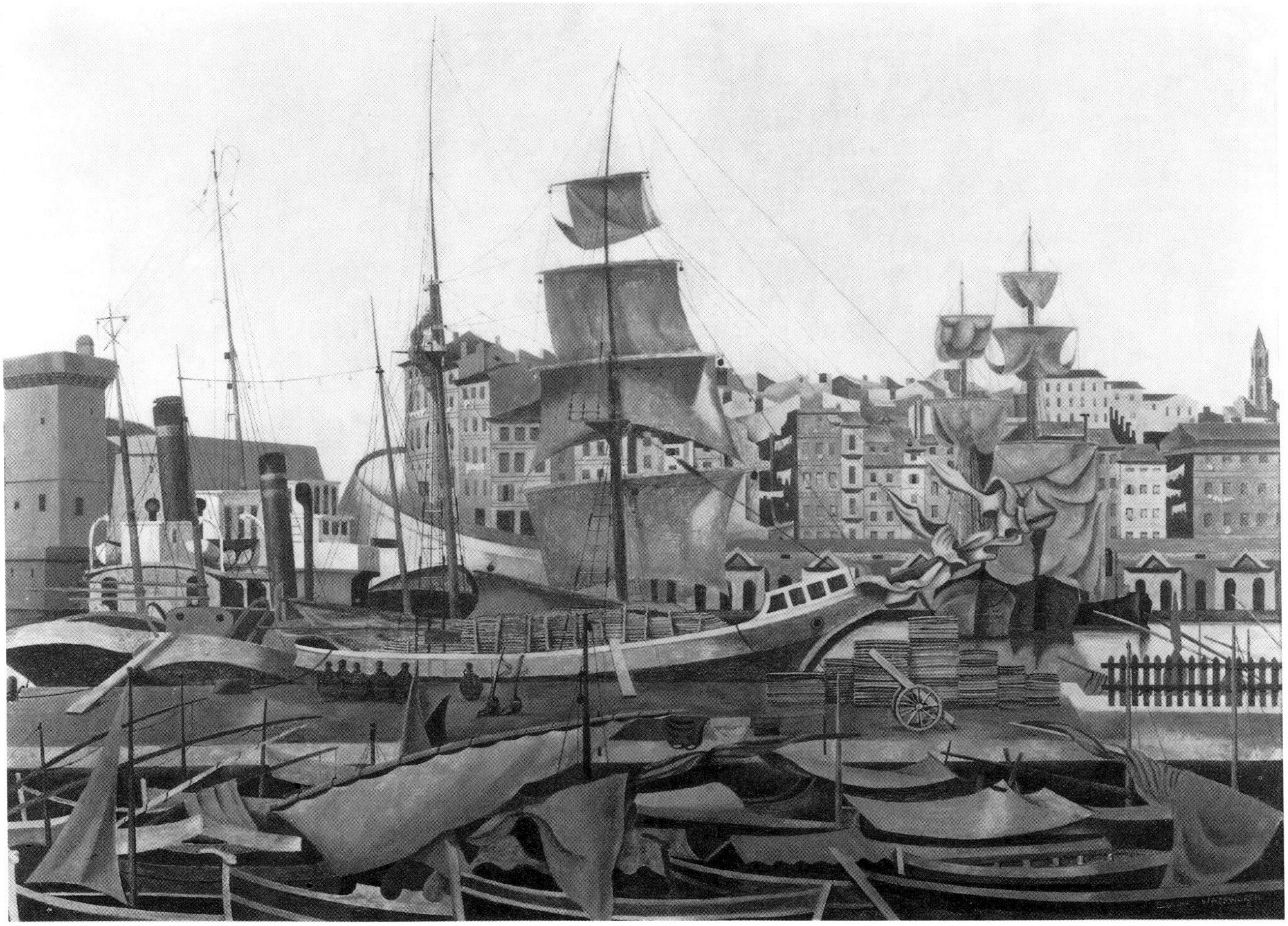

84. Quai du Port, Marseilles 1924

Jeremy Lewison

The Marine Still Lifes and Later Nautical Paintings

All I can say ... is that Wadsworth was an important artist: that as much as Old Crome was a genius of agricultural England, Wadsworth was a genius of industrial England (deflected, so I think, into nautical channels).
Wyndham Lewis.[1]

The sea is a point of consistency in Wadsworth's œuvre which outwardly appears to embrace a succession of different interests and styles. As early as 1918, when he was working on dazzle-camouflage for ships in Bristol and Liverpool, Wadsworth began to combine his passion for ships with a sense of the power of the object in a series of prints, and one large painting, in which the dramatic viewpoint was a principal device. This characteristic was to become of primary importance in the marine still lifes of the twenties, about which Lewis appears to have been somewhat disparaging, but which are now considered to have been of central importance to English modernism.

While some of the dazzle-ship works anticipate the marine still lifes in their adoption of a startling viewpoint and in the isolation of the object (the ship in the dry dock), the still lifes themselves developed fairly logically out of the sea and harbour scenes of the early and mid twenties. The first marine subjects such as 'The Cattewater, Plymouth Sound' 1923
Colour p.53
(80) represent distant views of ships and boats at sea organised within a linear structure of piers, jetties and promenades. In the early twenties Wadsworth appeared to have little interest in still life but, within one year, he started to bring the motif closer to the picture plane. Boats are piled up in a manner reminiscent of the compositional organisation of still lifes, with masts and boats at different angles, old-style rigged ships contrasting with tug boats, small fishing boats juxtaposed with ocean-going cargo ships. As Wadsworth moves closer to his subject, the details of port life become more important and he begins to incorporate still life elements. Thus in 'St Tropez (4)' 1925[2] two different anchors face each other in the middleground, with the bow of a sailing ship at the quayside to the left and a two-masted schooner approaching the port in the background. The painting is given a theatrical air by a folded sail or tarpaulin, situated on the picture plane, which occupies the entire height of the painting on the right and functions in the same way as drapery in Baroque portraits, softening the severity of the scene. In 'Quai du Port Marseilles' (84) of the same year, the dockside is occupied by trollies, containers, gangplanks and barrows, among other items, indicating future or past human activity. It becomes immediately apparent that Wadsworth's scenes are unpeopled and depersonalised, suggesting a sense of calm and detachment; the drama arises out of the compositional configuration. Even when he portrays boats at sea they appear to sail themselves or drift along in a crewless state like an unminded machine.

Other paintings of 1925 show a more marked interest in objects, for example 'Tarpaulins' (89), which depicts a heap of tarpaulins on the quayside behind which can be seen the masts, rigging, funnels and flags of a number of ships at rest. A crow bar, rope, table and crate form the still life elements in the foreground. Wadsworth's interest in materials such as tarpaulins and sails was extended to his paintings of the streets of Marseilles where sheets hang like theatre flaps, as well as like flags, waiting to be lowered and raised (see fig.17). Such paintings recall Monet's 'Rue Montorgeuil Decked Out with Flags' 1878 although the manner of depiction is entirely different.

The theatrical nature of Wadsworth's port scenes of 1925 and 1926 is a feature often remarked upon. 'St Tropez (1)' 1926 (89a) closely resembles a stage viewed from the front stalls. The scene is framed by a curtain-like sail or an awning held aloft by a rope. While the earlier port scenes appear to be relatively naturalistic, even if Wadsworth did make adjustments and additions to suit the composition of his paintings, a work such as 'St Tropez (1)' looks deliberately contrived. However, the view is probably that of a customer seated in a quayside café in the old port.

'St Tropez (1)' is additionally of interest for its emphasis on still life elements which now occupy the foreground of the painting, relegating the ship to a central but retiring position. Clearly by 1926 quayside objects were beginning to be Wadsworth's primary interest. As in the port scenes, this painting contrasts harsh rectilinearity with soft curvilinearity and the organic with the mechanical, juxtapositions which Wadsworth was to employ with great effect in the still lifes of the next two years.

His first marine still lifes depicted sea shells, some combined with classical columns, others with drapery or ribbons. Other props included plaster busts or fragments of ancient artefacts which were not necessarily associated with the sea. It was Wadsworth's practice to set up his compositions in the studio (fig.18) and to paint in front of the motif. To this end,

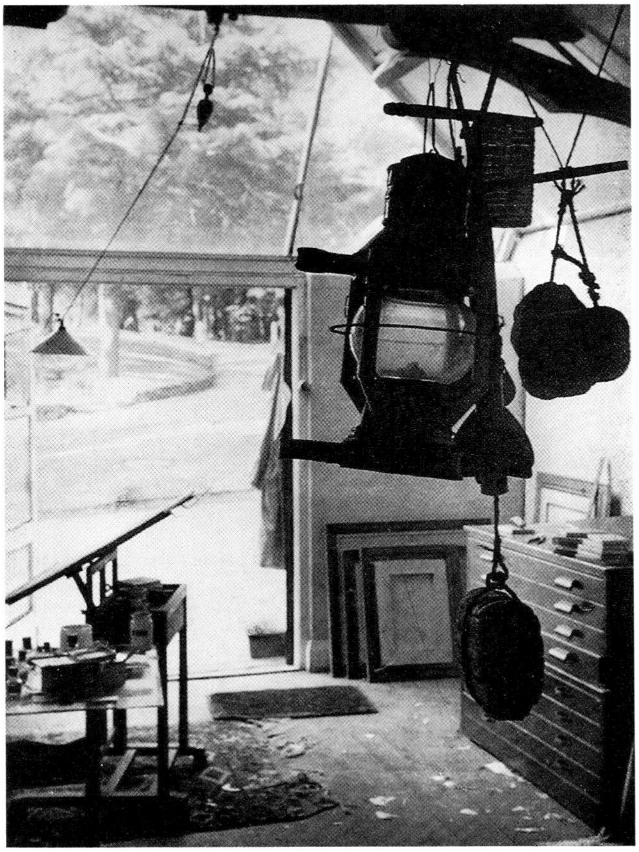

Fig. 18 Wadsworth's studio c. 1934 from *Unit One*

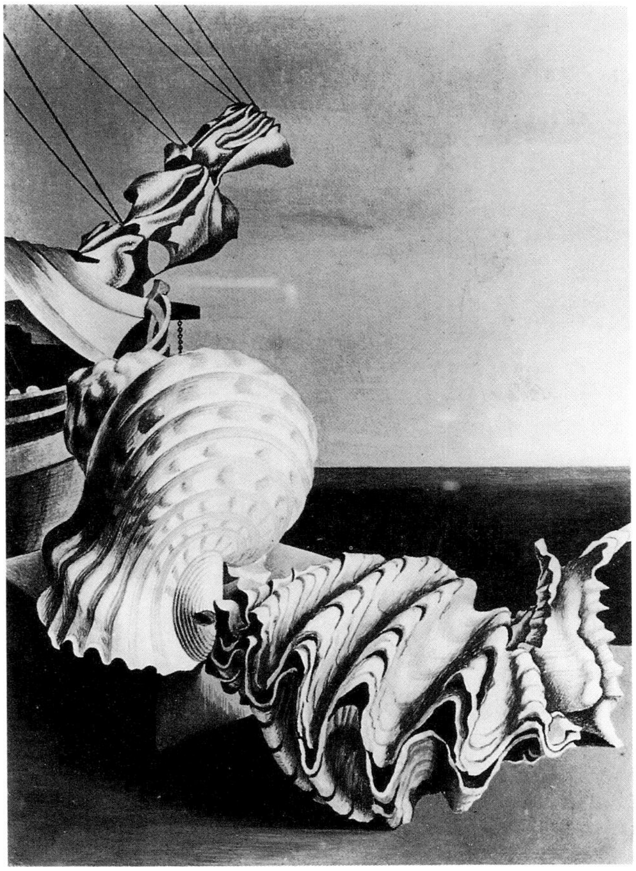

Fig. 19 *Conche and Bowsprit/Blue Horizon/Shells* 1926 (W/A 82), tempera, 53.3 × 38.1, private collection

he had a collection of maritime equipment, both old and new, as well as a plaster cast of a classical head. Only the seascapes in the background were imaginary.

The use of spiralling ribbons, sashes, drapery and cascading shells, as in 'Conche and Bowsprit' 1927 (fig. 19) or 'Coquillages' 1927 (93), is redolent of Rococo art which was enjoying a revival in England at the time. As Richard Morphet has pointed out,[3] this revival in contemporary painting was spearheaded by Rex Whistler. Whistler was close to the Sitwells – Osbert Sitwell had written the introduction to the catalogue of Wadsworth's exhibition at the Leicester Galleries in 1926 – who commissioned from Severini a sequence of frescos for their Tuscan castle depicting Commedia dell'Arte figures and formalised, lucid still-lifes of fruit and guitars. In addition, Rococo painting and nineteenth-century Rococo-influenced painting was prominently featured in magazines such as the *Connoisseur* in the mid twenties, which suggests that it was fashionable among collectors at this time.[4]

Colour p. 54

If the still lifes of the mid twenties have a Rococo character they also have a strong classicising tendency and in this regard relate closely to the works of Picasso and de Chirico. 'Fruits de Mer'[5] in the Stedelijk Museum, Amsterdam is Chiricoesque with its background of rectangular buildings and cylindrical lighthouse, its deep recessive space and its apparently casual arrangement of still life objects on a table in the foreground. The column which supports one of the four shells is the kind of prop frequently found in de Chirico's paintings and in Surrealist painting which, like Wadsworth's, laid particular emphasis on the isolation and aggrandisement of the object. It was also a device used in the display of consumer items in shop windows and in publicity photographs.[6]

The title itself may represent something of an homage to de Chirico whose 'Les Fruits de Poète', itself a marine still life, was reproduced in the *Bulletin de l'effort moderne* in October 1925, a magazine to which Wadsworth subscribed from

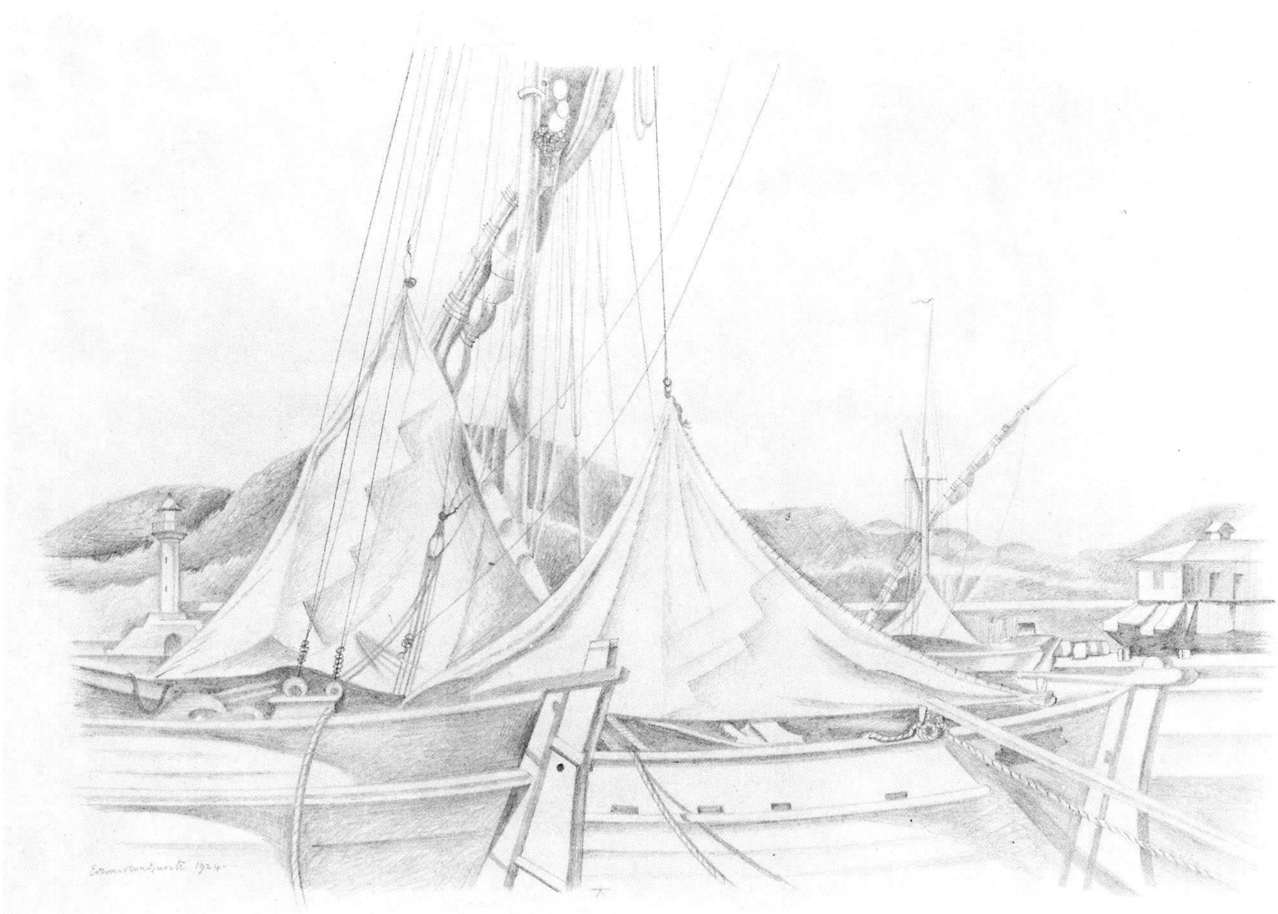

88. Study of Boats, St Tropez 1924

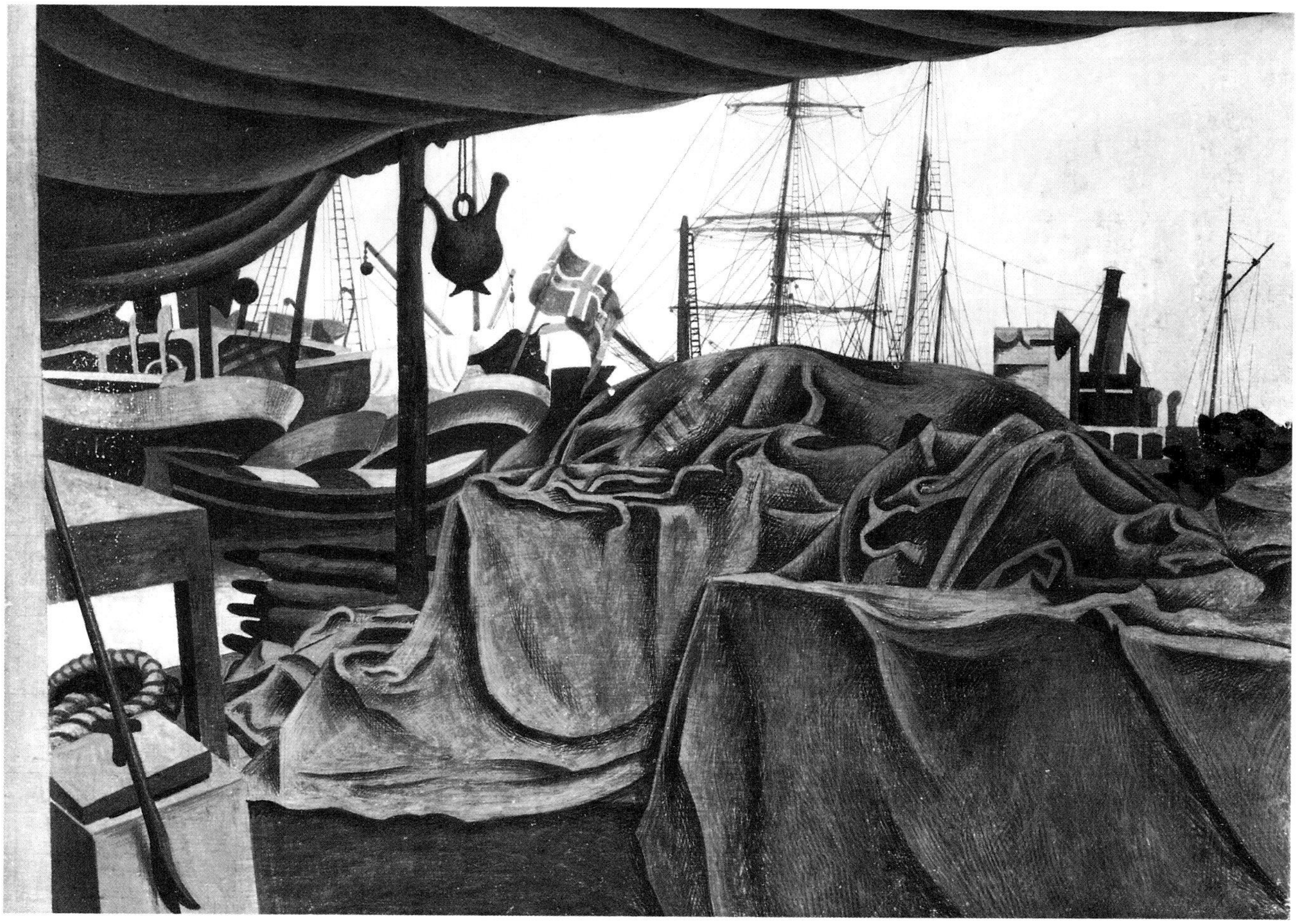

89. *Tarpaulins* 1925

January 1924 until December 1927. From the evidence of this and other paintings, Wadsworth was not interested in any one particular period of de Chirico's work but was stimulated by the whole range, including the most recent. De Chirico, who was also a practitioner of tempera painting, first exhibited in London in 1925 at the Lefevre Gallery in a show devoted to modern Italian art and contributed to an exhibition in Brighton in 1926. In May 1925 he held a one-man exhibition at Léonce Rosenberg's Galerie de l'effort moderne in Paris, and again in January 1928. His first one-man show in London was in October–November 1928 at Arthur Tooth and Sons, which by that time was representing Wadsworth. Although Wadsworth would have known de Chirico's work in reproduction, as well as through exhibitions, he was unlikely to have met him before 1927 when Wadsworth entered Rosenberg's circle (he was corresponding with de Chirico by June 1928 on the subject of tempera painting). It was in 1927 that Wadsworth's 'Coast Guards' was reproduced in Rosenberg's *Bulletin de l'effort moderne*.

In addition to some of the props which Wadsworth employed and his use of deep recessive space, another Chiricoesque feature of his paintings was the exaggerated size of the motif when viewed from close up. The depiction of still life objects (particularly modern ones) at close range was favoured by Jean Metzinger, Pierre Roy and Auguste Herbin as well as by de Chirico, all of whom were regularly featured in the *Bulletin*, for it endowed the objects with a Surrealistic quality making them seem larger than they were. While there is no suggestion that Wadsworth was a Surrealist he undoubtedly delighted in the metamorphic quality of the object when seen on a large scale and out of context, as was partially anticipated in the dazzle-ship works. Indeed many of the objects in the marine still lifes of 1926 and 1927 have anthropomorphic qualities, which did not go unnoticed by Waldemar George in his article published in the issue of *Sélection – Chronique de la vie artistique* devoted to Wadsworth in 1933:

> These objects exchange words. They act like actors in a drama. Talking objects, they force the attention of the spectator-medium, who is subjected to their strange spell and who participates visually in the dramatic action of which they are emblems.
>
> This passage from one state to another, this discovery of the lost paradise of composition, this tendency to make things speak, while waiting to make beings speak, reveals a latent wish to find again the sense of spiritual values and human values. Anthropomorphism is not a religion or a philosophy which belongs to ancient history. It is a vision of the world which in every way conforms to the great constants of occidental man.[7]

In the best of Wadsworth's still lifes the objects transcend their static nature and are animated by his dramatic sense of composition. This is particularly true of the works of 1928 such as 'Wings of the Morning' (98), Colour p.56 in which a ship's log[8] hovers over the composition while beneath it a table-cloth flutters like a butterfly. Wadsworth's ability to render a heavy object weightless by raising it is a device he used on a number of occasions, not only in 'Wings of the Morning' and 'North Sea' (94a), Colour p.55 but also in the works of the late thirties when he would suspend objects on ropes (see fig.18). The suspended object and the object displayed on a plinth are also commonly found in Surrealist painting, for example in Magritte's 'Menacing Weather' 1928 (itself a Wadsworthian title) where a chair, a tuba and a torso float in the sky above a rocky coast, or in the later 'Mountain Lake' 1937 by Dalí in which a telephone receiver is supported on a crutch. Other works by Wadsworth of the late twenties, however, are more static, emphasising the inert nature of the objects, for example 'Marine' (100) where the log lies on the table like a dead weight.

The contrast in the relative weights, textures and forms is one to which Wadsworth paid great attention. Thus in 'North Sea' we find steel juxtaposed with shell, glass, rope and cord, while in 'Wings of the Morning' steel is combined with shell, cloth, a delicate tassel and a fishing hook. Wadsworth appears to have been interested in arousing the tactile senses in a manner not unlike Dutch seventeenth-century still life. In 'Regalia' (96) Colour p.57 there is a distinct emphasis on sharp objects – the auger, the inclining sundial with needle-like feet and arrow-shaped indicators, the pointed fishing float which confronts the spectator in a slightly threatening manner – all of which endow the painting with an air of unease.

'Regalia' is one of Wadsworth's most imposing still lifes. Painted in 1928, it is one of the few compositions to include exclusively mechanical objects most of which are instruments of measurement. While many of them would still have been in current use, the two sundials were made no later than in the eighteenth century. It is probably no coincidence that the instruments depicted closely resemble the emblems and insignia of a king or queen which are used at coronations, for whatever the literal meaning of the painting, its title suggests a metaphoric value. For example, the glass fishing float relates to the orb, the auger to the sceptre, the surveyor's chain to the royal chain and the inclining sundial to the spurs. Although there is no evidence that Wadsworth intended such a close correspondence when titling the painting, there can be no doubt but that he paid great attention to his titles since they were so often changed in his lifetime. 'Lamentations' 1928 (fig.20) is clearly so named because of the 'weeping' flasks; in addition the flowers have a commemorative air and the moon is a waning crescent. In the previous seven years Wadsworth had experienced the loss of his father, his daughter Anne, an uncle, an aunt and his step-mother. In addition his cousin Norman Wallis, designer of the first

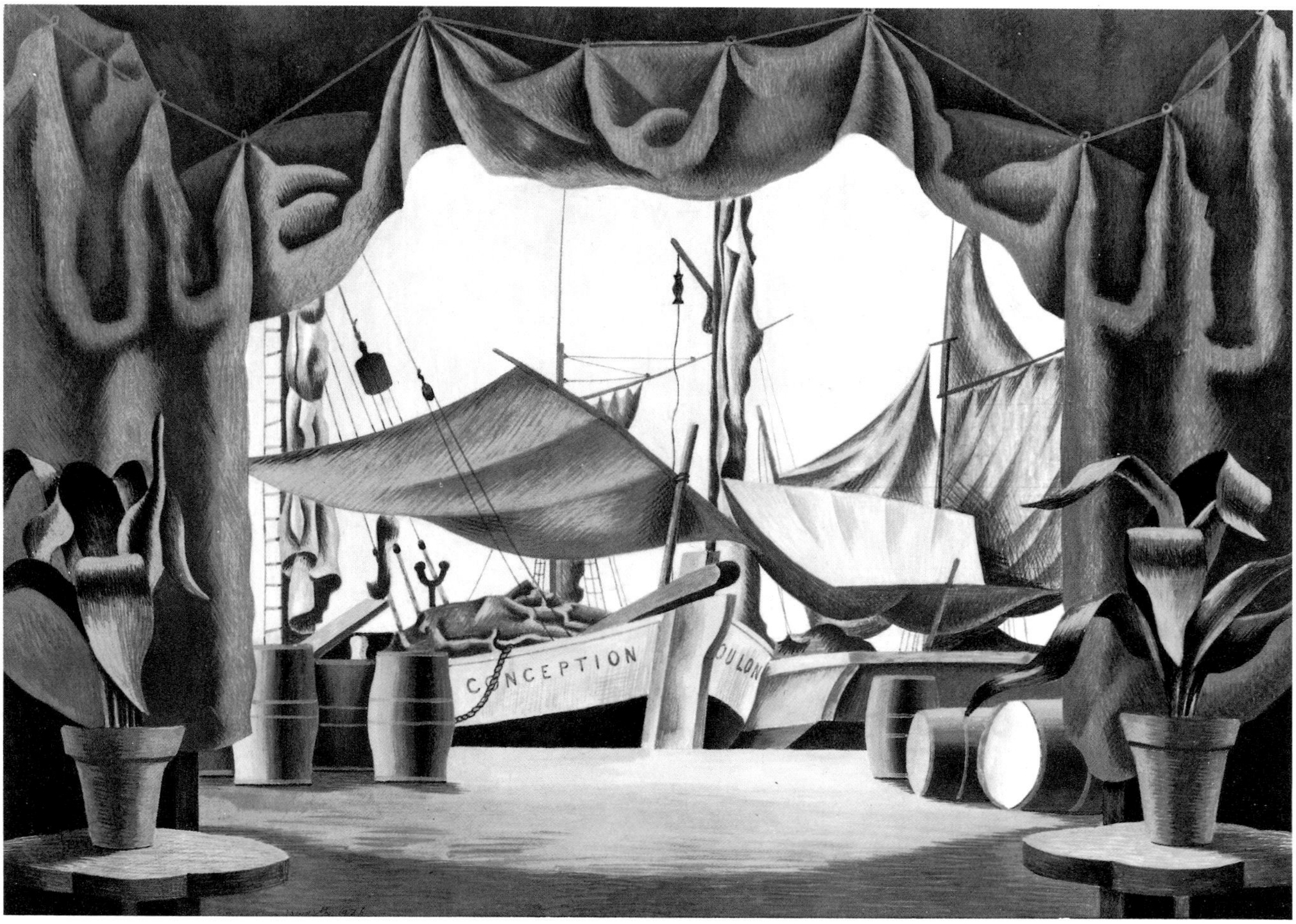

89a. *St Tropez* (1) 1926

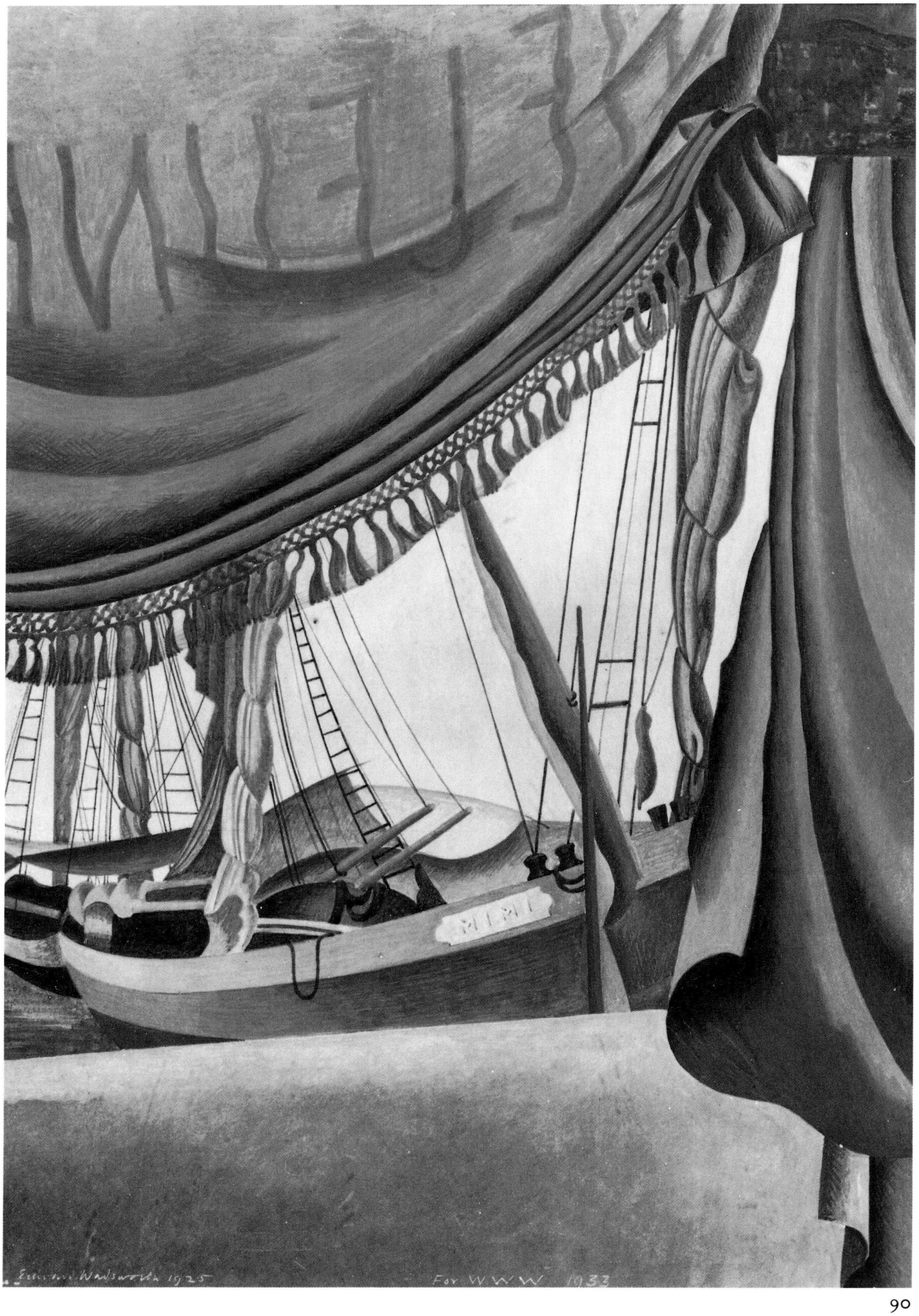

90

90. Quayside/St Tropez (3) 1925
94. Little Western Flower/The Poet's Darling 1928

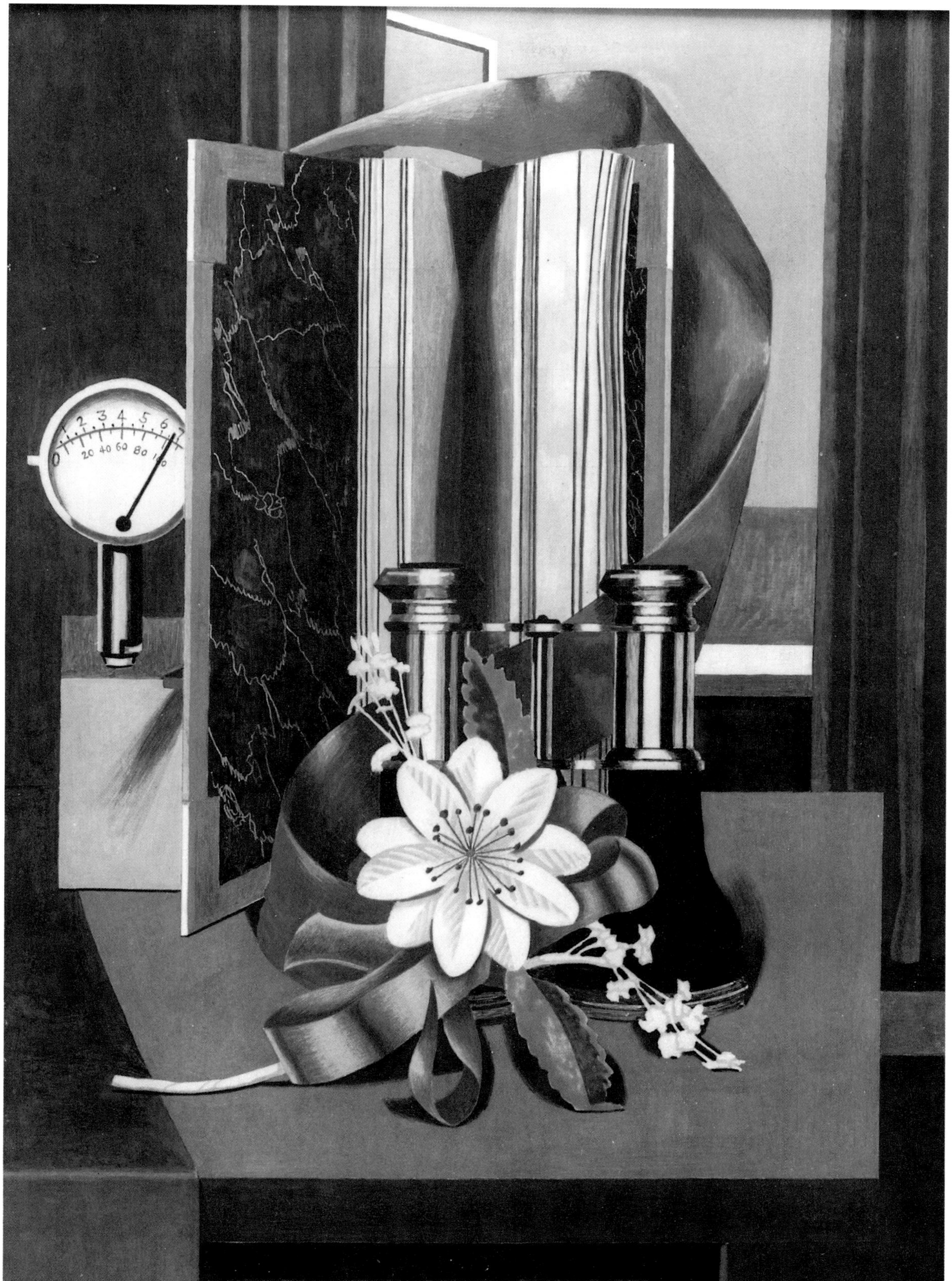

94

mahogany and white car body, died in 1927. One might speculate, therefore, that 'Lamentations' was in some respects a tribute to the dead, born of personal grief. The metaphorical aspect of Wadsworth's still lifes was a point not lost on Léonce Rosenberg when he wrote in the introduction to the catalogue of Wadsworth's exhibition at Tooth's in 1929, presumably with the artist's approval:

> It is not enough that a work should be constructed according to accepted principles to be beautiful. It is in the degree in which humanity radiates through the material (matter) that a production is worthy of interest.

The pyramidal, triangular construction which endows 'Regalia' with such dignity and strength, was one which Wadsworth favoured in the late twenties, and he may have been encouraged in its use not only by the still lifes of de Chirico (see fig.21), but by the many reproductions he would have seen in *L'Esprit nouveau*,[9] the organ of Purism edited by Ozenfant and Jeanneret (Le Corbusier) to which he subscribed. The magazine contained illustrations of paintings and architecture, which were subjected to structural analysis, and triangular compositions were given particular emphasis. The architectural nature of many of Wadsworth's compositions was remarked upon by Léonce Rosenberg when he wrote in the catalogue to Wadsworth's exhibition at Tooth's in 1929: 'For a constructor, the organisation rules the subject, for an imitator, the subject rules the organisation', thereby implying that Wadsworth was a 'constructor'. It should be said, however, that triangular compositions had been popular for many centuries but, following the flattening of the picture plane in the Cubist period, pyramidal compositions would have had a renewed appeal.

A further possible source for Wadsworth's interest in pyramidal construction, using plinths and blocks, may reside in publicity and display photographs of consumer items such as fine glass and ceramics found in the pages of *Studio* in the late twenties. For example, an article published in 1928 on modern Dutch products[10] illustrates displays of glasses and vases in pyramidal compositions using flowers to offset the harsh look, echoing a painting such as 'Little Western Flower' (94). Furthermore, the photograph of glass products by A D Coper (fig.22) is arranged in a planimetric format, the principal item being raised on a block, the block itself resting at an angle, all of which is paralleled in 'Regalia'. Although no claim is made for this photograph as a source, it perhaps indicates that Wadsworth's sense of design and composition was in line with contemporary ideas of design and presentation.

The overlap between art and design was prominently discussed in *L'Esprit nouveau* which was the forum for the debate surrounding the *rappel à l'ordre* and the return to the object.

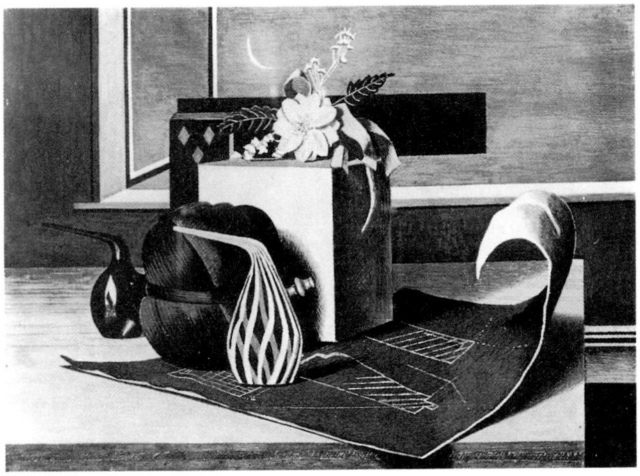

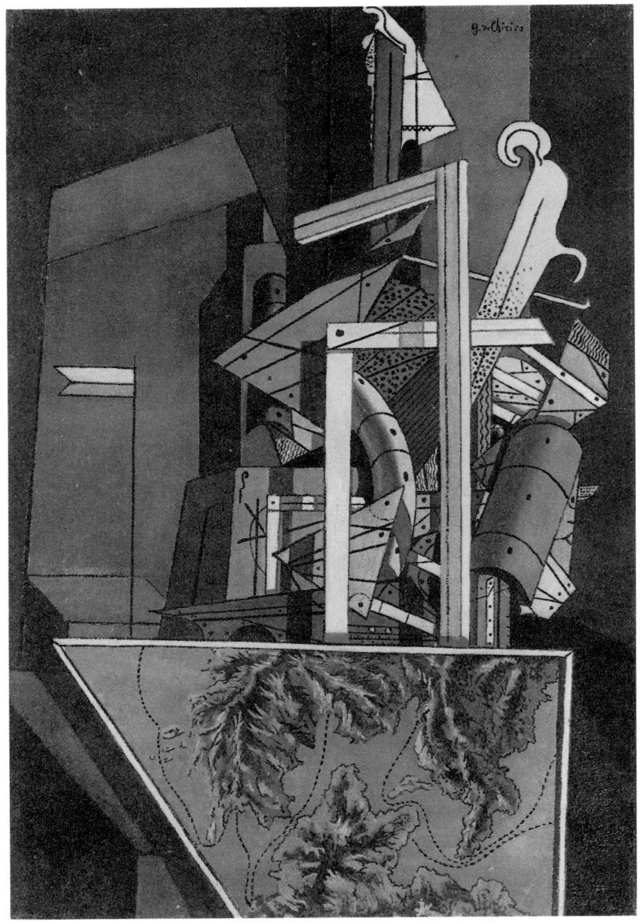

Fig.20 TOP *Lamentations* 1928 (W/A 96), tempera, 30.5 × 40.6, private collection

Fig.21 BOTTOM Giorgio de Chirico, *The Melancholy of Departure* 1916, oil on canvas, 51.8 × 36, The Trustees of the Tate Gallery

It placed great emphasis on Platonic notions of geometry and described a world which would increasingly value geometric form and proportion. Wadsworth's interest in depicting finely-designed, well-proportioned objects with clarity of light and construction should therefore be seen within a continental context. The still lifes of 1928, particularly those like 'Regalia', 'Parergon' (95), 'Marine' (100) and 'Log and Sextant' (fig.27) which consist solely of machine-made objects, have an affinity not only with de Chirico's still lifes incorporating instruments of measurement (see fig.21) but also with the paintings of Léger of *c.* 1924, for example 'The Siphon', and of Jeanneret in terms of their emphasis on clarity and their stress on the object. More importantly, however, there were many illustrations of manufactured objects in the pages of *L'Esprit nouveau* which were selected for their classical proportions, their fine design and their pure lines. The magazine also contained a number of advertisements illustrating finely engineered machines and consumer goods. Wadsworth's use of instruments such as the auger, the ship's log, the sundial and the compass may have been related to his reading of the magazine if not inspired by it, although it should be recalled that he was trained as an engineer and therefore had an innate liking for technical instruments. For example, issue number 10 contained the third part of Le Corbusier's article entitled 'Des Yeux qui ne vioent pas ...' and was devoted to automobiles (the first part, in issue number 8, was devoted to steamships which must surely have been of interest to Wadsworth). Within it were reproductions not only of elegant cars (fig.23), for which Wadsworth as the owner of a series of Rolls Royces must have had some interest (fig.24), but photographs of the interior of cockpits with instruments and gauges (fig.25), all of which were captioned. The caption beneath the Caproni-Exploration gauges stands out in particular as being relevant to Wadsworth: 'The word is not poetic. The poetry of facts is stronger. Objects which signify something and which are carefully and skillfully located create a poetic effect', a statement which could easily describe a painting such as 'Regalia'. These articles also included photographs of exemplary buildings such as the Parthenon, thereby juxtaposing the new with the modern just as Wadsworth does within his still lifes. Similarly *L'Esprit nouveau* contained reproductions of organic objects and organisms, sometimes setting them beside mechanical items as Wadsworth was to do in his paintings. His interest in shells and organisms may have been stimulated further by D'Arcy Thompson's *On Growth and Form* published in 1917, a book which was popular among artists and which contained diagrams and reproductions of many different kinds of shell.

The correspondence of mechanical to natural forms and their respective perfect geometries must have been among Wadsworth's principal interests. Léonce Rosenberg, writing in the catalogue to Wadsworth's exhibition at Tooth's in 1929 touched on this theme when he stated:

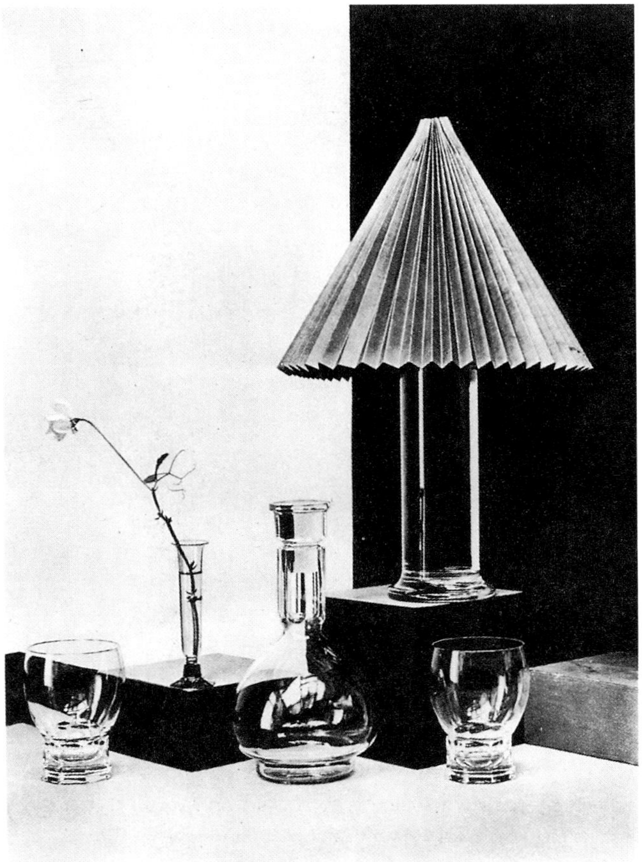

Fig.22 *Lamp, Decanter, Glasses and Small Vase* by A D Coper from Studio, April 1928, p.289

> A ballet where the dance confines itself to the imitation of music is only illustrated music. The art of the composer consists in creating, out of the accordance of two equivalent but not similar elements – music and dance – a new unity, namely a ballet.

By taking real objects from different areas of life and combining them in unexpected ways, Wadsworth achieved more than 'realism'; he created a poetic fusion. As Rosenberg continued: 'The art of Wadsworth intends simply to reach unity in finding the exact relations between equivalent but different elements associated.' 'Objects' 1928 (fig.26) is a clear example of this in which the form of an Ammonite parallels the twists in a ball of twine.

The object was also of central importance to Léger. In the first issue of the *Bulletin de l'effort moderne* he wrote:

> I consider that plastic beauty, in general, is totally independent of sentimental, descriptive and imitative qualities. Each object, picture,

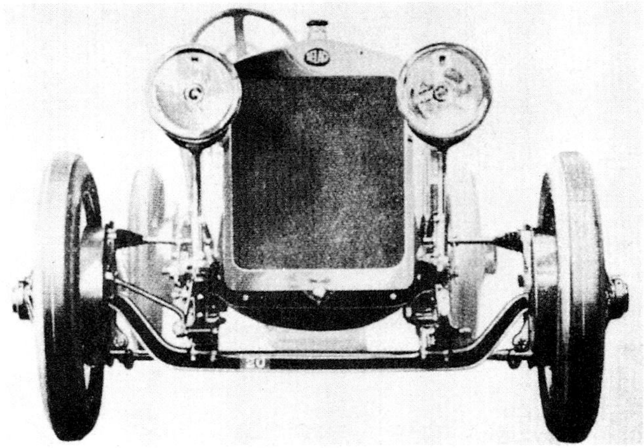

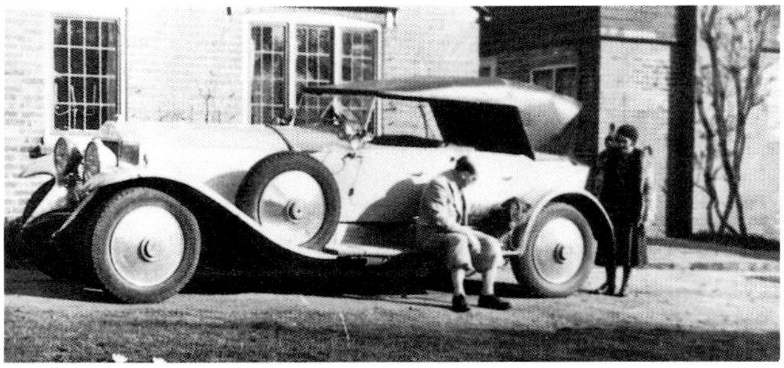

Fig.23 TOP *Delage* from 'Des yeux qui ne voient pas ... III: Les Autos', *L'Esprit nouveau*, no.10

Fig.24 BOTTOM Edward and Fanny Wadsworth at Maresfield, c.1932

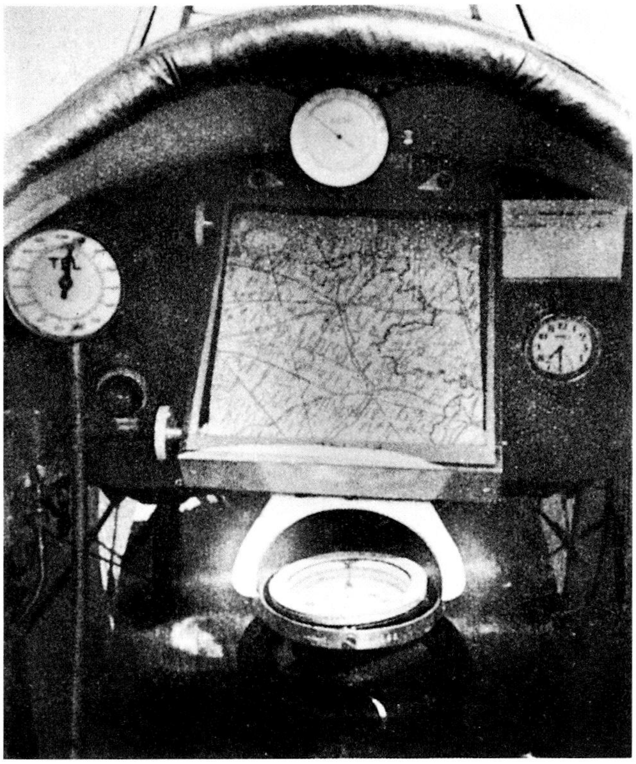

Fig.25 *Caproni-Exploration*, from 'Des yeux qui ne voient pas ... III: Les Autos', *L'Esprit nouveau*, no.10

building, ornamental arrangement has its own value, strictly absolute, independent of what it represents.

A machine or manufactured object can be beautiful when the relationships of the lines which define the volumes are balanced in an order equivalent to those of earlier buildings.[11]

Such a statement was typical of Léger's beliefs with which Wadsworth would undoubtedly have been familiar. The architectonic nature of many of Wadsworth's compositions and his accurate, clinical depiction of objects indicate that he must have had a particular interest in Léger's work and an affinity with his aesthetics. Indeed, some time after 1928 he purchased two paintings by Léger from Léonce Rosenberg, 'Les Clés' 1928 and 'Carte et pipe' 1928 (see fig.37), now in the collection of the Tate Gallery, both of which are of a kind that had a considerable impact on Wadsworth's paintings of 1929 and 1930 when his still lifes became abstracted and close to Purism.

Although Léger believed in the autonomy of the object and its independence from sentimental value, there can be no doubt but that Wadsworth was interested not only in the object in its own right but as a means to creating a particular atmosphere. Thus while 'Regalia' has a regal air and 'Bright Intervals' (97) buzzes with activity, 'Little Western Flower' (94) is redolent of a wreathed memorial. However, since the title is taken from *A Midsummer Night's Dream*, the painting is possibly an elegy on the subject of love, given the context of the passage in Oberon's speech to Puck, where the sleeping eyelids to which he refers may correspond to the binoculars lying in disuse.[12]

Colour p.57

Some of Wadsworth's paintings convey a sense of veiled threat, for example 'Log and Sextant' (fig.27), which resembles a composition of instruments of torture with its mace-like ship's log reminiscent of an instrument of war – strangely anticipating the V1 and V2 bombers – its 'hangman's' noose, its vice-like sextant and its disturbingly pointed weight.[13] 'North Sea' has a similar feel with its icy blues and greys. Less menacing is 'Wings of the Morning'[14] in which the same log, minus the noose, is suggestive of a Zeppelin (these airships were commonly illustrated in magazines and newspapers in the early decades of the century),

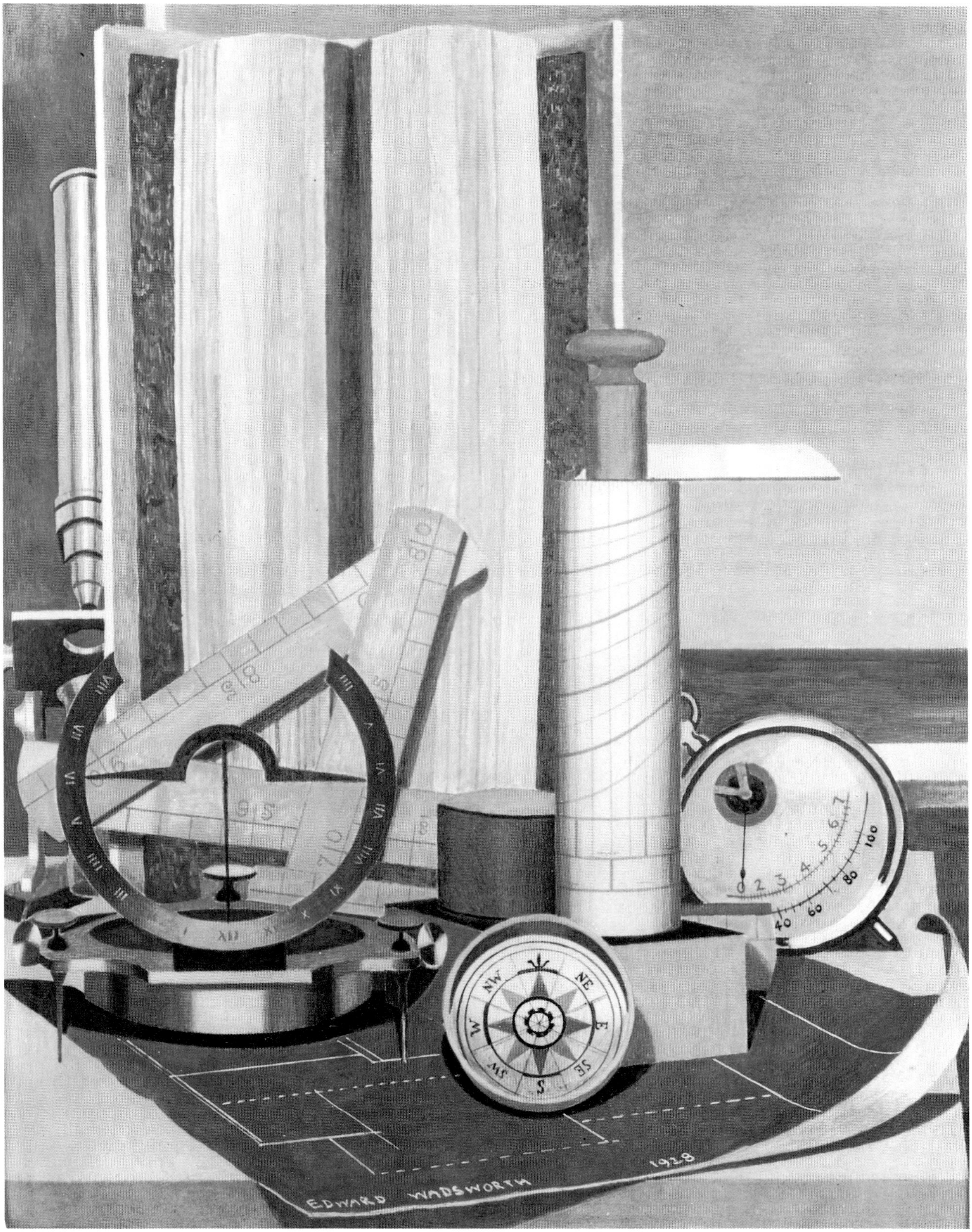
EDWARD WADSWORTH
1928

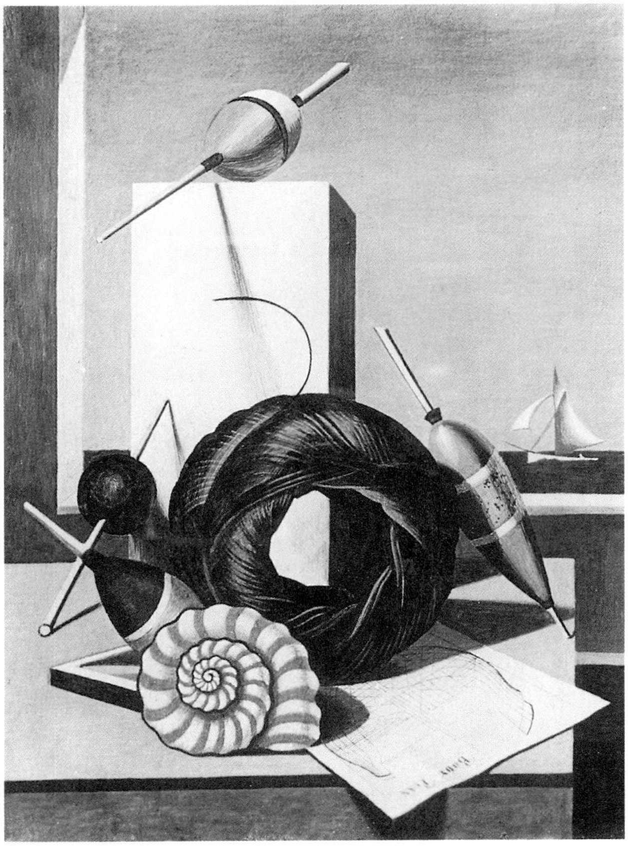

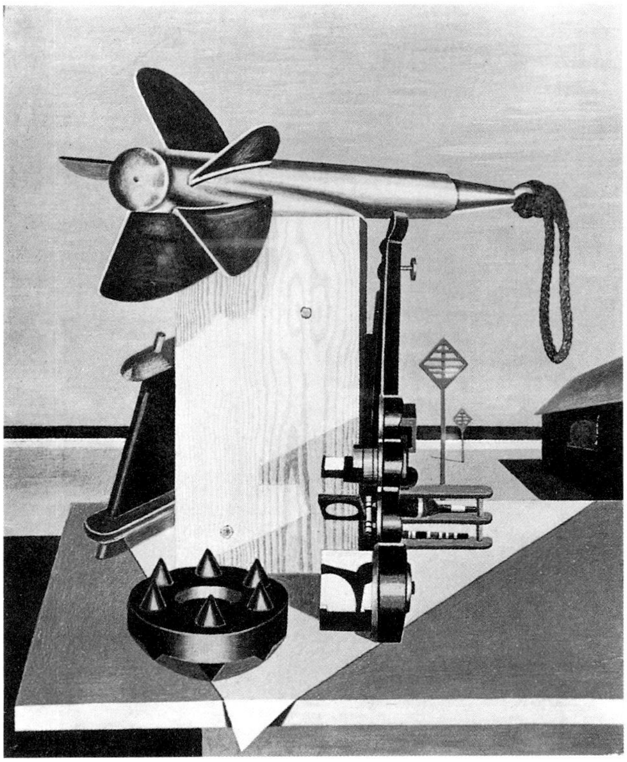

and combines with a vicious little fishing-hook to create an atmosphere of foreboding somewhat mitigated by the glowing pink shell. The conjunction of the phallic log with the vaginal shell also endows this painting with an erotic quality.

Much of the tension in Wadsworth's paintings is created by the palette of colours he employed. After receiving a piece of technical advice from de Chirico in 1928,[15] and following a three-month stay in Paris where he would have seen the richly coloured paintings of Metzinger among others, he adapted his cool palette, which as many contemporary critics remarked was influenced by Italian primitive painting, to include more saturated colours. The confrontational character of this new range, which included a strident red, is exacerbated by the manner in which the objects startle and surprise by their enlargement and decontextualisation. They assume almost human proportions and begin to threaten the viewer's space in a manner normally associated with sculpture. Indeed they become invasive. The enlarged object was a feature not only of de Chirico's work but also of the paintings of Pierre Roy (fig.28), with whom Wadsworth became acquainted probably early in 1927 when the latter exhibited at the Galerie Barbazanges, Paris in February of that year. Roy also knew Roger Fry, Clive Bell, P G Konody and Boris Anrep among others and was a regular visitor to England. Wadsworth owned two paintings by Roy although it is not certain when he acquired them. Nevertheless they were exhibited at the Brummer Gallery, New York in 1930 as belonging to him. Furthermore, possibly as early as 1926 and certainly by 1928, Roy visited Wadsworth to learn how to paint in tempera. There is some dispute, however, as to when this actually took place. The painting which Wadsworth made as a demonstration, 'Still Life' c.1926, is in the collection of the Tate Gallery but according to Barbara Wadsworth it was more likely painted in 1928.[16] Stylistically and compositionally, however, this painting may have been painted before 1928.

The other artist who appears to have made a particular impact on Wadsworth was Jean Metzinger whose works were regularly reproduced in the *Bulletin de l'effort moderne*. In particular Metzinger's 'La Roulette' c.1926, reproduced in the January 1927 issue of the *Bulletin*, may be of some relevance to 'Regalia'.[17] 'La Roulette' (fig.29) depicts a table-top still life before a window overlooking a landscape. Among other objects the still life comprises a roulette wheel, in the centre,

Fig.26 ABOVE LEFT *Objects* 1928 (not in Barbara Wadsworth op. cit), tempera (dimensions and whereabouts unknown)

Fig.27 LEFT *Lowestoft Scores/Log and Sextant* 1928 (W/A 102), tempera, 40.7 × 35, private collection

97a. Still Life, Dungeness 1928
99. On est bien au bord de la mer 1928-9

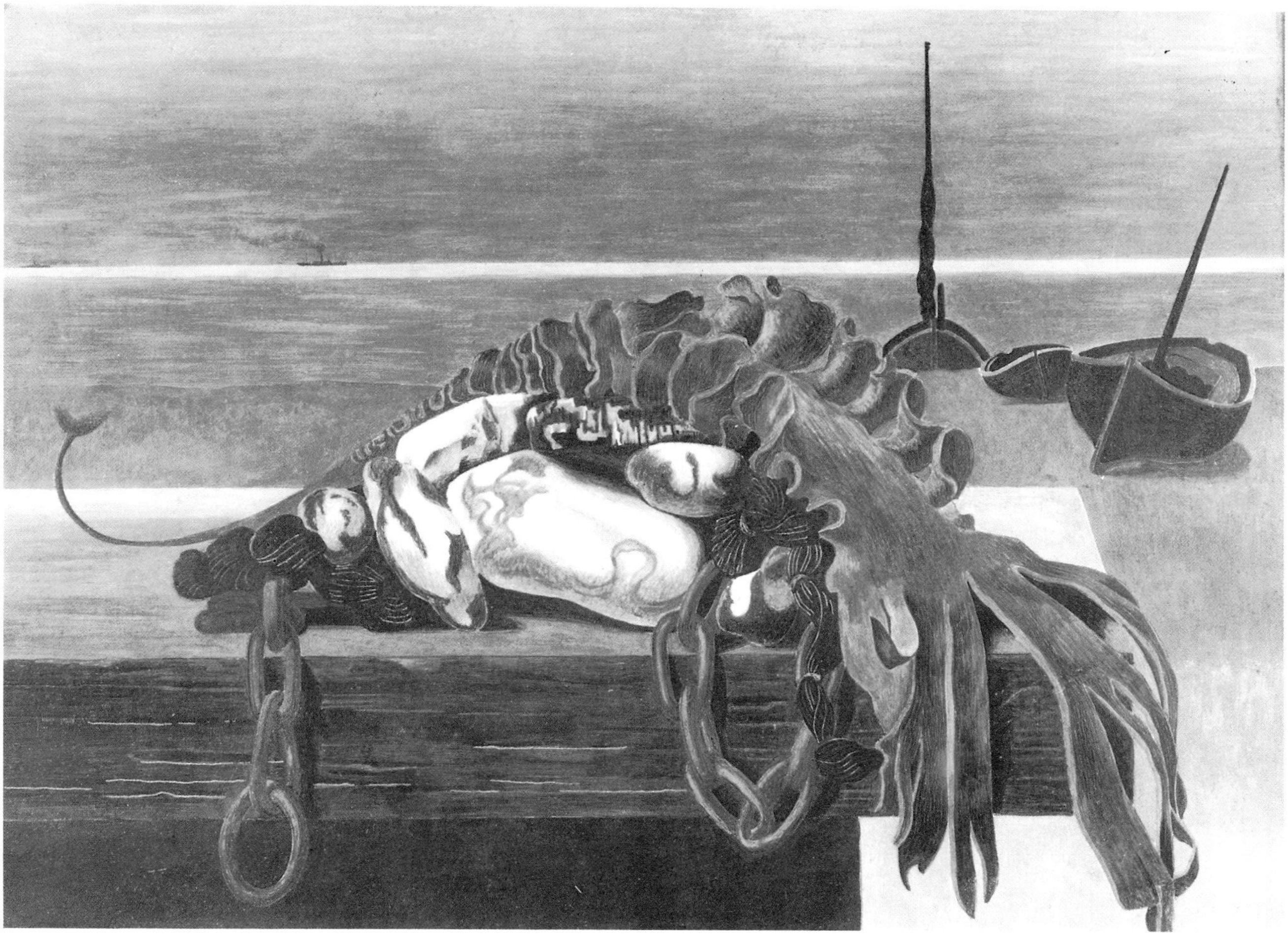

97a

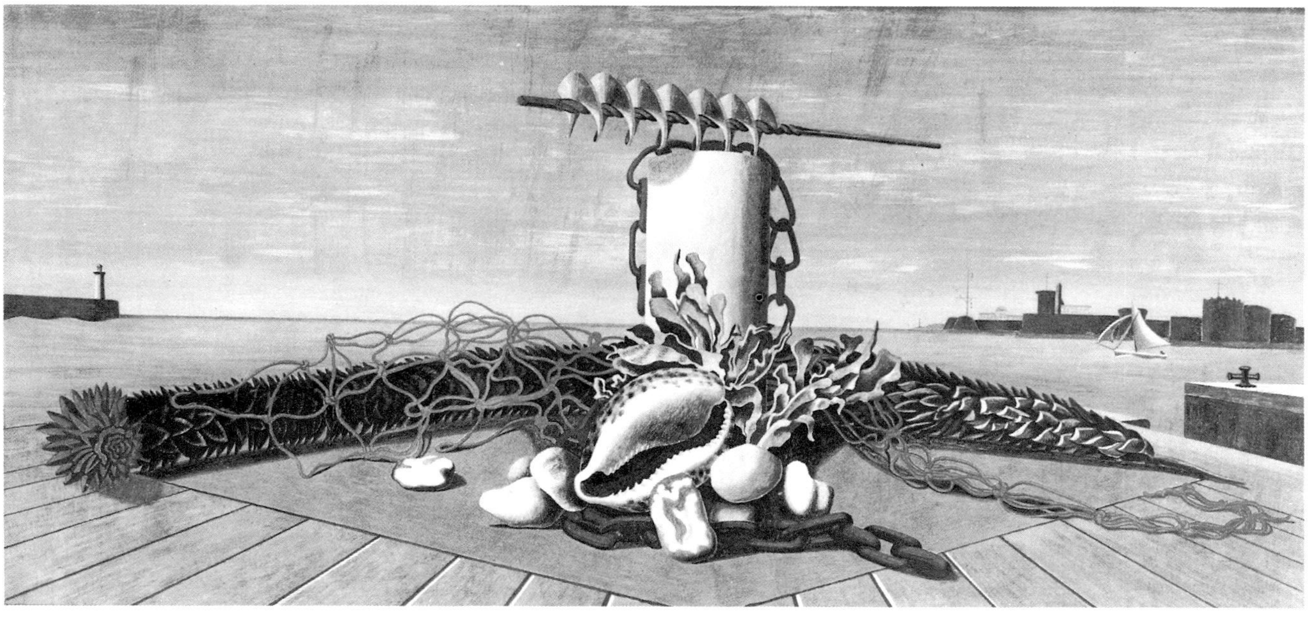

99

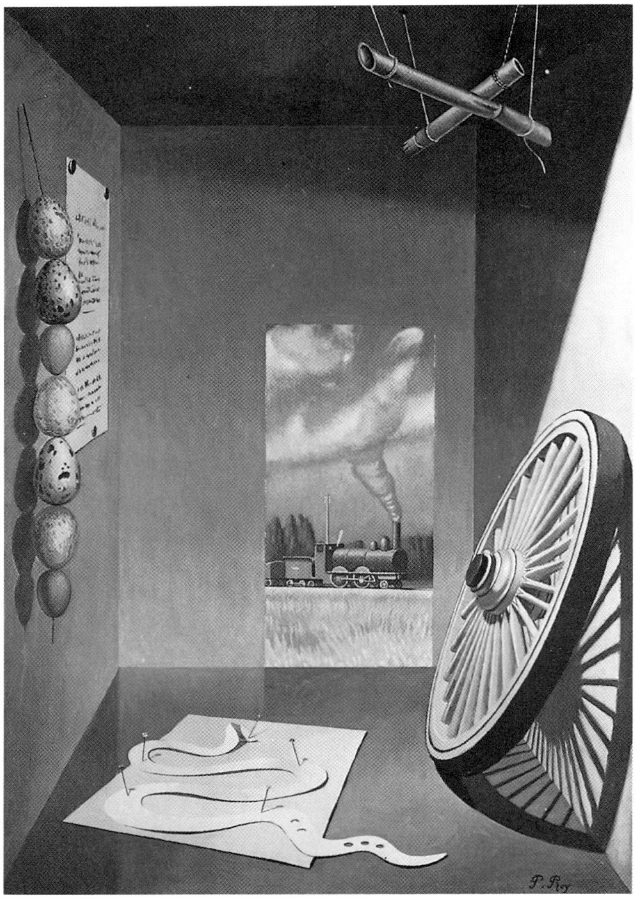

Fig.28 Pierre Roy, *Le Cabinet du naturaliste* 1928, oil on canvas, 92 × 62.5, The Trustees of the Tate Gallery

placed on a green baize cloth which protrudes beyond the front edge of the table. These aspects may be directly compared with the inclining sundial and the harbour signals chart in 'Regalia'. Furthermore, 'La Roulette' is painted predominantly in red and yellow, the keynote colours of Wadsworth's painting. While Metzinger's picture may not have been an actual source for 'Regalia', Wadsworth would have known it in reproduction, if not in actuality, and it is typical of the kinds of works by Metzinger which were to be found in the pages of the *Bulletin* and which laid emphasis on the depiction of objects. Furthermore Metzinger painted a number of marine allegories, for example 'Astrologie' and 'Allégorie maritime',[18] both of 1927, the latter being of particular interest since it depicts instruments of measurement. Another possible source for the composition of 'Regalia' was Jean Lurçat's 'Fruits on a Table' 1927,[19] although Lurçat's expressive paint-handling is far removed from the precision of Wadsworth's style. By 1930, however, Lurçat was painting still lifes of tools and objects set in the landscape, as though viewed at close range, indicating that there may have been some interchange of ideas at some point. It should also be acknowledged that the depiction of objects on an unusual scale was a practice adopted by Paul Nash who, like Wadsworth, was a keen admirer of de Chirico. Nash and Wadsworth were friends although for a certain period in the twenties they fell out. By 1928, however, they had patched up their differences.

Nash and Wadsworth were also united in their interest in the concepts of time and distance. Both stressed the relationship between objects near and far – in Wadsworth's case the latter might be a small yacht – joining them together by means of a device such as the beam of a lighthouse, as in 'Reunion' 1928,[20] or by the echoing of forms as in 'Punch Balls' 1942 (129) where the spinakers and punchballs mirror each other. The depiction of binoculars in some paintings metaphorises the telescoping of distance, which parallels the compression of time achieved through the juxtaposition of new and old marine instruments, of products of engineering with products of nature or of classical masks with modern steamships. The enormous temporal and geographical contractions within each painting enliven the outwardly static nature of still life.

The still life theme itself was common in British art in this period since, as a relatively neutral genre, it provided the basis for stylistic experiment. It was, moreover, not only a vehicle of modernist art but a genre frequently adopted by artists associated with the *rappel à l'ordre*. The still life before a window was regularly to be found at exhibitions of the Seven and Five Society and was favoured, among others, by Ben and Winifred Nicholson, Christopher Wood and David Jones, all of whom were interested in the transition between inside and outside and activity and rest.

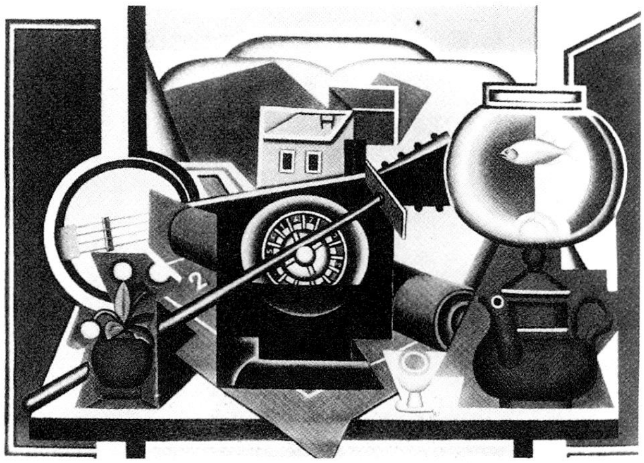

Fig.29 Jean Metzinger, *La Roulette* c.1926, oil on canvas, 97 × 146 (whereabouts unknown)

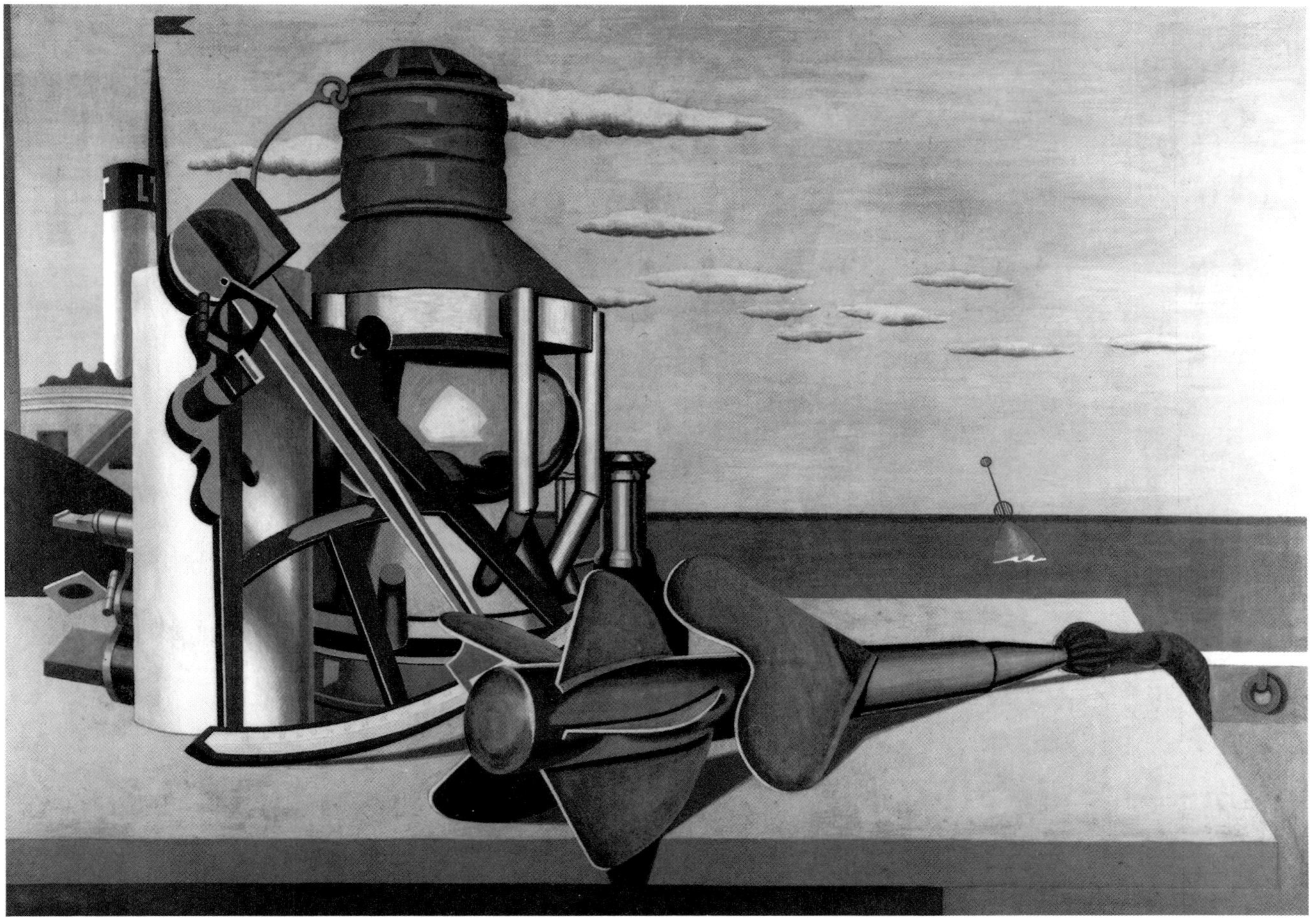

100. *Faithful Servants/Marine* 1928

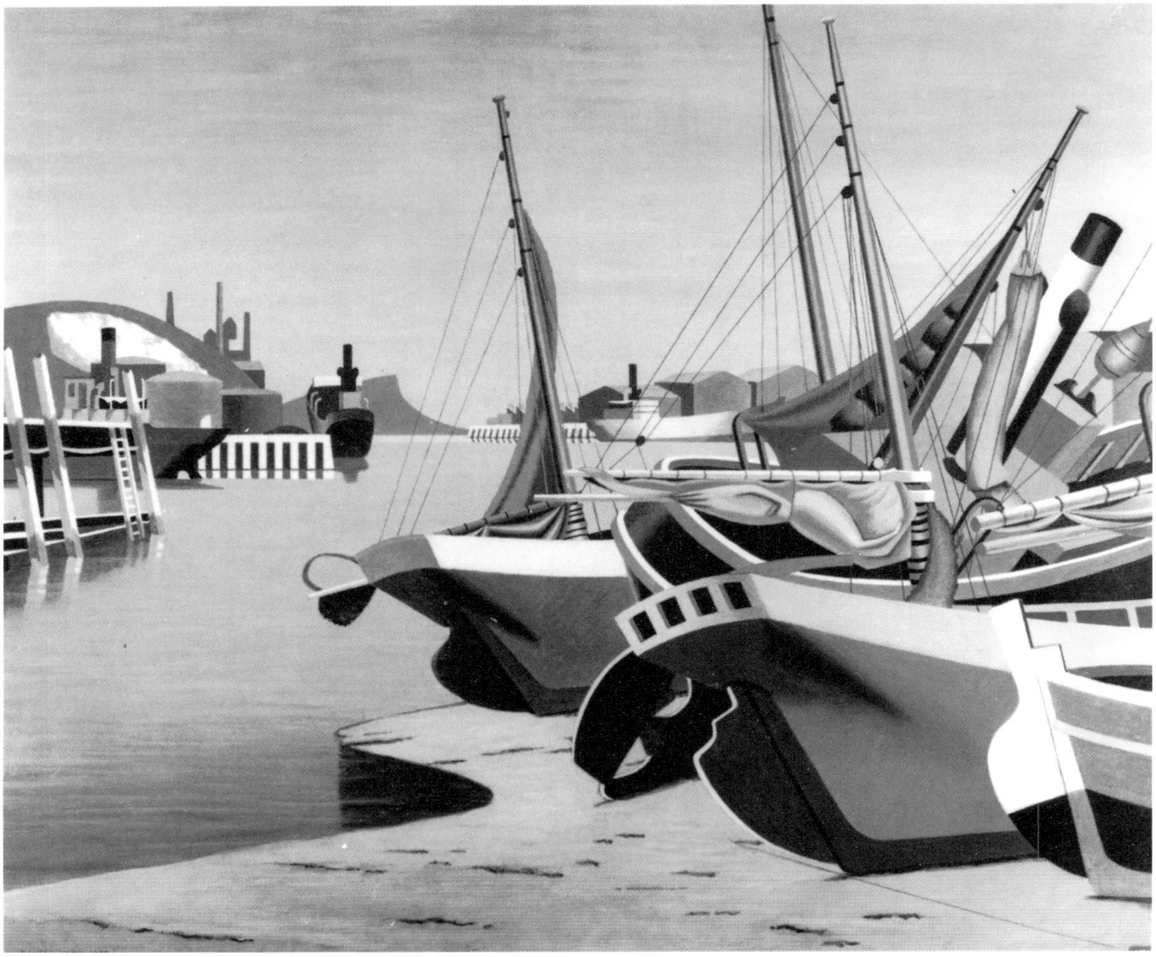

113. Slump 1935

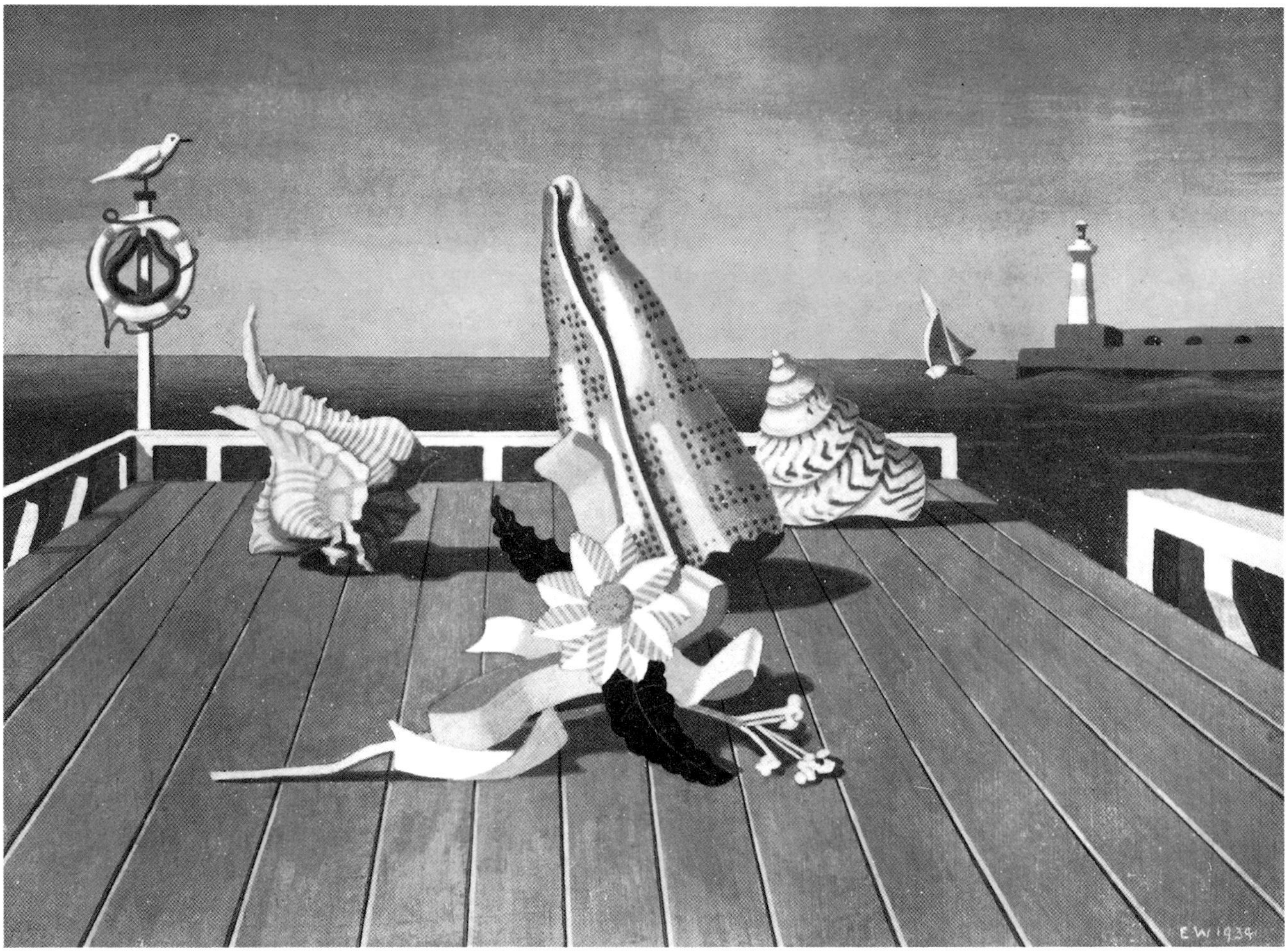

111. *World of Happy Days* 1934

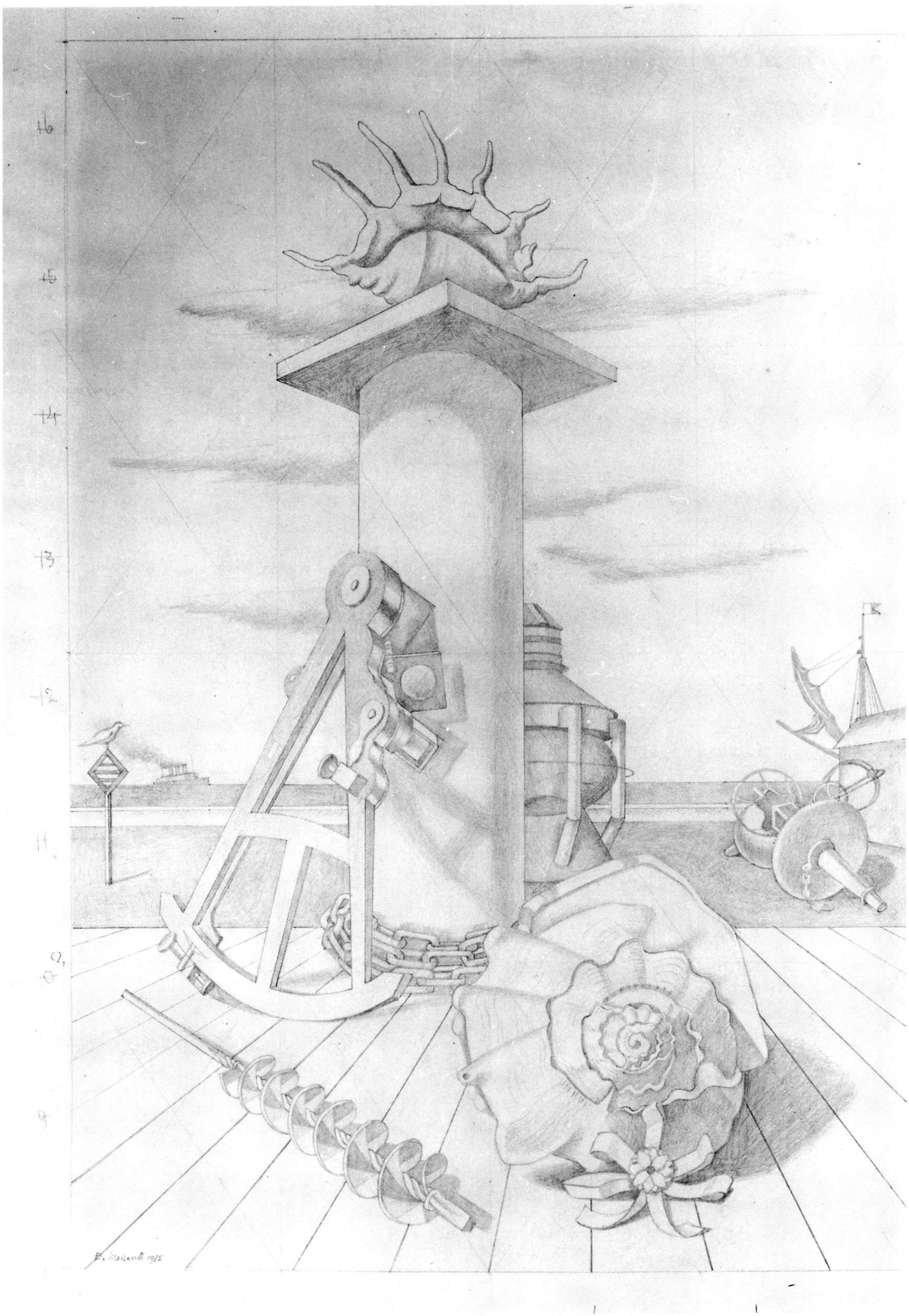

115

115. Cartoon for 'Offing' 1935
114. Offing 1935

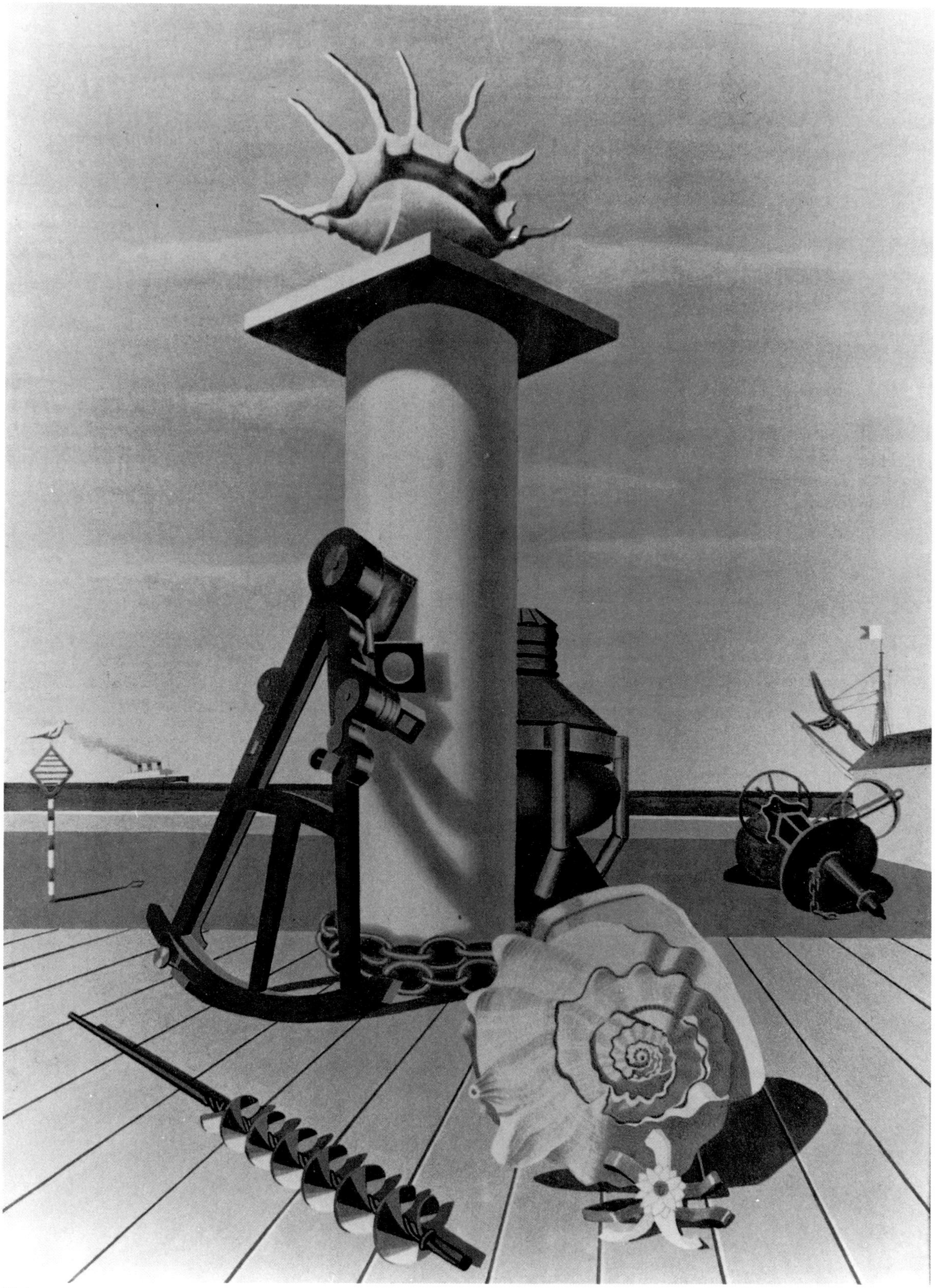

114

The relationship of Ben Nicholson's work to Wadsworth's is worthy of comment. Both were passionately interested in Italian primitive art and both were well travelled. Indeed some aspects of Wadsworth's still lifes coincidentally anticipate, in an illusionistic way, some of the areas Nicholson was to make his own in the thirties. For example, the barometer in 'Bright Intervals' is emphatically a circle within a square, a combination much favoured by Nicholson from 1933 onwards, and the different planes and depths suggested by the conjunction of the carpenter's straight edge and the white block anticipate Nicholson's interest in rectilinear relief carving. Further, the signals chart in 'Regalia' has an affinity with the diamonds and circles of Nicholson's compositions of the early thirties. Finally, both artists were deeply concerned with precision.

Precision and clarity were characteristics found in the paintings of many artists in this period and although the connection with Nicholson is important, and was to be more so when they were both members of Abstraction-Création and Unit One in the thirties, Wadsworth's paintings had greater points of contact with those of other British artists such as William Roberts, whose tubular figures were painted with a sharpness similar to the clarity which characterised Wadsworth's paintings. Among other artists who painted images of a high resolution were Algernon Newton, David Bomberg in his Jerusalem paintings, Wyndham Lewis, John Armstrong and Maxwell Armfield with whom Wadsworth conducted an extensive correspondence from 1929 onwards on the subject of tempera painting. As Richard Morphet has pointed out,[21] impersonal lucidity was a characteristic that united artists across the whole spectrum from avant-garde to orthodox.

The emphasis on clarity was international in the twenties and thirties to the extent that it is found in German *Neue Sachlichkeit* painting (Dix, Schad, Schrimpf), Surrealism (Tanguy and Dalí), Parisian art (Balthus, Derain, Picasso, Cocteau), American Precisionism (Sheeler, Demuth, Crawford) and in Italian Magic Realism (Carra, Severini, Funi, Casorati, Donghi). Interestingly, Waldemar George invoked the name of Magic Realism, albeit when referring to Wadsworth's connection with de Chirico, in his article published in *Sélection*, and it may be that Wadsworth saw the works of those painters characterised as Magic Realist when he visited Italy in 1923. He surely would have known Severini not only from before the war but because Severini continued to exhibit in Paris and was deeply influential in the classical revival. Léonce Rosenberg wrote a series of paragraphs in Wadsworth's 1929 catalogue which clearly linked him to prevailing continental trends:

> Individualism, here, is the enemy.
>
> From the day when an artist begins to be in front of his work instead of behind it, art ceases to be universal, noble and durable. It is the start of decadence: tradition is lost and a new faith, a new enthusiasm will be necessary to find tradition again and to make it revive under hitherto unknown forms.
>
> Wadsworth is, in the world, one of the very few heroes of the new faith ...
>
> During all great periods, the aim of the artist's effort has always been not the ideal nor the reality, but the truth (la vrai).

In the case of the avant-garde the desire to delineate the object sharply may have been a reaction to the chaotic destruction of war and what might have been perceived as the earlier disintegration of the object in the Cubist epoch. The spirit of reconstruction was exemplified in the return to order adumbrated in *L'Esprit nouveau*. Tonal and compositional clarity may also testify to the considerable influence of the Italian primitives on British art in this period. As Morphet points out, however, there was a tradition of such lucid painting within British art stretching back to the Pre-Raphaelite Brotherhood and which was to be taken up more extensively in the thirties, not only by figurative artists such as Edward Burra and Meredith Frampton, but also by Ben Nicholson in his paintings of circles and rectangles. To this we might add that the whiteness of Nicholson's white reliefs and Hepworth's white marble carvings were another extension of the pursuit of clarity, although their use of white should be seen within the context of modernist architecture.

When Wadsworth returned to marine subjects in 1933 after his biomorphic phase, he continued to paint with the utmost clarity, although towards the end of the thirties he broke up the evenness of the surface by adopting a *pointilliste* style. Clarity was of course a function of his use of tempera, a medium which demanded precision and allowed for little overpainting.[22] If the means did not change, however, the subjects did. The return to this general theme resulted partly from a feeling that abstract painting was not sufficiently expressive nor particularly suited to the medium of tempera, which historically was associated with the figure and the object. In 1933 he wrote in 'The Abstract Painter's Own Explanation' that

> At no period has the aspect of things been a main consideration in my painting, although admittedly I have from time to time been stimulated by certain landscapes or objects, the realistic appearance of which I have promptly subdued in order to emphasise qualities which I considered more important.[23]

Although this statement suggests that he was interested in the formal aspect of the object it may also imply that his paintings did indeed have symbolic or metaphoric content, as S D Cleveland confirmed in 1943 when he wrote that Wadsworth's fascination with nautical objects resulted from 'their aloof, symbolic and often nostalgic qualities'.[24]

Some of the marine subjects of the thirties and forties

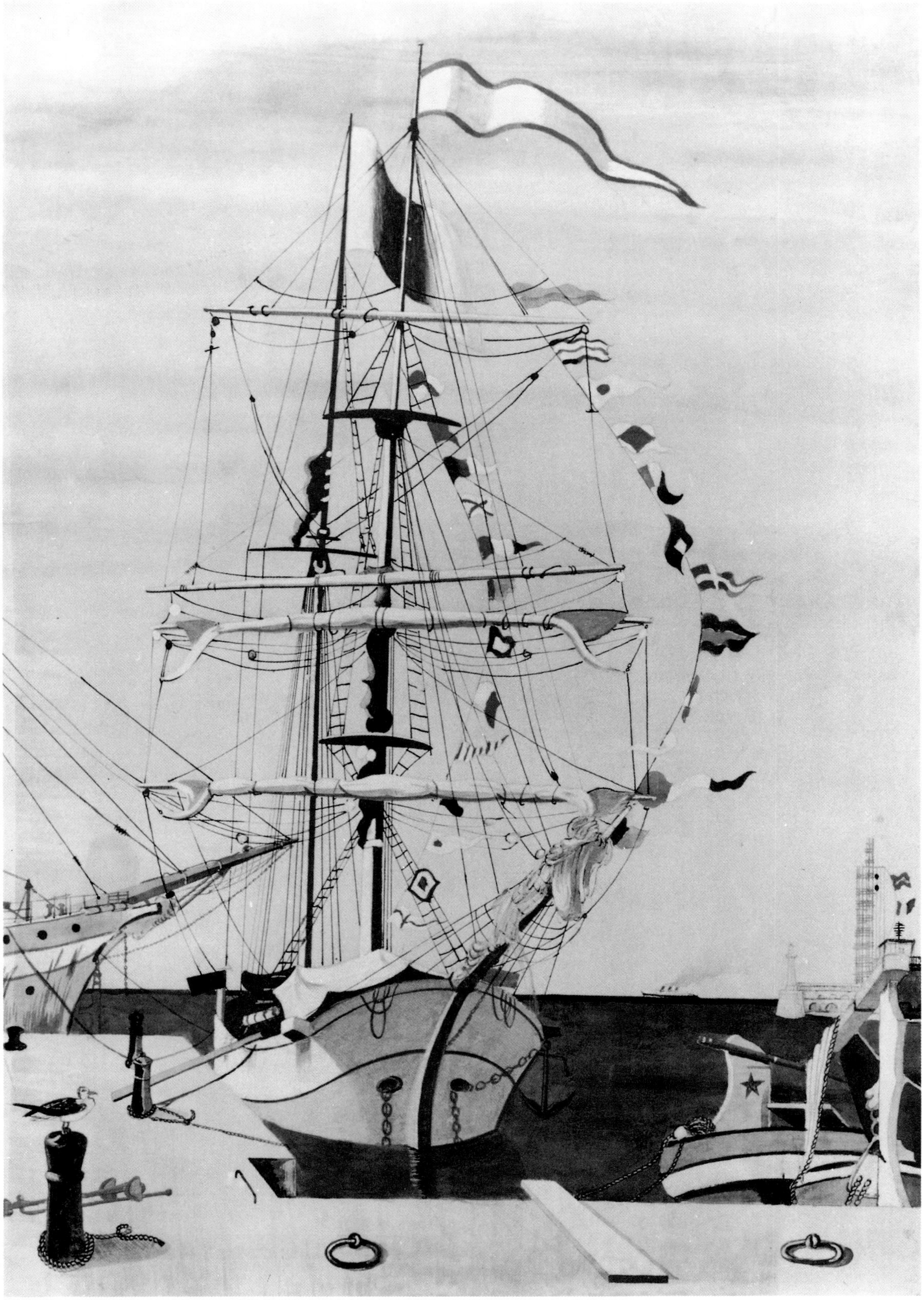

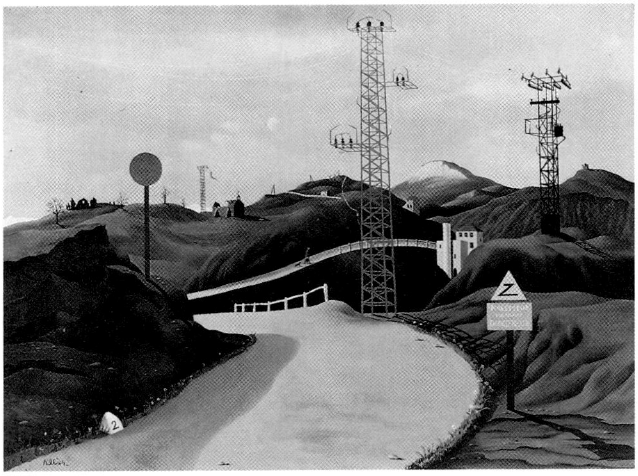

Fig.30 Tristram Hillier, *La Route des Alpes* 1937, tempera on canvas, 59.7 × 80.6, The Trustees of the Tate Gallery

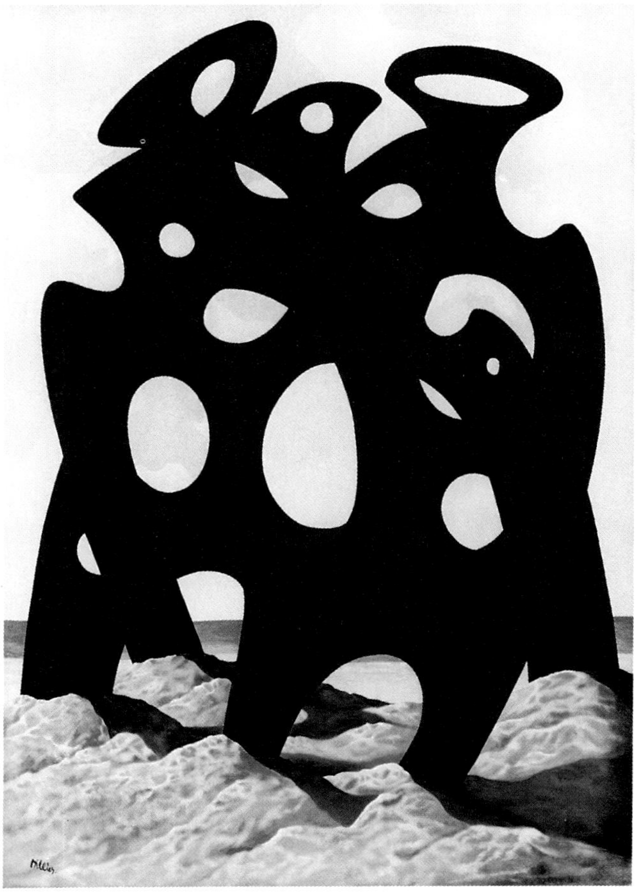

Fig.31 Tristram Hillier, *Variation on the Form of an Anchor* 1936-7, oil on canvas, 150.2 × 109.2, The Trustees of the Tate Gallery

made open reference to external events. 'Light Sections (3)' 1940 (128) appears not only to refer to boat building but to wartime destruction while 'Requiescat'[25] c.1940 (128a) is a moving memorial to loss of life at sea. 'Bronze Ballet' 1941 (127a), painted to the sound of the bombardment of Abbeville, Boulogne and Calais, is unusual in its depiction of a choppy sea, suggesting perhaps the turbulent times in which it was painted. 'World of Happy Days' 1934 (111), painted as a wedding present for his daughter, is reminiscent of the works of the late twenties. While it is undoubtedly an expression of pleasure at a happy event, it also suggests a nostalgic longing for the atmosphere of the previous decade and was painted at a time when Europe was experiencing the rising tide of totalitarianism, of which Wadsworth would have been only too well aware since his son-in-law was a German national. One of the sources of his later unhappiness was the order imposed upon him during the war to remain outside the coastal zone, as a result of his daughter's marriage and his son-in-law's internment. Such a deprivation would have been very hard to bear for a man for whom the sea was of such cardinal interest.

Apart from the wartime still lifes which appear to be related to topical events, the still lifes of the late thirties are distinguished by a lack of gravity both literally and metaphorically and by an increasing emphasis on animism and metamorphism, for example the tarpaulin stretched on the quayside in 'Le Havre' 1939-45 (135a) which looks like a large bat. Many of the objects in his later paintings are depicted suspended in the air or almost floating. In 'Bronze Ballet' the propellor blades appear to be taking off into the distance; the fishing floats in 'The First of the Ebb' 1938 (122) are hanging in mid-air. The same is true of 'Punch Balls' c.1942 (129) and 'Souvenir of Fiumicino' 1937 (121) in which Wadsworth depicts a sculptural construction of nautical and fishing objects hanging from ropes in a manner reminiscent of Alexander Calder's mobiles and stabiles. Wadsworth had met Calder while he was staying in Paris in 1930 and both were members of Abstraction-Création. A series of equally sculptural constructions is depicted in the earlier 'Visibility Moderate' 1934 (112)[26] which, like 'Bright Intervals' (97), refers to a phrase frequently used on the shipping forecasts. The composition of this painting indicates the extent to which Wadsworth remained an admirer of de Chirico even after the former's biomorphic abstract phase, for the depiction of furniture, and specifically chairs, in outdoor settings was a feature of some of de Chirico's paintings of the mid twenties. Wadsworth shared this interest with Paul Nash whose work of this period was quite close in a number of aspects. Another artist with whom Wadsworth can be compared in the thirties is Tristram Hillier who was undoubtedly influenced by Wadsworth's paintings of the

Colour p.63 p.62

Colour p.61 p.57

118. *Marine Set* 1936

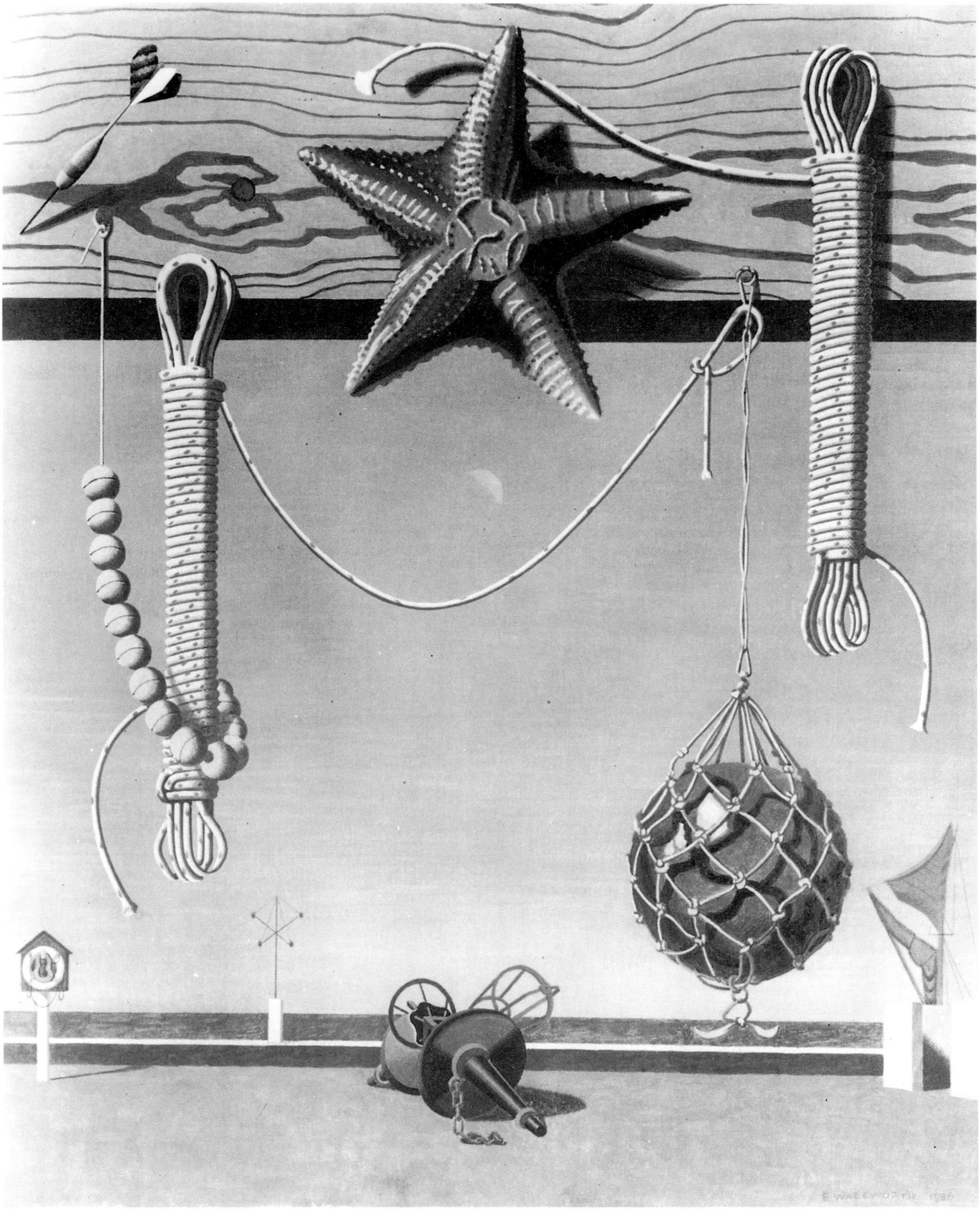

twenties. Hillier's 'La Route des Alpes' 1937 (fig.30) may owe a debt to Wadsworth's use of signs in 'Log and Sextant' but anticipates a work such as 'Top of the World' 1942-3 (130). His 'Variation on the Form of an Anchor' 1936-7 (fig.31) shares Wadsworth's characteristic close-up view as well as the depiction of a marine subject. De Chirico and Lurçat were clearly of importance to Hillier but, like Wadsworth, he was not a Surrealist.

Although Wadsworth was never a Surrealist – he did not exhibit at the International Surrealist Exhibition in 1936 but was described by many contemporary critics as a Surrealist – these marine paintings of the thirties are as near as he ever came to such a categorisation. However, they do not fit into any neat category for they are barely still lifes. Generally speaking, still lifes are collections of objects on tables or grouped together on the ground. The later works eschew such a category and in many respects anticipate the interests of recent British sculpture. For example, 'Light Sections (3)', 1940 (128) is suggestive of the themes of skin and container explored by Richard Deacon, while 'Omega and Alpha' 1944 (fig.32), in its assemblage of discarded industrial materials, footwear and domestic objects, anticipates the sculpture of Tony Cragg and David Mach while renewing an interest in waste previously evidenced in the Black Country drawings of the twenties. This disturbing vision of destruction and obsolescence, found in other works of the period such as 'Pastorale, Chailey, Sussex' c.1942,[27] is rendered benign by brilliant and cheerful colours which echo the optimistic note set by the accompanying text. Beneath this colourful veneer, however, lies a fundamental antiheroic, negative attitude to life induced possibly by the effect of the war and the erosion of values within society.

'Omega and Alpha' was commissioned by ICI as part of a series entitled 'Services of an Industry' and used as an image of propaganda in specialist and non-specialist magazines to proclaim their advances, owing to wartime need, in the 'chemistry of salvage'. The campaign was devised by Sidney Rogerson whose intention was 'to produce an advertisement which should be an embellishment to the paper in which it appears, and which was designed to please, interest, and finally instruct the public'.[28] According to Joyce Watkins, the theme was carefully specified so that the image would dovetail with the accompanying text which, in view of the poor opportunities for sales, was designed to promote the company's achievements, its contribution to the war effort and to raise the company's profile.[29] The text states:

> In one sense a salvage dump is an end, the last resting place of tyres, rusted iron, boots, paper, rags and bones. In another sense it is a beginning, for, to the chemist, matter is not only indestructible but reconstructible. By his magic, new forms arise from the scrap-heap like the Phoenix from its own ashes.[30]

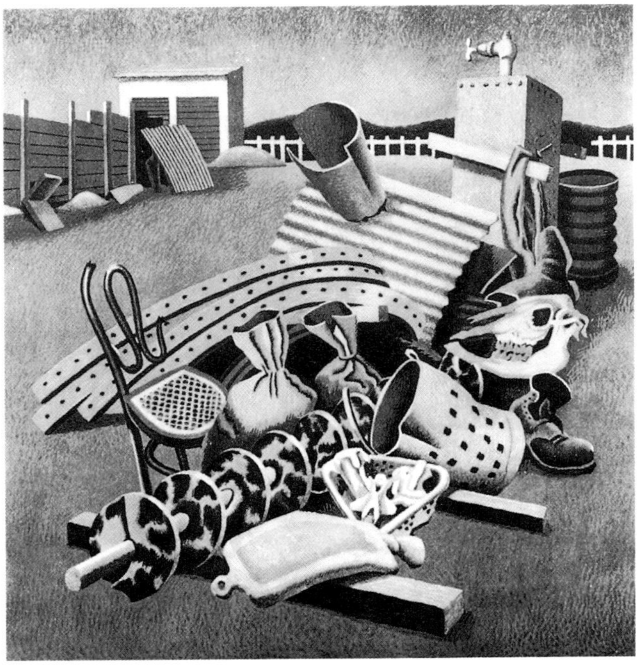

Fig.32 *Omega and Alpha* 1944 (W/A 139), tempera on paper, 40 × 38.7, collection ICI

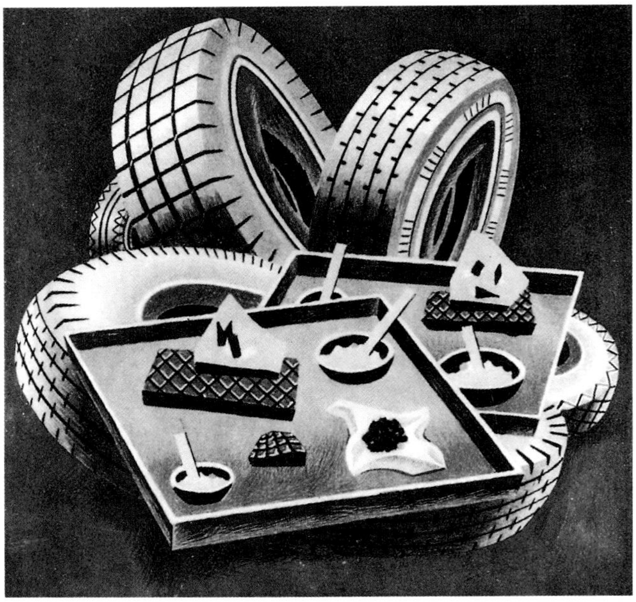

Fig.33 *Measured Tread* 1942-4 (W/A 132), tempera on paper, 27.9 × 30.5, collection ICI

This almost Baudelairean passage announces the themes of recycling and alchemy both of which are topical today. Another painting from the same campaign, entitled 'Measured Tread' 1942-4 (fig.33), narrating the need to collect and reuse old rubber and to develop synthetic rubber, heralds the work of Pop artists in its still life of tyres with different treads and its objects on trays all displayed in a matter of fact, non-hierarchical manner. An image from another campaign, entitled 'Cold Steel',[31] seems to anticipate the work of Roy Lichtenstein in its simple, sharp shapes and its almost comic-like depiction of small figures dwarfed by large sheets of steel.[32]

Although no connection can seriously be made between Cragg, Deacon or Pop Art and Wadsworth the resemblance is certainly noteworthy, as is the highly sculptural nature of Wadsworth's illusionism. Wadsworth was not a particularly innovative artist but his work was highly individual and distinctive and, as these late works clearly demonstrate, in spite of their inescapable period look, his paintings remain highly relevant to the present.

Notes

1. *Listener*, 30 June 1949.
2. Reproduced in André de Ridder (ed.) 'Edward Wadsworth', *Sélection – Chronique de la vie artistique*, 13, Antwerp 1933, p.44.
3. 'Le Réalisme anglais entre les 2 guerres', *Cahiers du Musée national d'art moderne*, nos.7-8, Paris, 1981.
4. More research is needed on the Rococo revival in England at this time, which also embraced the theatre. I am grateful to my colleague, Richard Morphet, for signalling its importance to me.
5. Repr. *Sélection*, op cit, p.46.
6. For further discussion of the relationship of such publicity photographs to the paintings of Wadsworth, see below.
7. 'L'Art d'Edward Wadsworth', *Sélection*, op. cit, p.12.
8. The propellor-like object is a ship's log used to measure distance travelled.
9. *L'Esprit nouveau* was published in twenty-eight undated numbers between 1920 and 1925 issued at regular intervals.
10. Dora Hedges, 'Leerdam', *Studio*, April 1928, pp.286-9.
11. January 1924, p.5.
12. 'Yet marked I where the bolt of Cupid fell | It fell upon a little western flower, | Before, milk-white; now purple with love's wound: | And maidens call it 'love in idleness'. | Fetch me that flower – the herb I showed thee once. | The juice of it on sleeping eyelids laid | Will make or man or woman madly dote | Upon the next live creature that it sees.' (Act II, scene I, vv.165-72).
13. The author has been unable to identify this object.
14. The title is taken from Psalm 139 which affirms God's inescapability, his ubiquitous presence and his greatness. It appears to have no direct correlation with the image other than in the mention of the sea and in the suggestion of wings in the cloth: 'If I ascend up into heaven, thou *art* there: if I make my bed in hell, behold, thou *art there*. | If I take the wings of the morning, and dwell in the uttermost parts of the sea; | Even there shall thy hand lead me, and thy right hand shall hold me'. (vv.8-10).
15. De Chirico suggested to Wadsworth that he adopt a rich egg emulsion in a letter of 8 June 1928, quoted in Christine Boyanoski, 'The Art of Edward Wadsworth', unpublished MPhil thesis, University of London, Courtauld Institute of Art, 1981, p.64.
16. See the entry on 'Regalia' in *Tate Gallery 1982-84. Illustrated Catalogue of Acquisitions*, 1986, p.349.
17. See the entry referred to in the previous note, p.349.
18. Both repr. in the *Bulletin*, 36, June 1927.
19. See *Tate Gallery*, 1986, op cit, p.349.
20. Repr. in *Sélection*, op cit, p.55. Not listed in the appendix of Barbara Wadsworth, *Edward Wadsworth: A Painter's Life*, Wilton 1989.
21. *Cahiers du Musée national d'art moderne*, op cit, 1981.
22. As Richard Cork points out in his earlier article on Wadsworth's woodcuts, Wadsworth wrote that he liked the woodcut medium because 'it leaves nothing to accident'. Precision, preplanning and deliberateness were always important to Wadsworth.
23. *Studio*, November 1933, p.275.
24. 'Recent Tempera Painting', *Studio*, June 1943, p.175.
25. The title is taken from the *Confessions of St Augustine*: 'Fleisti nos ad te et inquietum est cor nostrum, donec requiescat in te'. Thou hast created us for thyself, and our heart cannot be quieted till it may find repose in thee. (Book I, chapter 1).
26. Now known as 'The English Channel'. Barbara Wadsworth does not list the alternative title, 'Visibility Moderate' in the appendix of Barbara Wadsworth, op. cit.
27. Repr. *Studio*, December 1942, p.206. This painting depicts three steamrollers lying in disuse surrounded by scrap metal and junk, suggesting the appropriation of manual labour by conscription.
28. Quoted in Joyce Watkins, 'The Advertiser as Patron', *Studio*, April 1942, p.108. This article is devoted to the wartime advertising campaigns devised by ICI to involve artists.
29. See previous note.
30. I am grateful to Philip Winterbottom, currently working on the ICI archives, for making available to me the album devoted to this campaign from which this extract is taken.
31. Repr. in article cited in note 28, p.111.
32. The depiction of figures was very rare in Wadsworth's painting.

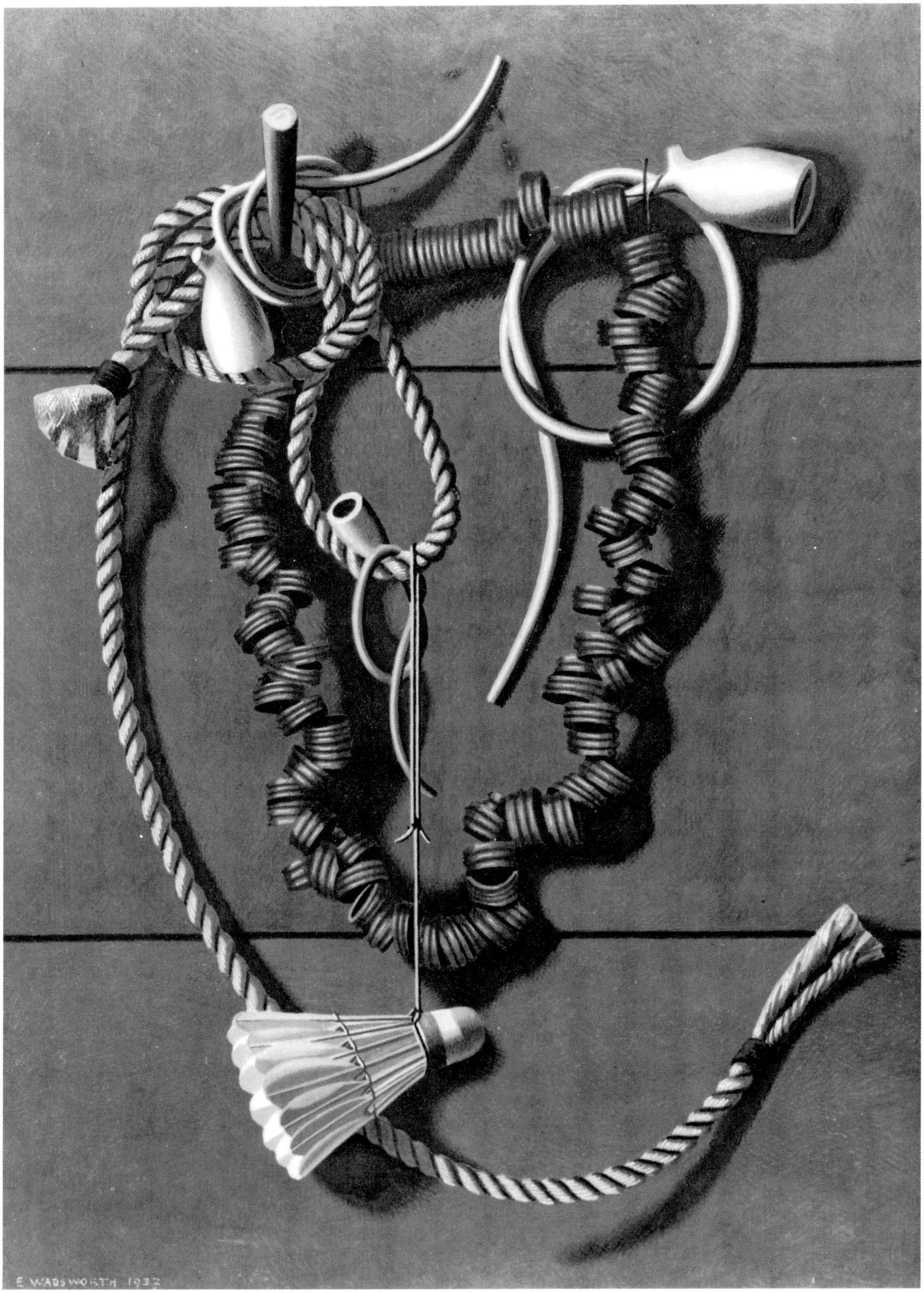

123

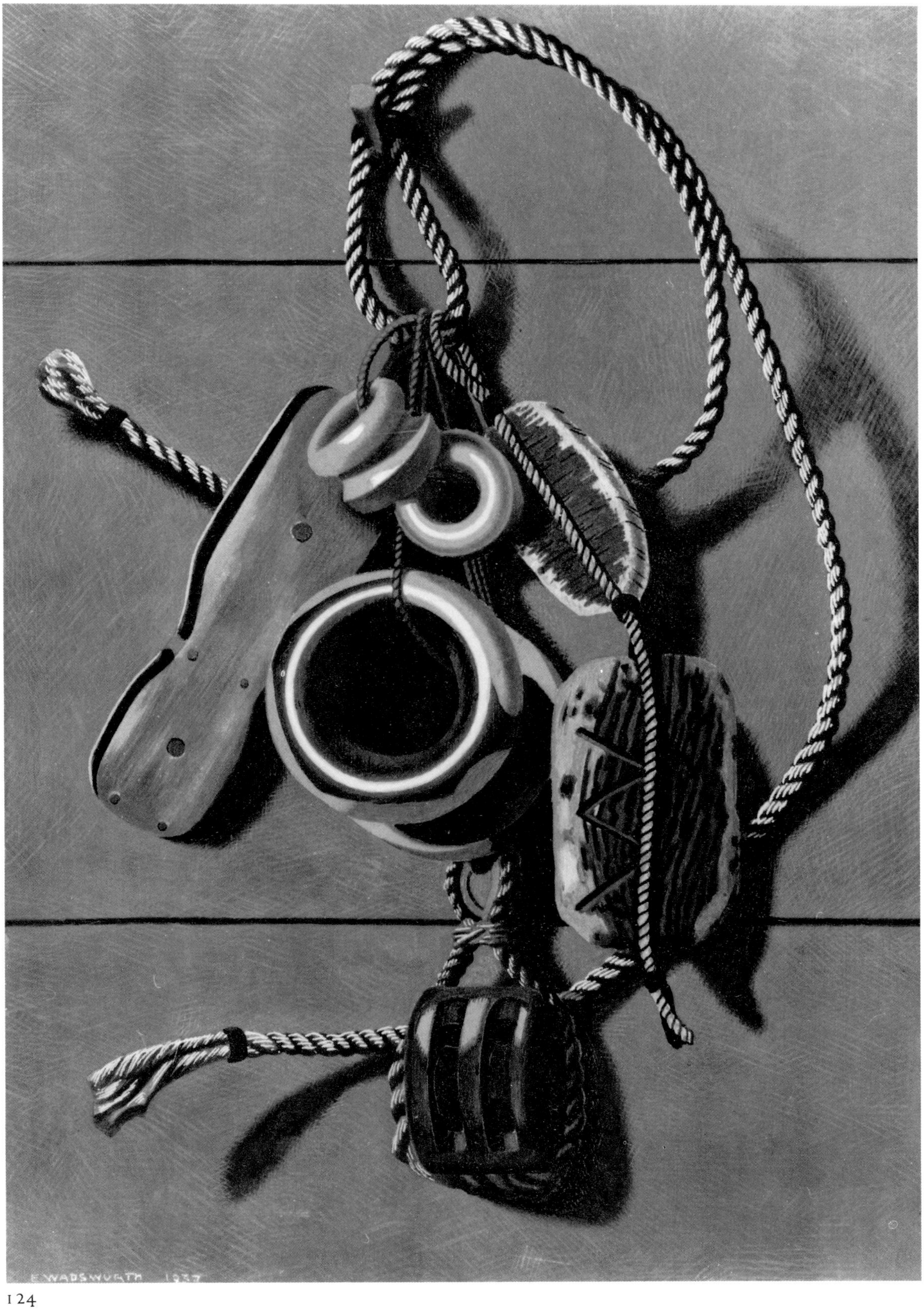

124

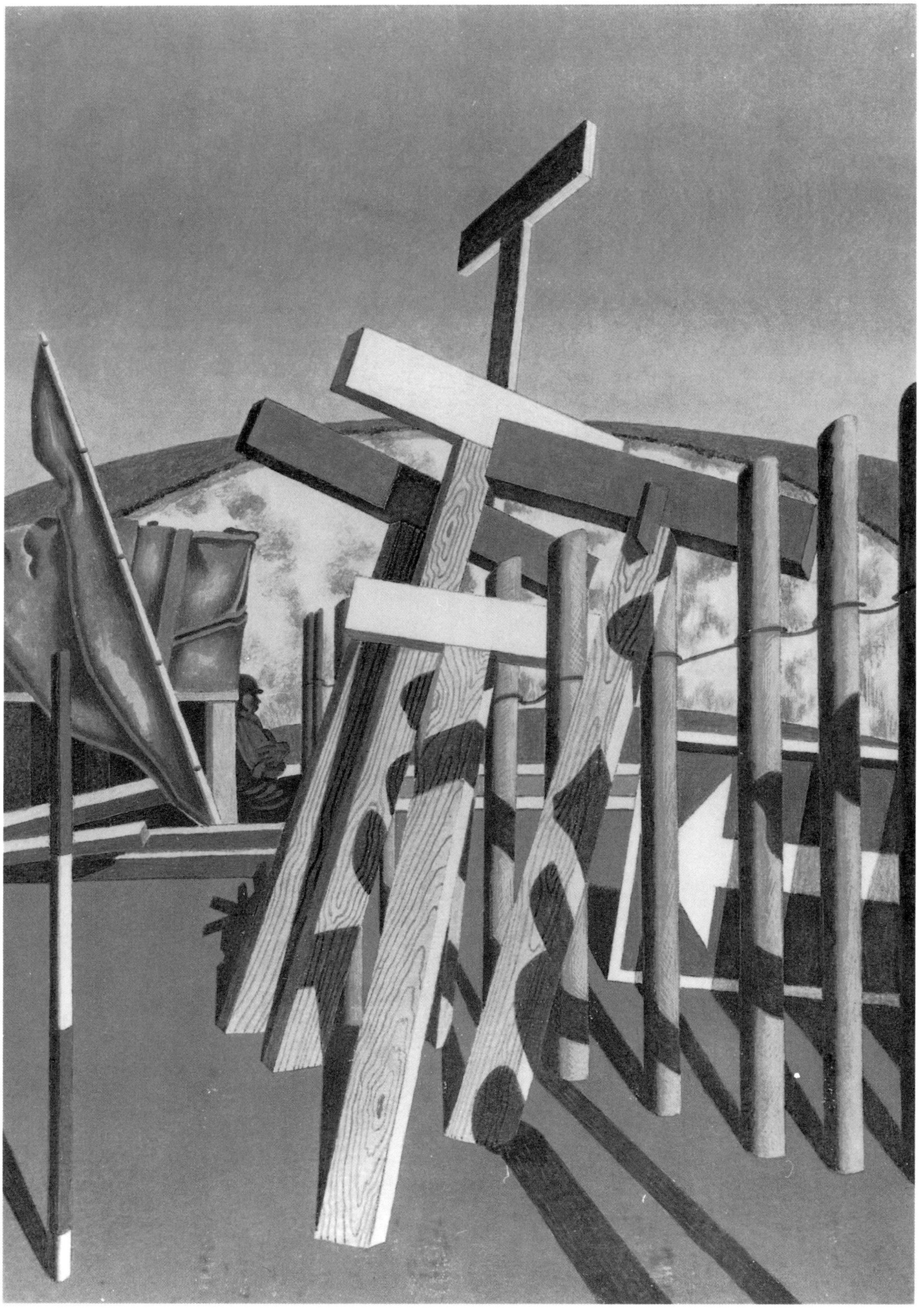

125

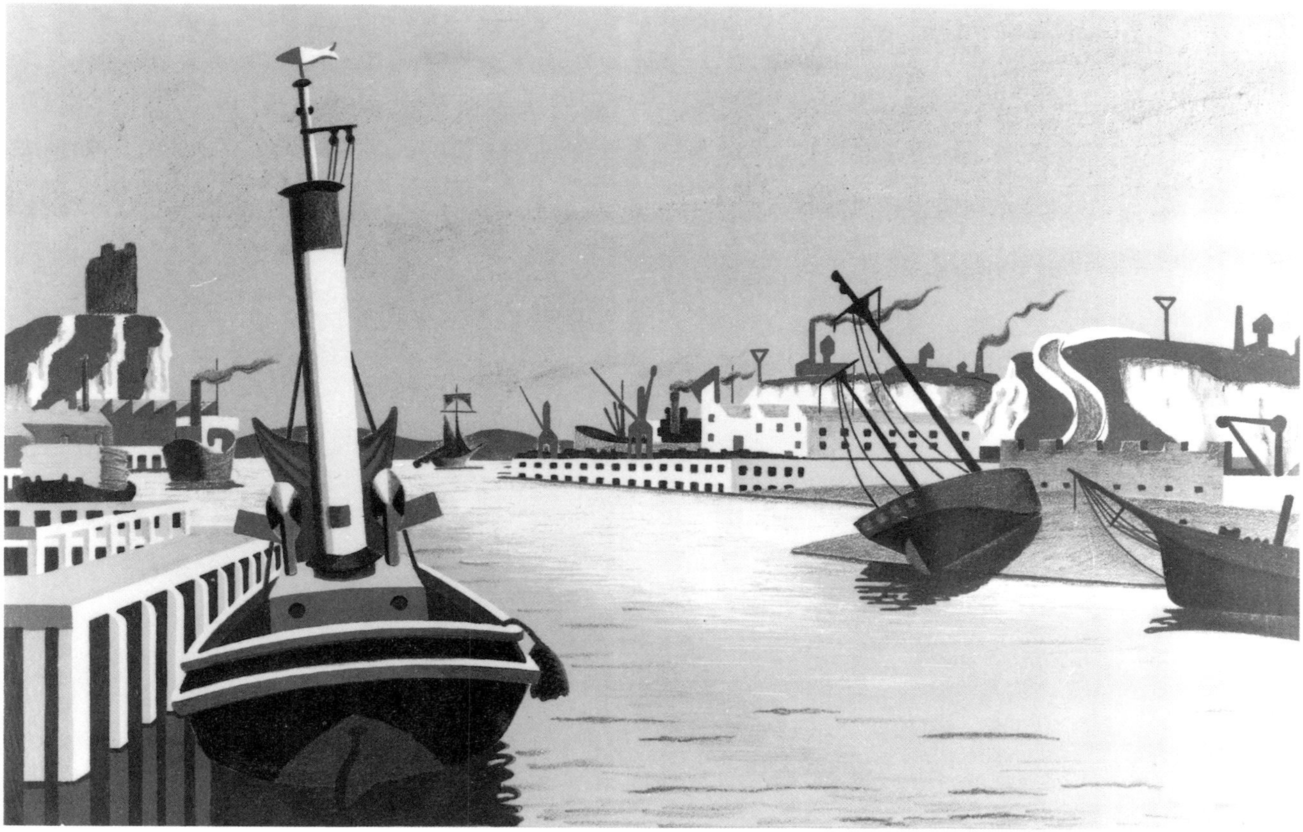

126

125. *Sussex By-pass* 1937
126. *Imaginary Harbour* 1938

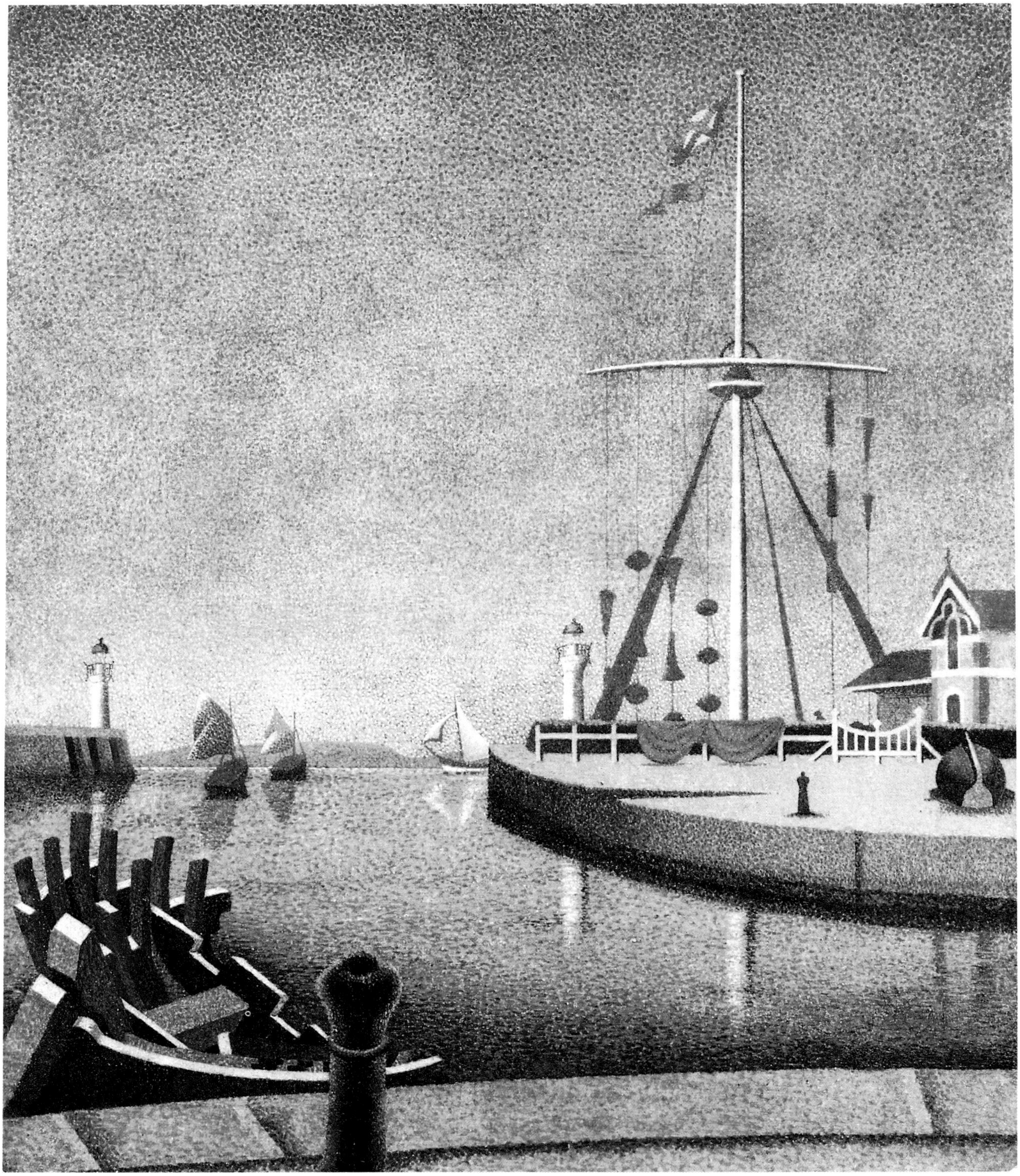

127

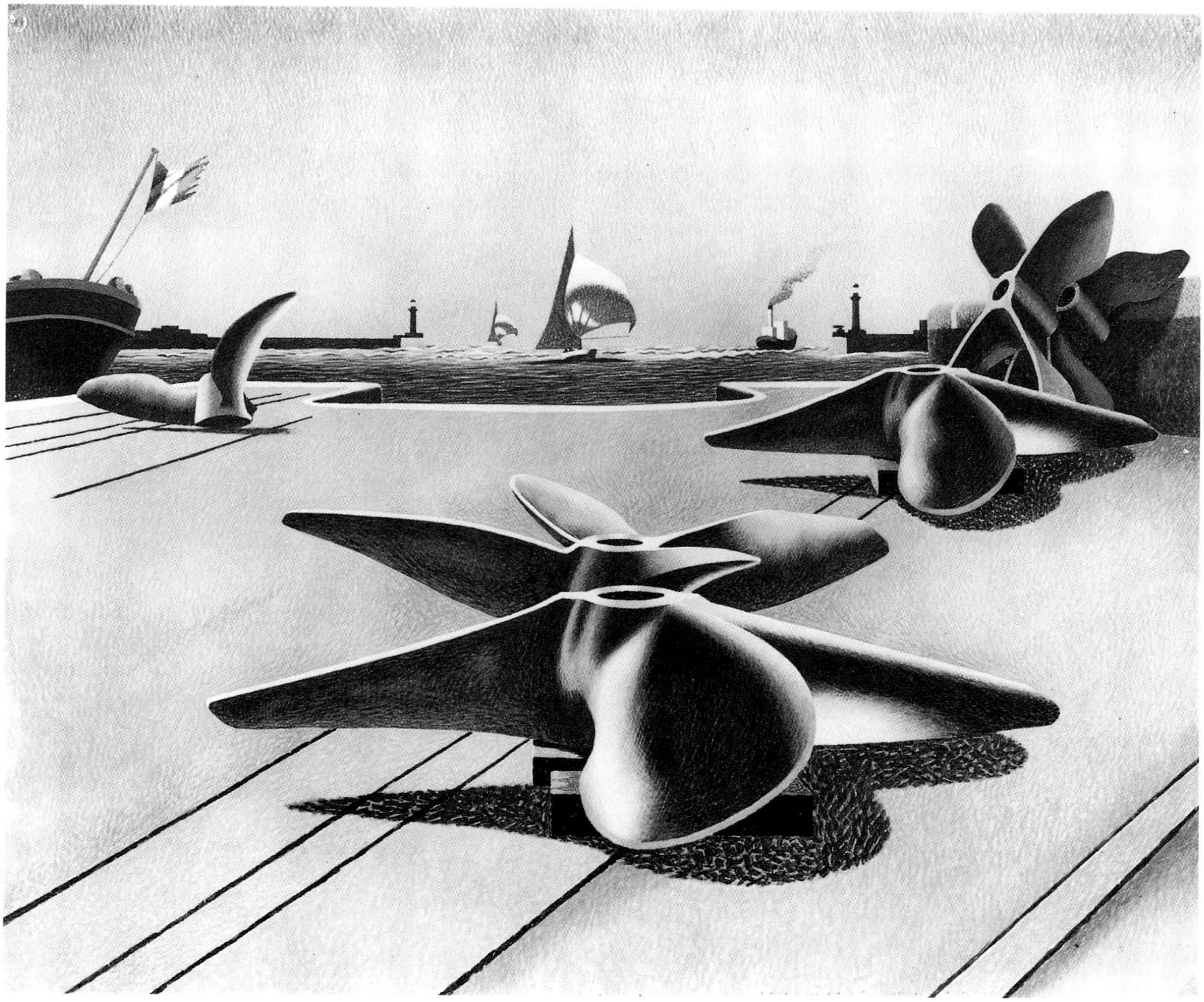

127a

127. *Honfleur – Entrance to Harbour* 1939
127a. *Bronze Ballet* 1940

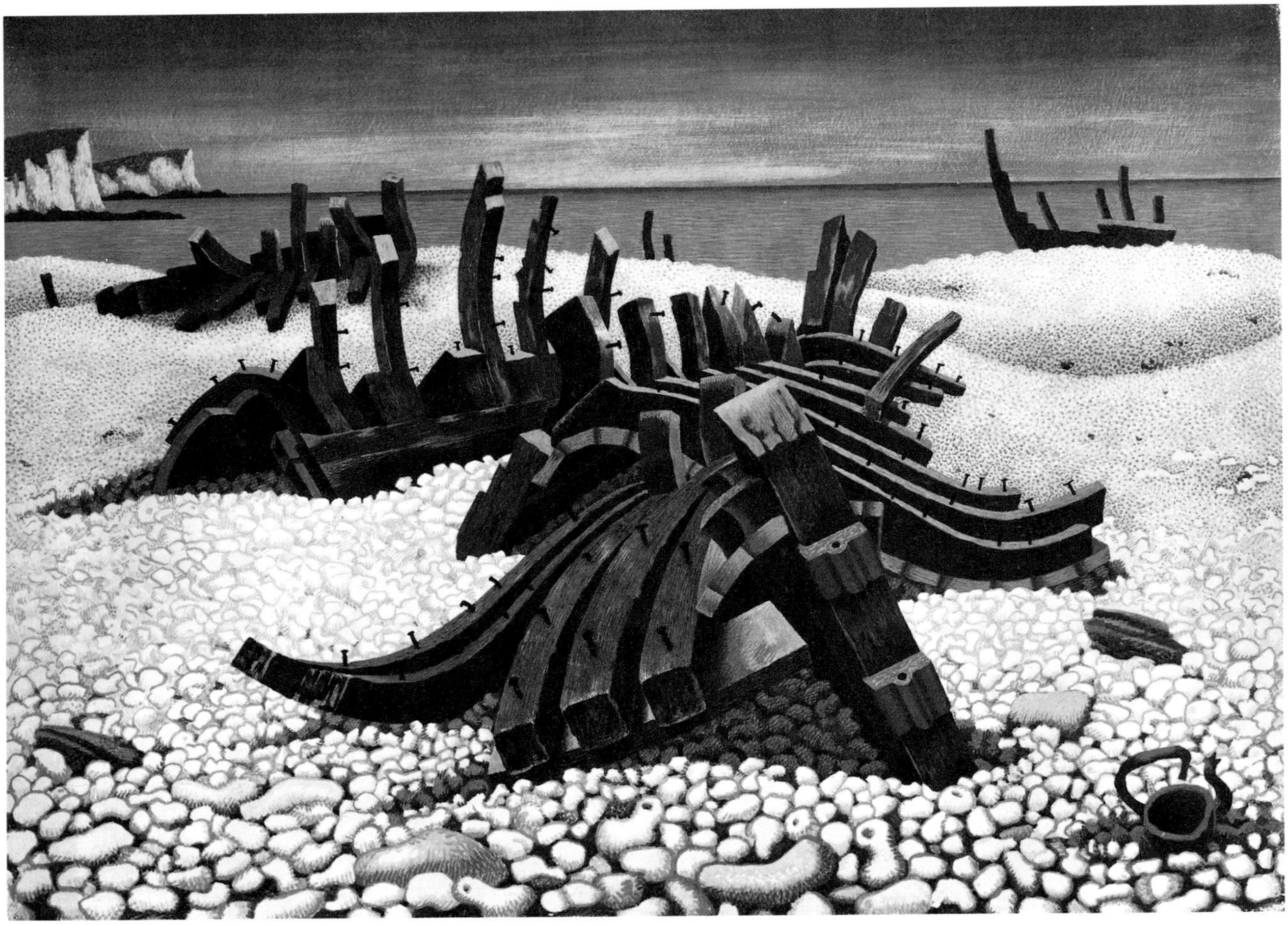

128a

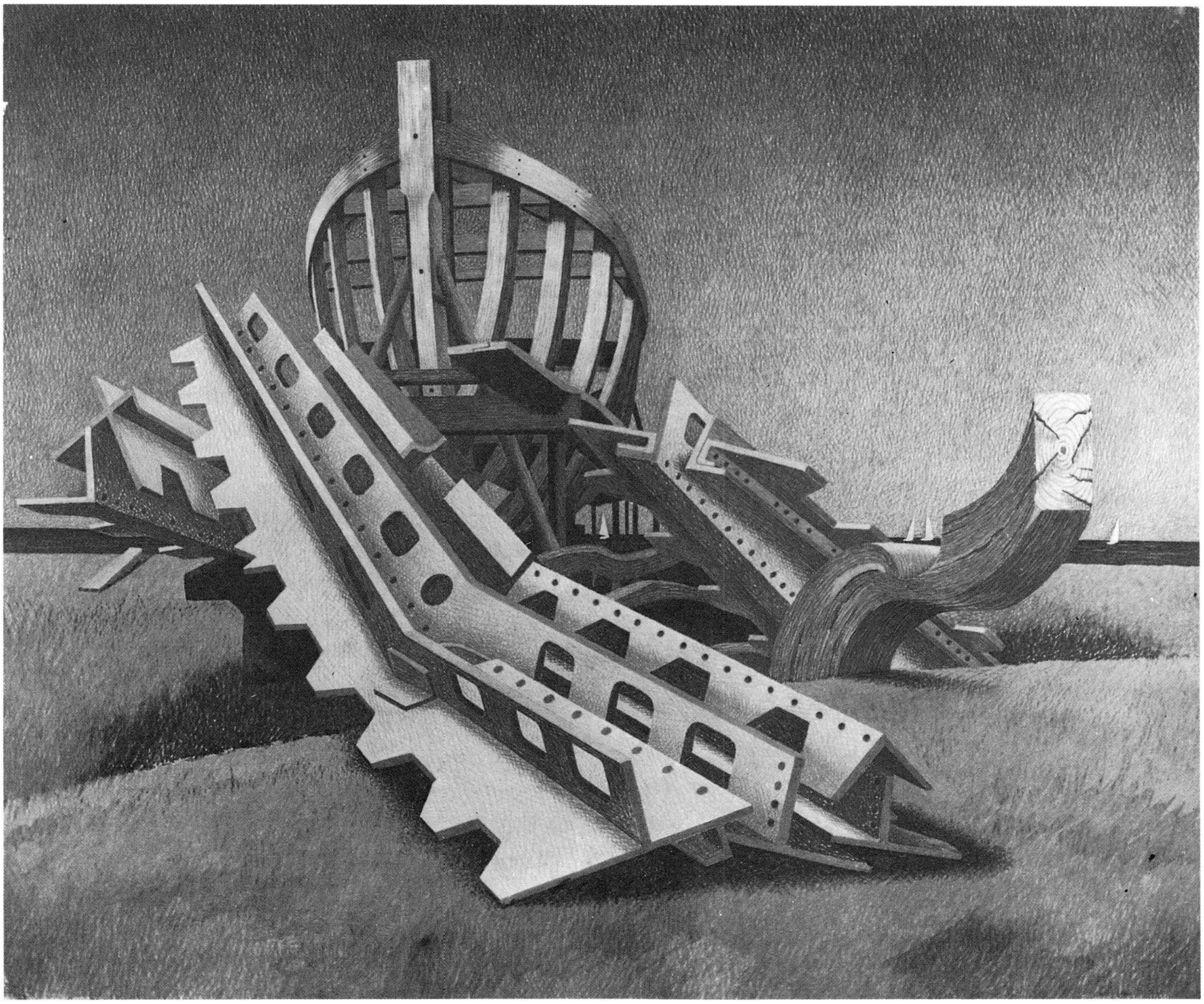

128

128a. *Requiescat* c. 1940
128. *Light Sections (3)* 1940

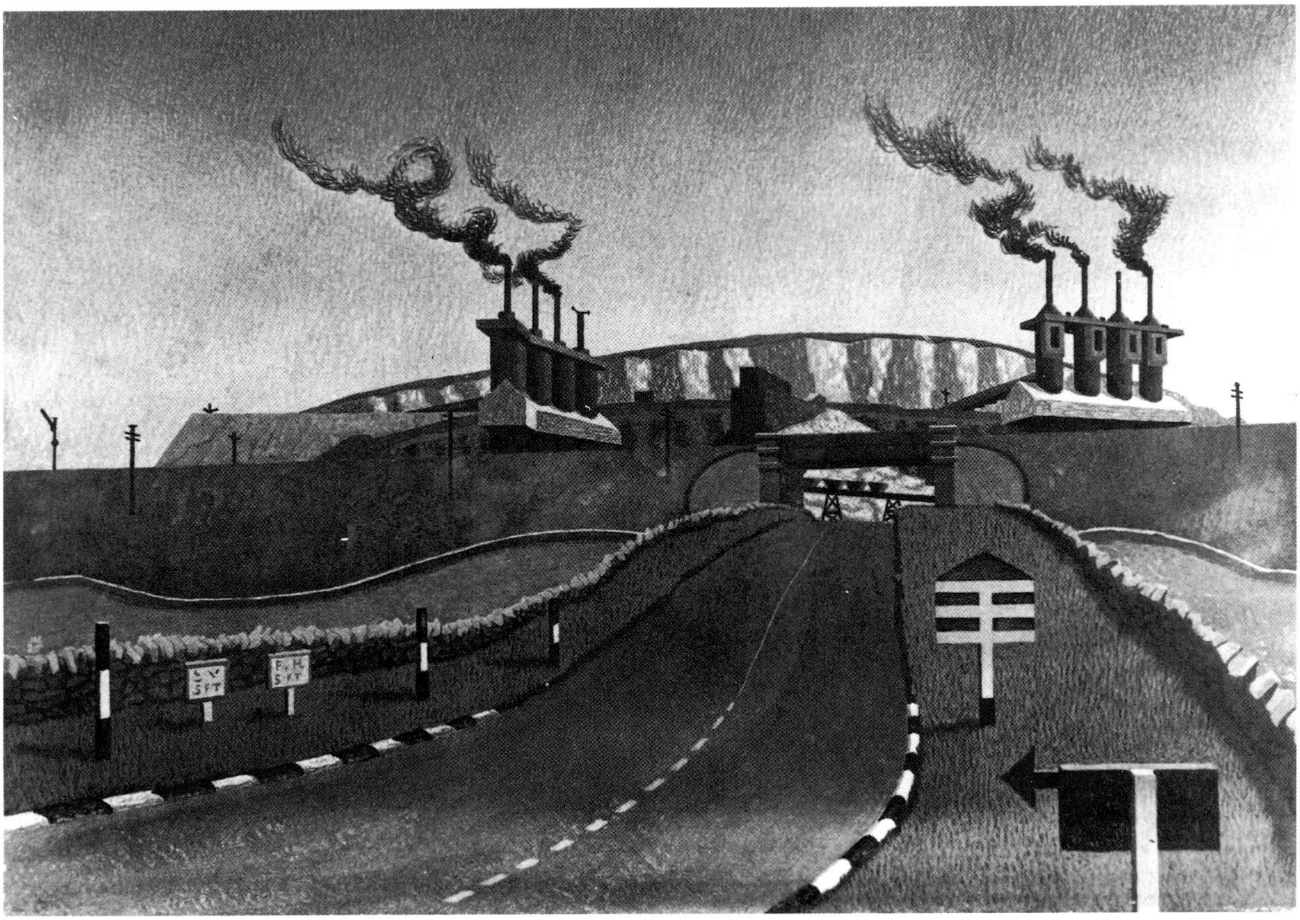

130

130. Top of the *World* 1942-3
129. Pendent/Punch Balls 1942

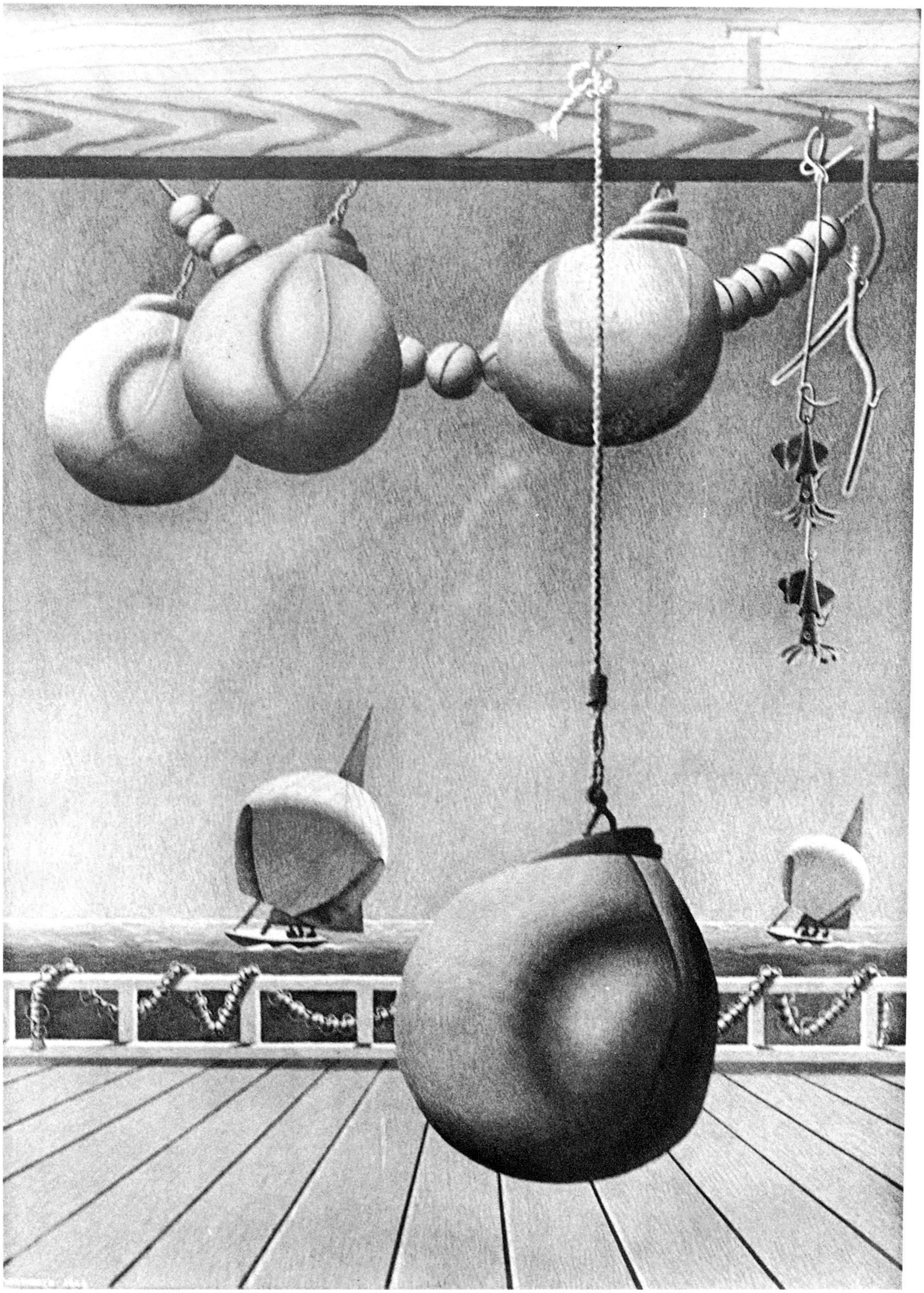

129

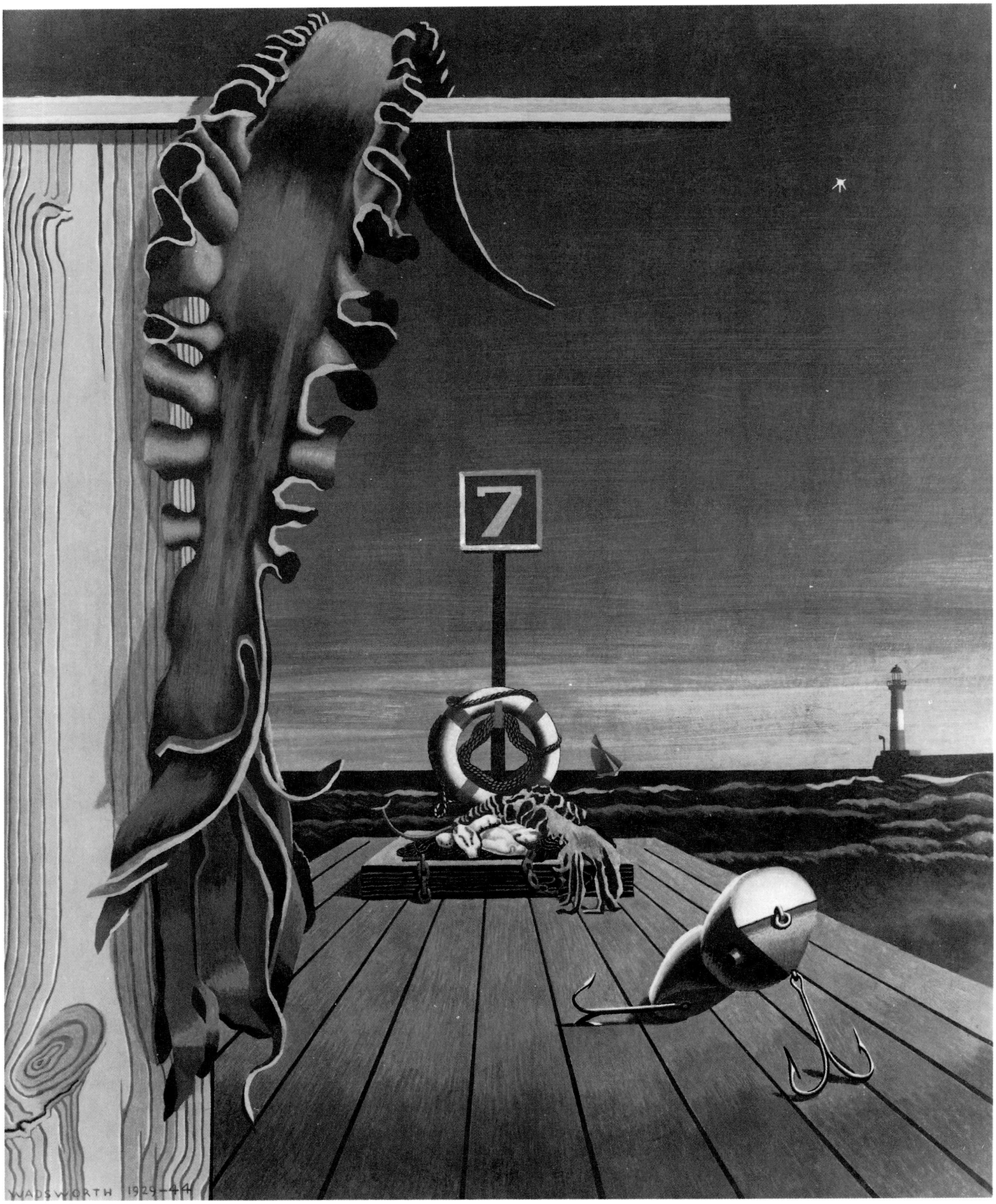

131

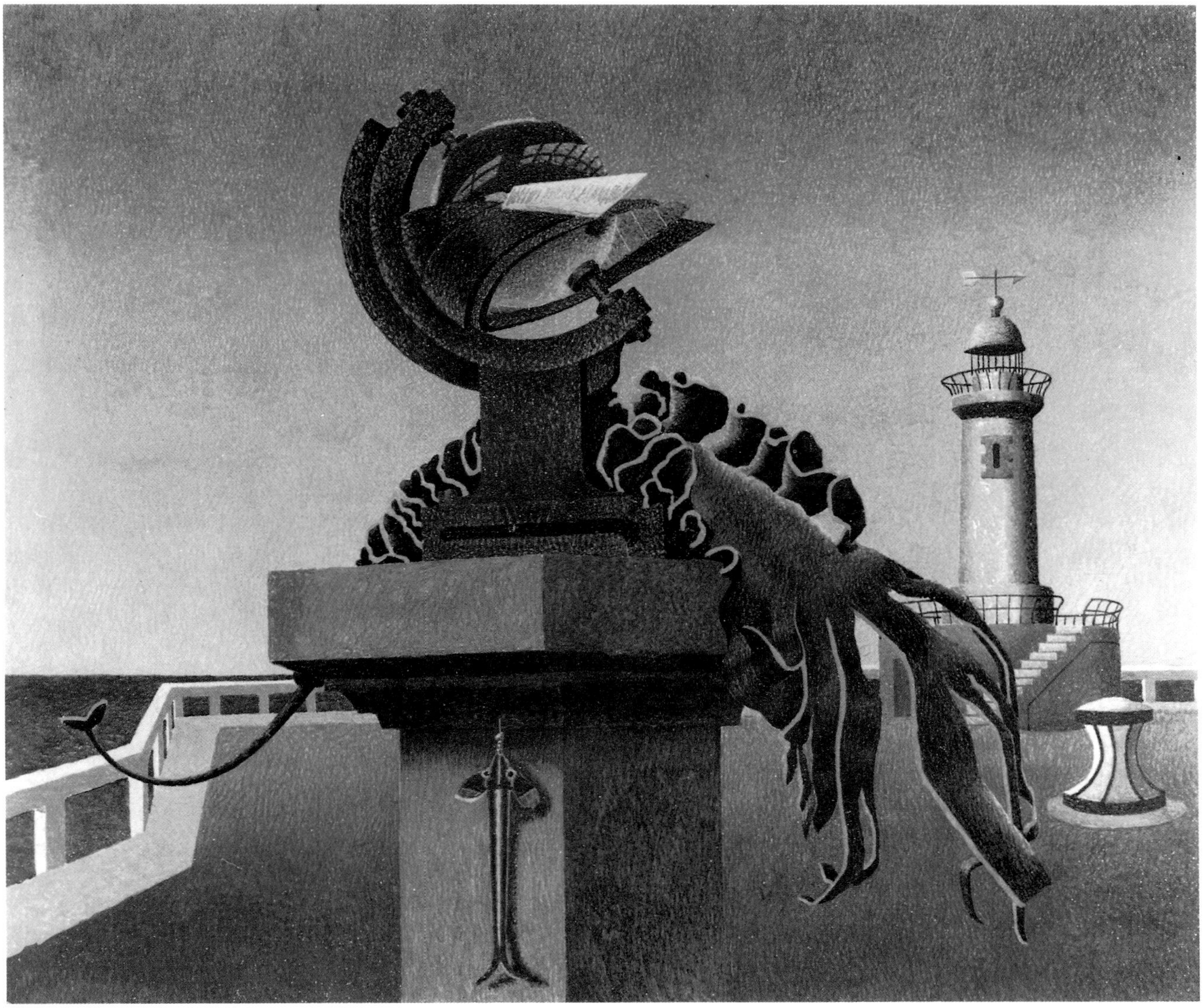

132

131. *Tomorrow Morning* 1929-44
132. *Anticyclone* 1943

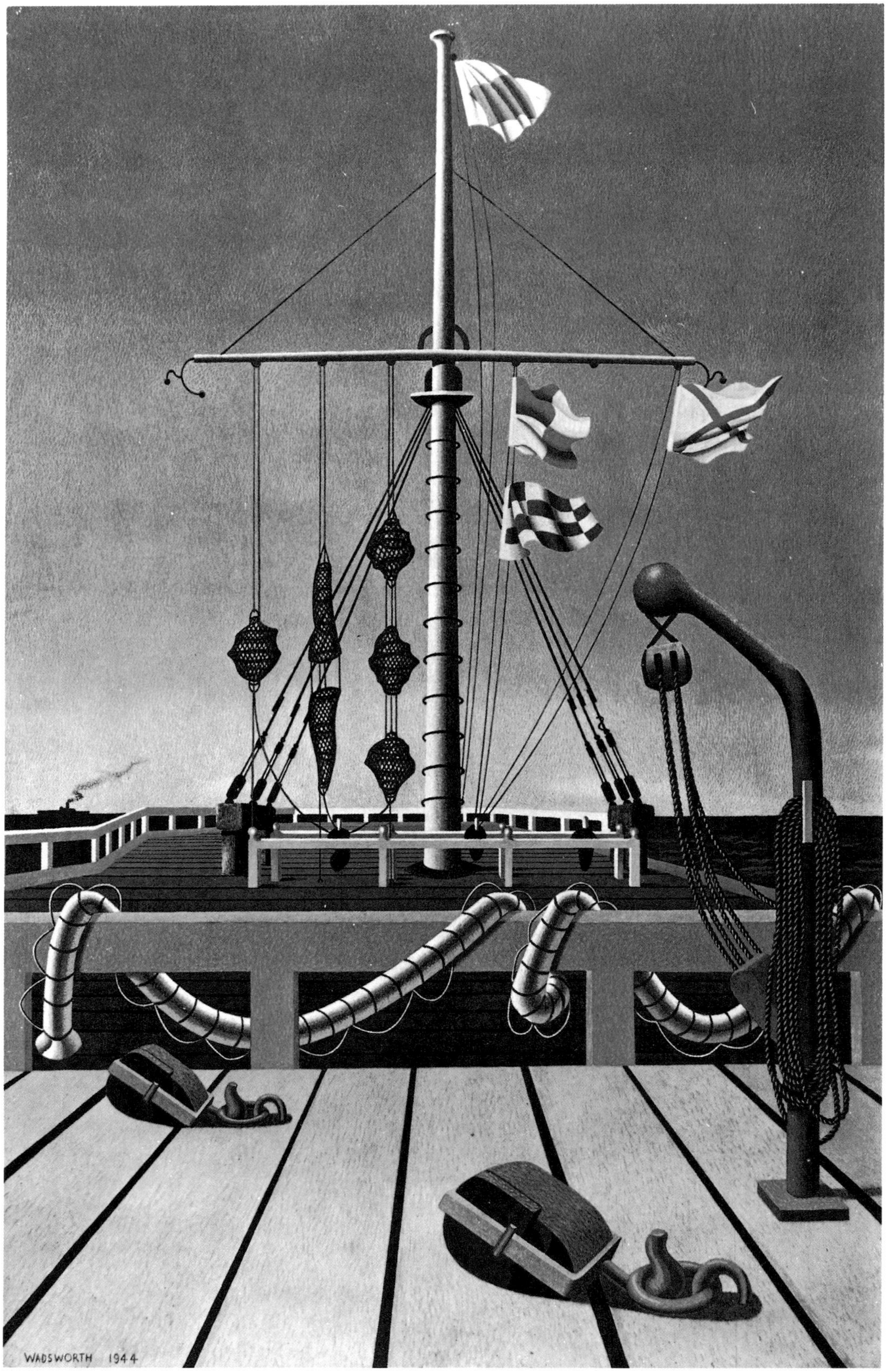

134

134. *Signal Station/The Jetty* 1944
135a. *Le Havre/Harbour Entrance/Boats in Harbour* 1939–45

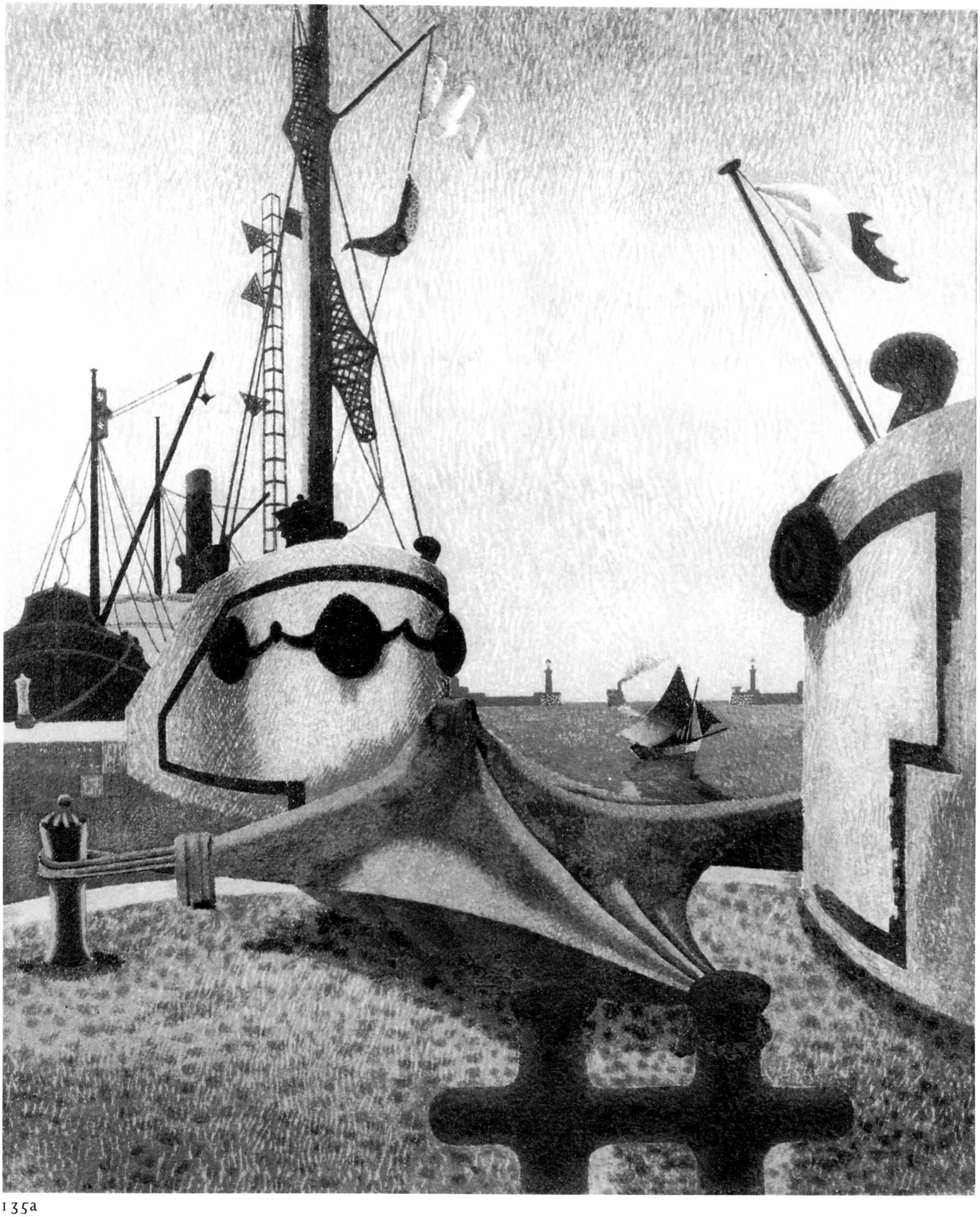

135a

Serge Fauchereau

Abstraction-Création, Unit One ... Permanent Change

As a student at the Slade School of Art, Edward Wadsworth was a figurative painter but in his espousal of Vorticism, in the year that preceded the outbreak of the Great War, he became one of England's first radically abstract painters. Following the war, however, he reverted for some ten years to what is conventionally known as figurative painting and even to a certain realism. The term 'Surrealist' has been applied to some of his paintings of unusual arrangements of objects – but they are never as obviously heteroclite as those which appear in the work of, say, Pierre Roy. Yet by the beginning of the thirties, Wadsworth was so deeply immersed in abstraction that he was perceived by his continental counterparts as Britain's leading exponent of the style. This remained the case until 1934 when for a further ten years he again reverted to figurative painting. At the time of his death in 1949, however, his art was undeniably abstract.

Described in these terms, Wadsworth's career appears to have been a series of sudden about-turns. Indeed this was not unusual for artists of his generation. For example, before Auguste Herbin became the leading figure in Abstraction-Création, he had been a *fauve* painter of figurative subjects and then an abstract artist; he subsequently returned to figurative art in the twenties before finally adopting an abstract style. The comparison between Wadsworth and Herbin, however, gives a false impression of the former's approach to painting. For Wadsworth, figuration and abstraction were not mutually exclusive and in that sense he is, perhaps, closer to Robert Delaunay, who quite happily painted both figurative and abstract works throughout his career.

Even if we restrict the present discussion to Wadsworth's last two abstract periods, a brief look at his earlier career may explain why the 'abstraction or figuration' dilemma was never a problem for him. In the twenties he arranged and constructed his still lifes without striving for exact verisimilitude. This is obvious even in early landscapes inspired by specific places. The paintings of La Rochelle (81 and 82), for instance, are reconstructed from elements that have been taken from various locations within the harbour and then reassembled to make a picture. As anyone who has lived in La Rochelle will point out, it is in fact impossible to stand by the outer harbour and see simultaneously the towers at the entrance to the tidal dock, the lighthouse, the Gabut customs house and the inner floating dock, to say nothing of the building of the quai Duperré (see figs. 34-6). However, verisimilitude is largely irrelevant since the painting is magnificent as it stands. The truth of a painting lies in the painting itself. With considerable ease Wadsworth made the transition from landscapes reconstructed from real and recognisable elements to completely imaginary landscapes, in which the foreground is made up of objects, used on repeated occasions, which have been chosen and arranged at will in front of a seascape of no precise location; in other words, a move away from realism. In 1929, he moved further away from it by treating the object in an increasingly stylised manner, distorting the perspective to such an extent that it no longer existed. Michael Sevier described this perfectly in 1933:

> It was not really until 1929 that ... objects and motifs, which were individualised in their natural substance, located in a three-dimensional perspective and which were formerly replaced by their visual equivalents, gave way to forms with purely ideographic contours situated in an ideal space which was everywhere and nowhere. Shells became cones, drills became spirals, columns became cylinders, tables became square surfaces, and so on.[1]

Wadsworth himself had long since realised that abstraction represented an extension of pictorial language: 'The necessity for expressing oneself exclusively with forms that are based on nature is only a temporary limitation.'[2]

In Wadsworth's work the transition from a figurative to an abstract style, or vice versa, was gradual but was always reversible over both short and long periods. He did not distinguish between the aims of either style (in fact, the division of his work into periods is simply a matter of convenience). The shells and metal-shavings which he had begun again to paint in perspective, but now combined with abstract structures, gave way in 1930 to flat forms which were more or less distant memories of spirals and triangles. He continued to paint shells in preference to other objects because their regularity lent itself to a geometry of form in perfect harmony with strictly geometric figures; for example 'Composition with Shell' 1930 (104). We might speculate that Wadsworth was encouraged to adopt a more abstract style by the example of Willi Baumeister, who was to become a friend, and especially by the series of 'Machines' he painted in the twenties, but Wadsworth's paintings of 1929-30 are, perhaps, more strongly reminiscent of painters like George Valmier, whose work he cannot really have known. In fact the example common to all these painters was

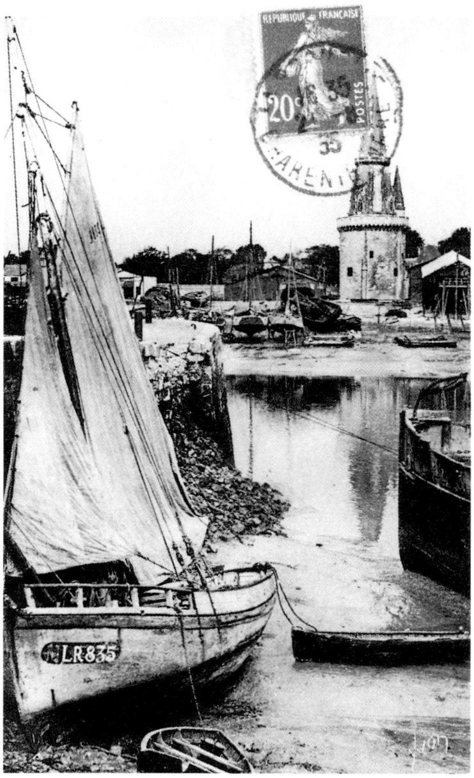

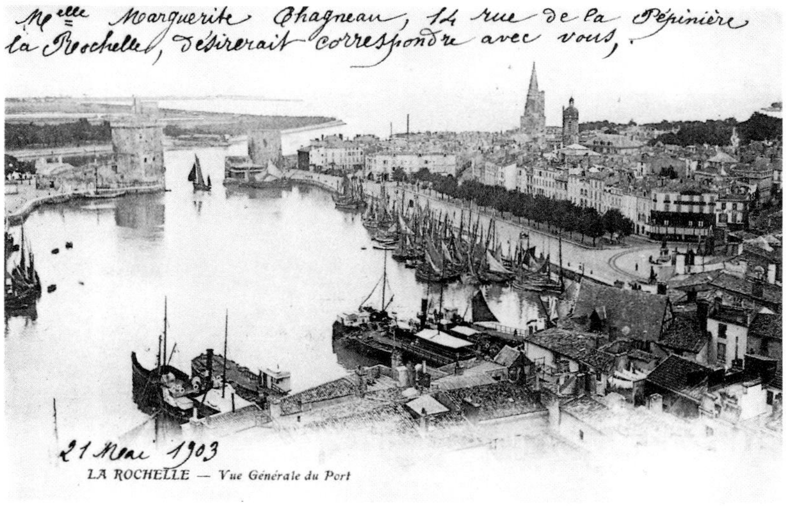

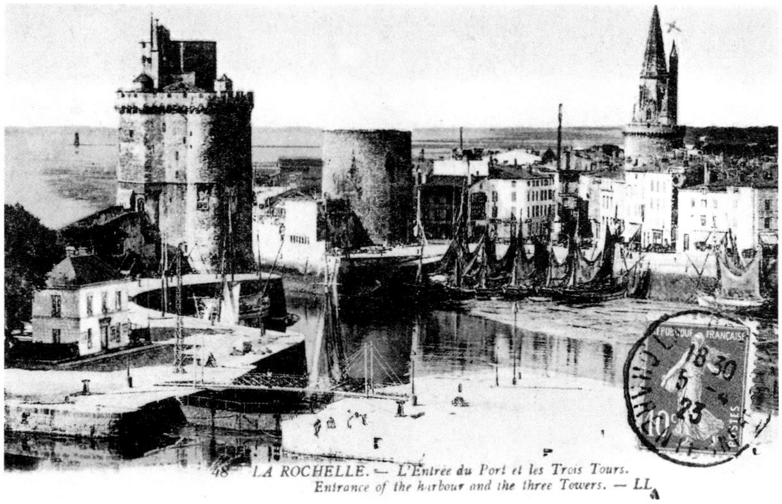

Fig.34 ABOVE *La Rochelle, le chenal et la tour de la lanterne*, postcard postmarked 1935

Fig.35 RIGHT, TOP *La Rochelle, vue générale du port*, postcard postmarked 1903

Fig.36 RIGHT, BOTTOM *La Rochelle, l'entrée du port et les trois tours*, postcard postmarked 1923

set by Fernand Léger (see fig.37), a senior figure for whom Wadsworth always felt a real admiration. Several of Wadsworth's 'Composition' paintings were painted in the spirit of Léger in that they were still based upon forms taken from the real world, in this case pocket knives with either open or closed blades. The sectarians of Abstraction-Création, however, saw no trace of realism in them, since two of these paintings were reproduced in the first issue of their journal in 1932.

At the instigation of Herbin, Hélion, Vantongerloo, Kupka and a few others, Abstraction-Création came into being in Paris in 1931. It aimed avowedly to promote abstract art and less overtly to oppose, on the one hand, all kinds of realism and, on the other, Surrealism, which had in recent years been a very active force in art, literature and even politics (not that this prevented an artist like Arp from continuing to have close links with the Surrealists). All tendencies were represented, from Brancusi to Mondrian, Kandinsky to Delaunay. Abstraction-Création was intended to provide as international a platform as possible stripped of all political loyalties. 'There was very little internal politics in Abstraction-Création', Jean Hélion wrote in his memoirs, although he went on to state that 'Herbin and I inclined towards Communism'.[3] As politics was obviously never one of Wadsworth's major concerns, the purely aesthetic stance of the association must have suited him.

Precisely how Wadsworth came into contact with Abstraction-Création is not very clear. It was certainly not through Ben Nicholson or Barbara Hepworth, who also joined the group, since their work did not feature in the first issue of the journal *Abstraction-Création*, whereas Wadsworth's was well represented. It seems unlikely that either Herbin or

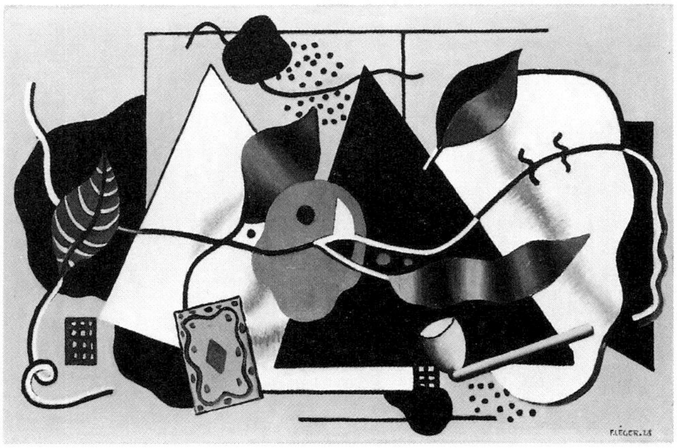

Fig.37 Fernand Léger, *Carte et pipe* 1928, oil on canvas, 60 × 91.5, The Trustees of the Tate Gallery (formerly collection Edward Wadsworth)

Hélion introduced him to it. Perhaps it was Baumeister. It was unusual for English painters to join international associations in 1932. British writers and artists have rarely been inclined to collaborate with foreigners, their traditional American allies being an exception to the rule; hence the importance of the encounter – which predates Surrealism – between Wadsworth, and then Hepworth and Nicholson, and the very cosmopolitan Abstraction-Création group. A footbridge, if not a roadbridge, had been built between Britain and the Continent. Until then, Great Britain had languished in a 'slumbering provincialism', to use Herbert Read's damning words.[4] It is true that until the mid thirties, there was a certain isolationist attitude in the British art world, although it was not always manifested in British works of art. In spite of being based on the Futurist model, Vorticism itself was an expression of a desire for complete self-sufficiency and a wish to denigrate all foreign influences (Nevinson's alliance with the Italian Marinetti was only temporary).

When he joined Abstraction-Création, Wadsworth himself was a completely abstract painter. While there may be some evidence of perspective in 'Composition on a Red Ground' 1931 (106) one would be hard put to say just what stylised object is suggested by those shapes. In 1927 Wadsworth definitely exhibited at the Galerie Barbazanges but, although his 'Coastguards' 1927 was reproduced in Rosenberg's *Bulletin de l'effort moderne* that year, the press paid little attention to his work. In the early thirties, his works began to appear in various group shows and he began to be talked about. In 1931, Michael Sevier, a critic and occasional painter, devoted an article to 'Tendances modernes en Angleterre' in the *Cahiers de Belgique*: the only illustrations were of works by Wadsworth. Curiously enough, they were 'Dunkerque' 1924 and a 'Painting', both of which were obviously figurative, whereas the author was arguing the case for non-figuration: 'It is in the domain of pure abstraction that painters like Wyndham Lewis, Ed. Wadsworth and John Selby Bigge have found the elements they needed for an intense and direct expression of their aesthetic conceptions.'[5] In spite of his odd choice of paintings, Sevier was well informed about recent developments in the work of Wadsworth who had completely abandoned figuration and was in the process of doing away with all effects of perspective. The descriptive title of 'Composition, Crank and Chain' 1932 was probably chosen more to distinguish it from other paintings than because the forms, vaguely reminiscent of Léger, resemble actual mechanical parts.

Wadsworth usually gave his paintings neutral titles which evoked no visual associations. There are, for example, a series of numbered 'Compositions' and several 'Dux et Comes' (108, 109, 110). These paintings were probably well thought of in Abstraction-Création, as they related to the lyrical organic forms celebrated by Herbin (for example Wadsworth's 'Composition IV', 107) and Arp (for example 'Dux et Comes'). Two paintings entitled 'Dux et Comes' of 1932 were in fact reproduced in the second issue of *Abstraction-Création* in 1933. There is always a certain element of biomorphism in Wadsworth's abstract paintings, with their clean forms and flat tones, and he never adopted the rectilinear geometric style of Mondrian or van Doesburg. Although painted in the spirit of Abstraction-Création, 'Composition on a Blue Ground' 1932-3 is very unusual: the juxtaposition of the amoeba-like forms, the scalloped pink and white shapes juxtaposed with the irregular and vigorous elliptical lines gives the whole work a rare dynamism.

In Europe, Wadsworth tended to be seen as the leading light in British abstraction; in May 1933 he was paid an exceptional tribute, which very few twentieth-century English painters have received, when the Antwerp-based publishers of *Sélection* devoted one of their periodical *cahiers* to his work. The idea for this monograph may have come from Georges Marlier, the former editor in chief of *Cahiers de Belgique* who was then the secretary of *Sélection*, and from the editor, André de Ridder, in collaboration with Michael Sevier. Baumeister, who had also been the subject of a *cahier*, can only have approved of the interest they took in his English friend. Whoever was behind the idea, the publication was, for its time, quite sumptuous; forty-four of the eighty pages carried photographic reproductions. Five woodcuts were reproduced in text. It also included three essays; 'L'Art d'Edward Wadsworth' by Waldemar George, Michael Sevier's 'L'Evolution du peintre Edward Wadsworth', and 'Homage à Edward Wadsworth' by the sculptor Ossip Zadkine. Zadkine ended his essay, which is as personal as it is friendly,

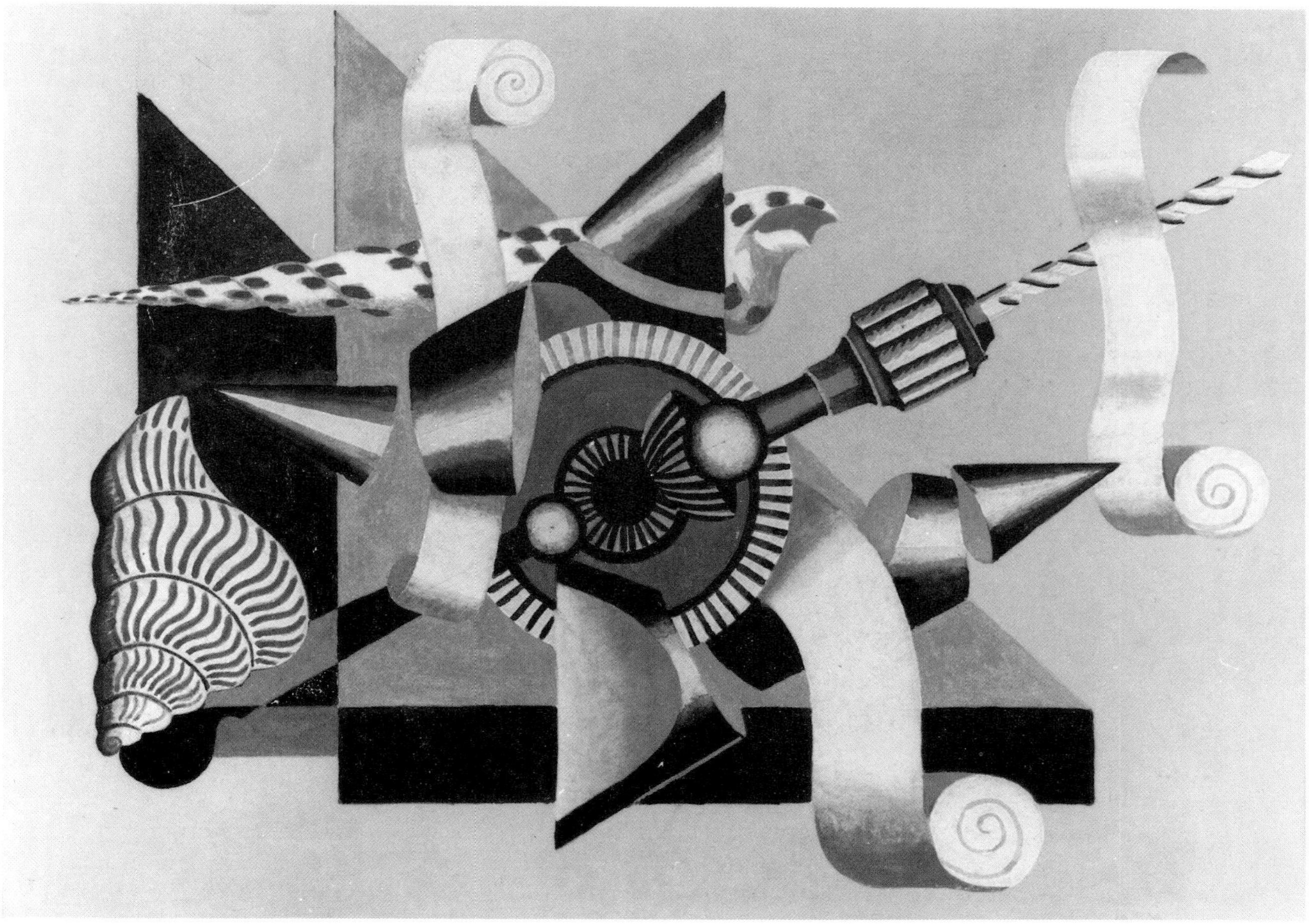

102

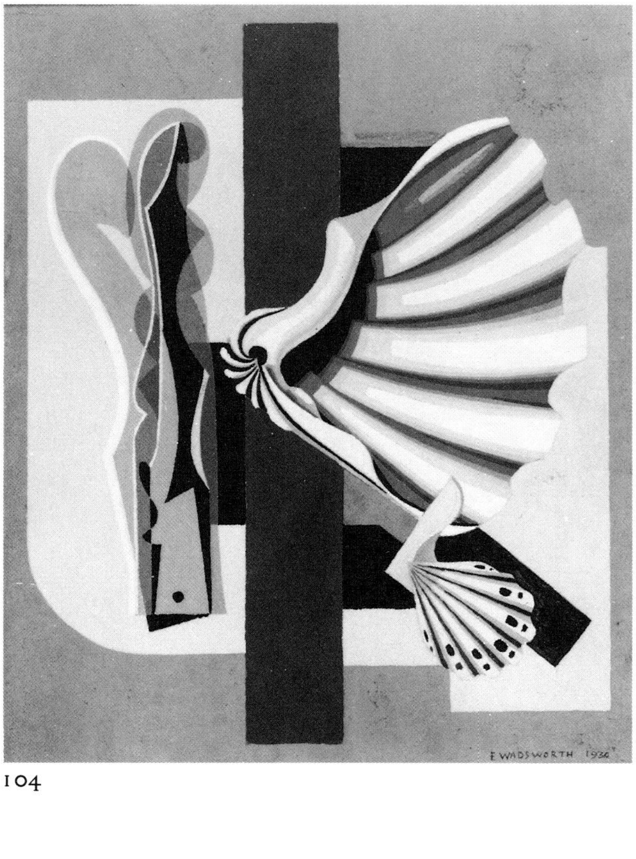

104

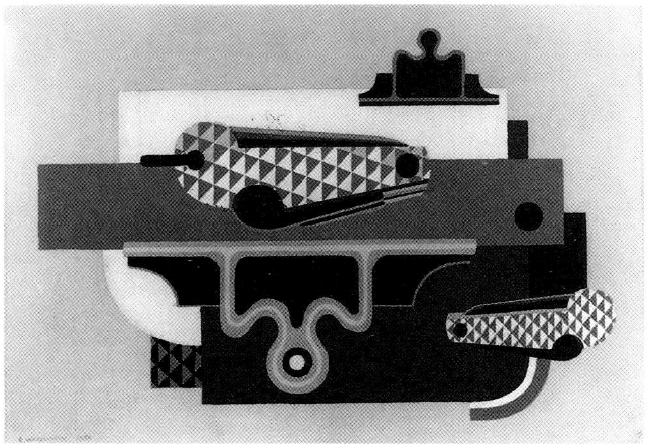

105

102. *Cones, Spirals and Triangles* 1930
104. *Composition with Shell* 1930
105. *Composition on a Pink Ground/Abstract Design with Claspknife* 1930

by saying that: 'Love of determinate objects which can be known and named is finally staggering towards liberation. The painter composes, dissects and then recreates his world. Then, the curtain falls. Behind the laboratory window, a man seeks and thinks.' One could not hope for a better account of this stage in Wadsworth's development.

1933 was also the year in which a group of British artists came together to form Unit One. They were the painters John Armstrong, John Bigge, Edward Burra, Tristram Hillier, Paul Nash, Ben Nicholson and Edward Wadsworth, the sculptors Barbara Hepworth and Henry Moore, and the architects Colin Lucas and Wells Coates. The group did not really have any coherent aesthetic, which no doubt explains why it was so short-lived and, whilst abstract painters were in the majority, Nash was more of a Surrealist and Burra an Expressionist. There are obviously many explanations for the emergence of the group but they all relate to a wish to make common cause against the conservatism that was so widespread in contemporary British art and to do more to improve the difficult material and moral position of avant-garde artists. In Britain as in other countries, the years that followed the financial crash of 1929 were both troubled and turbulent. Intellectuals found it difficult to situate themselves within the context of the political and social climate. The choices they made were not particularly far-sighted; 1933 was the year of publication of W H Auden's *Dance of Death* and Stephen Spender's *Poems*. Wyndham Lewis, for his part, published an essay on Hitler. At a time when Stalin and Hitler were becoming absolute tyrants, there was little to choose between the Communist commitment of the former and the reactionary stance of the latter. The members of Unit One had little liking for brutal ideologies and their aesthetic and social options (insofar as they were expressed) led them to choose the mid-ground. In the group's collective publication *Unit One*, published in 1934, the year in which they all exhibited together at the Mayor Gallery in London, Wadsworth adumbrated a formalist position by giving a revised or more dynamic version of Maurice Denis's definition of a painting: 'A picture is primarily the animation of an inert plane surface by a spatial rhythm of forms and colours.'[6] A few months earlier, he had been asked why he had abandoned figurative art. His reply took the form of a major text published in the *Studio* on 6 October 1933. The following paragraphs are a good expression of the painter's credo:

> In my opinion the tree 'does' a tree much better than your artist can 'do' it and I repeat again that the artist is concerned with pictures – not with trees …
>
> At no period has the aspect of things been a main consideration of my painting, though admittedly I have from time to time been stimulated by certain landscapes or objects, the realistic appearance of which I have promptly subdued in order to emphasise qualities which I consider more important …
>
> The aim remains the same – the animation of surfaces by forms and colours – only the means are different. And they are different because we live now in 1933. Neither in the arts nor science nor philosophy are we concerned with the problems that were so vital in the past. The past has solved its problems – always with a little bit of an eye on the future – let us do the same. The only permanent thing in life is change.[7]

Change is what fascinated Wadsworth, who was reluctant to go on using the same means of expression indefinitely, no matter how up to the minute they had become. In 1934, therefore, he reverted to a figurative style similar to that of his paintings of the twenties, or to what Michael Sevier called his 'magic realism'. Yet the statement cited above remains valid: no matter whether it is figurative or abstract, art has nothing to do with nature and is not in competition with it. As Mondrian was fond of saying, 'Art is artificial'. Since for Wadsworth, figuration and abstraction were simply different, but not mutually exclusive, means to the same end, he was represented at the Exposition Universelle in Brussels in 1935 by the radically abstract 'Composition on a Blue Ground' 1933. He was also on very good terms with Myfanwy Evans and John Piper, whose publication *Axis* was largely devoted to abstract art. The first issue contained a reproduction of an abstract 'Composition' painted in 1932.

In the easel paintings done after 1934, Wadsworth returned to 'magic realism' but other works from the same period have more to do with abstract art than with any form of realism. These were large-format works for public buildings, including the mural of 1935-6 for the De la Warr Pavilion which had recently been built by Erich Mendelsohn and Serge Chermayeff. Wadsworth juxtaposed in a single plane a few objects seen in perspective but which were schematic in terms of their forms and colours. In addition to some unrepresentational geometric figures one can recognise some fishing and navigation gear: shells, a marine chart, a hook, fishing lines and floats. The manner in which a group of objects is detached from a flat ground which supplies no context might be reminiscent of Léger, were it not that they are mere utensils with none of the insistent presence of the French painter's objects. The objects assembled by Wadsworth are distributed so as to cover a vast space without overloading it and they wittily trace gracious forms and rather precious lines across it. Yet Wadsworth's preoccupations are closer to those of Léger than the Mexican muralists whose aesthetic views he did not share and whose names he probably did not know.

In Paris, the years 1935-6 marked the most acute phase in what was then known as the 'quarrel over realism'. However, whilst most painters were torn by the figuration or non-figuration dilemma, Léger and a few others regarded it as a non-problem (it goes without saying that Wadsworth would have shared his opinion). For Léger, as for Delaunay,

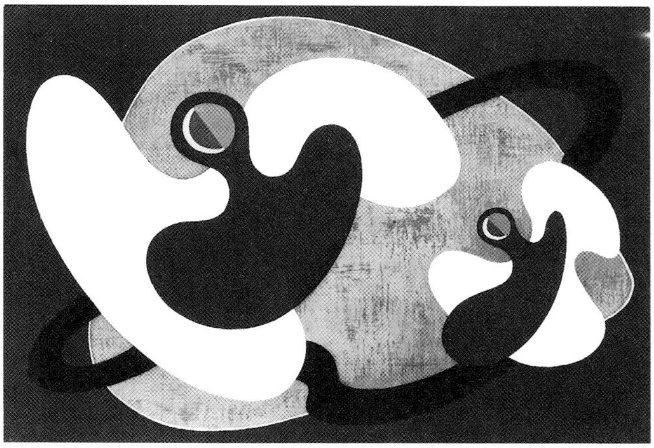

107

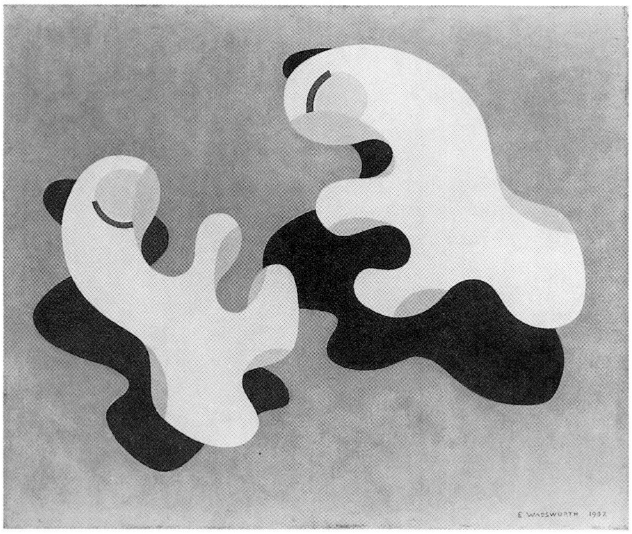

108

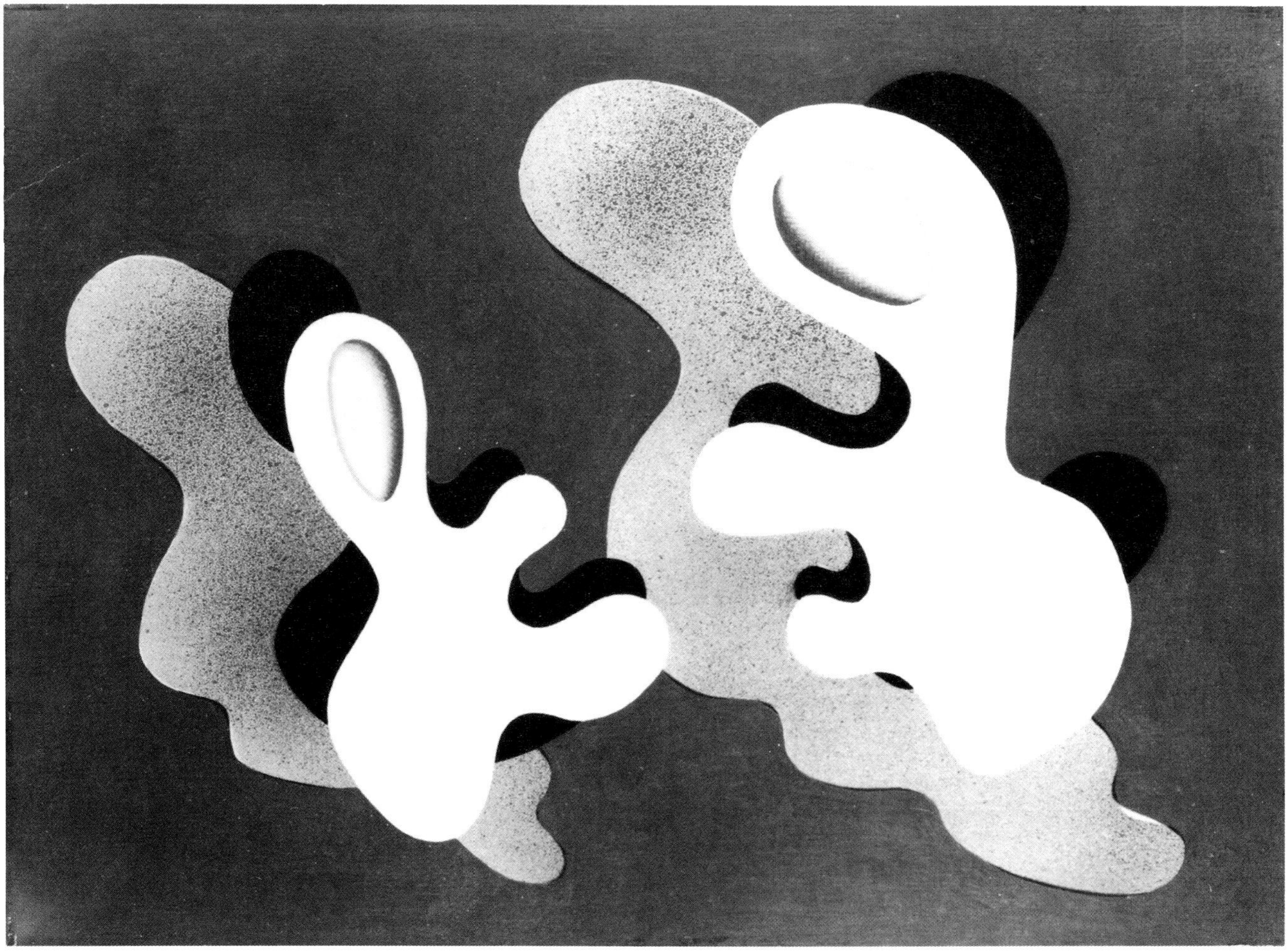

110

107. Composition *IV* 1932
108. Dux et Comes (1) (Rebuff) 1932
110. Dux et Comes (7) (Exhalation, 1) 1932

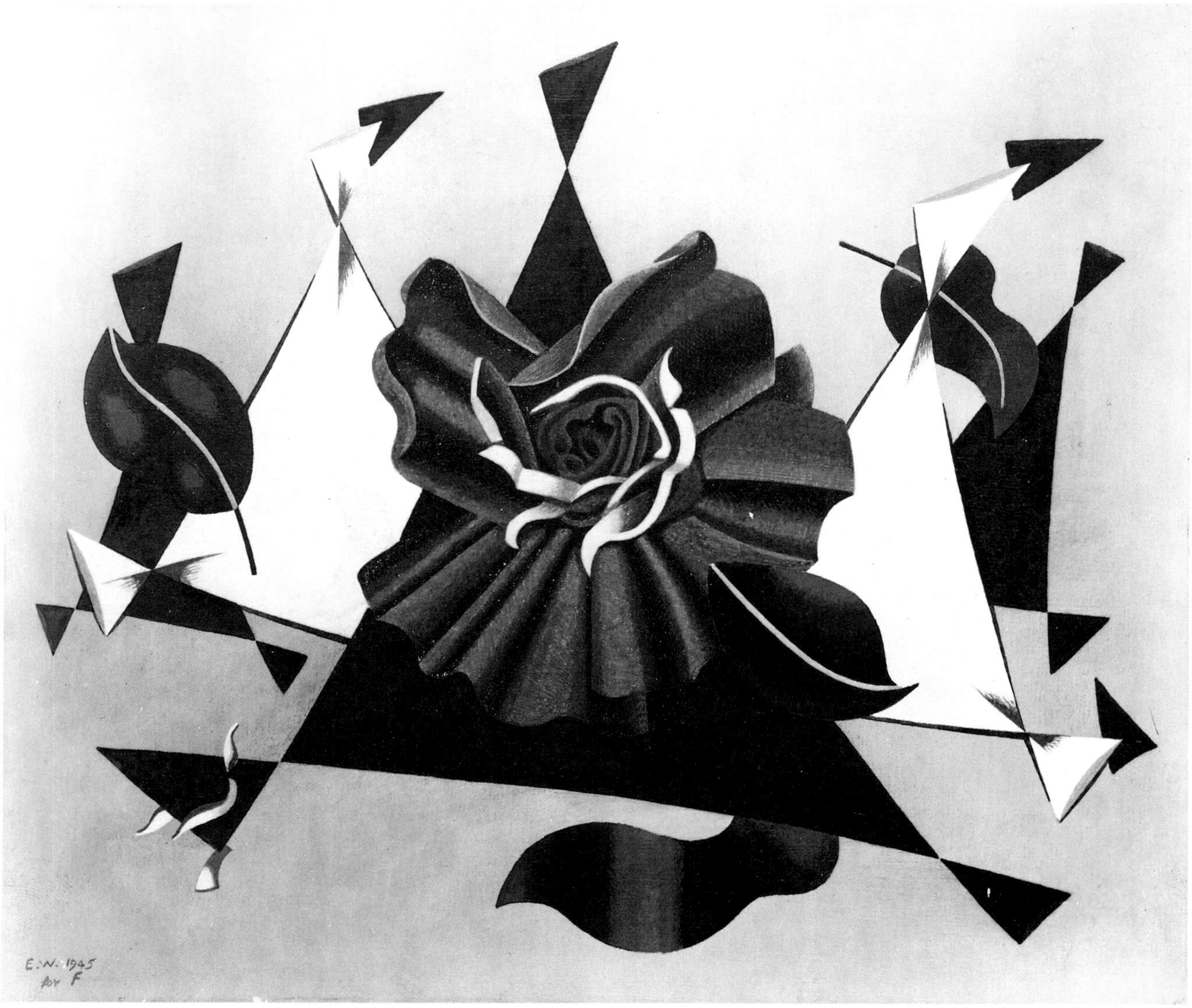

136

136. *Abstract with Rose* 1945
139. Single Dahlia 1946-7
140. Composition, Invention/Flower and Shell 1946
142. Tapestry of Starfish and Shells 1948-9

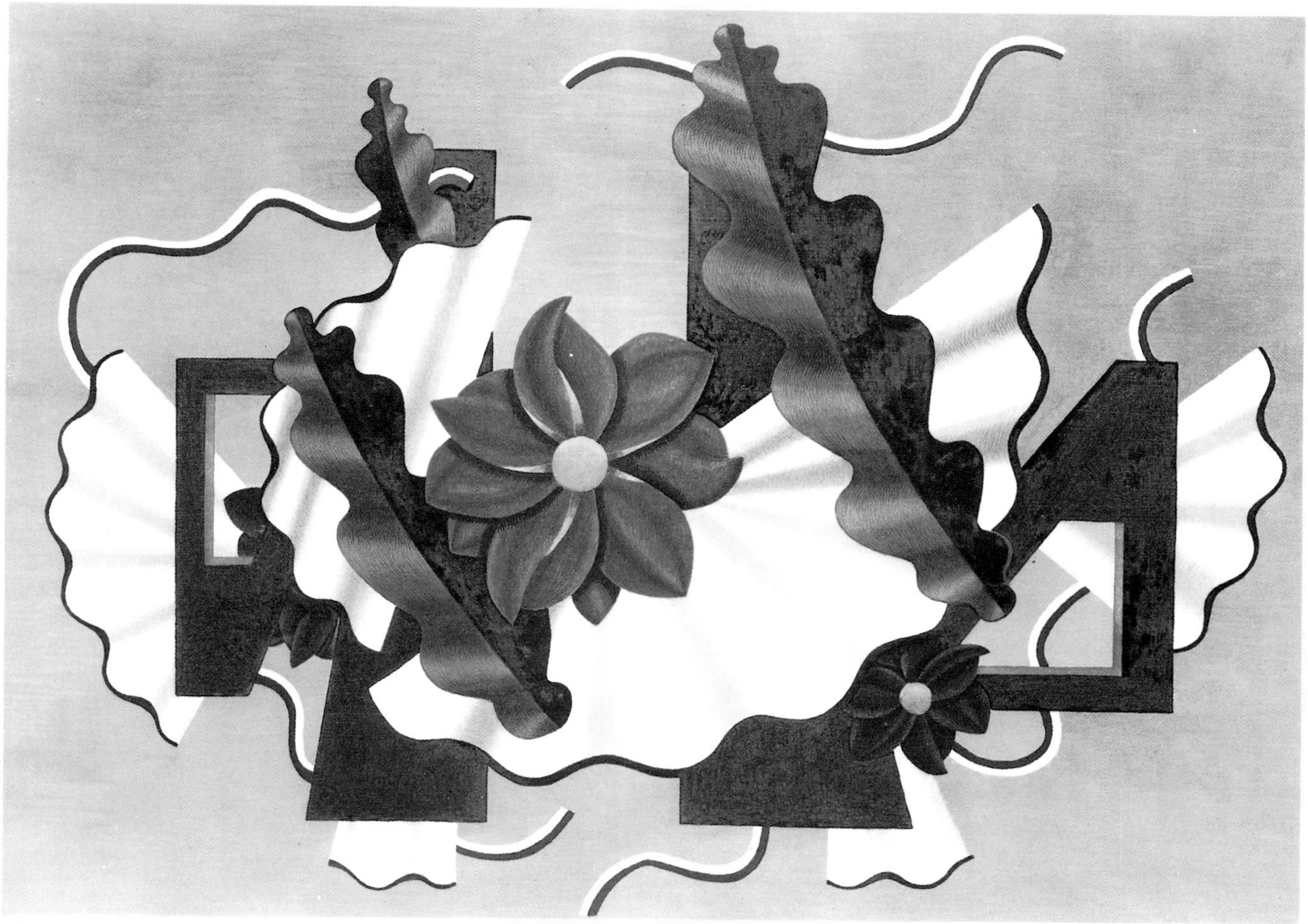

139

140

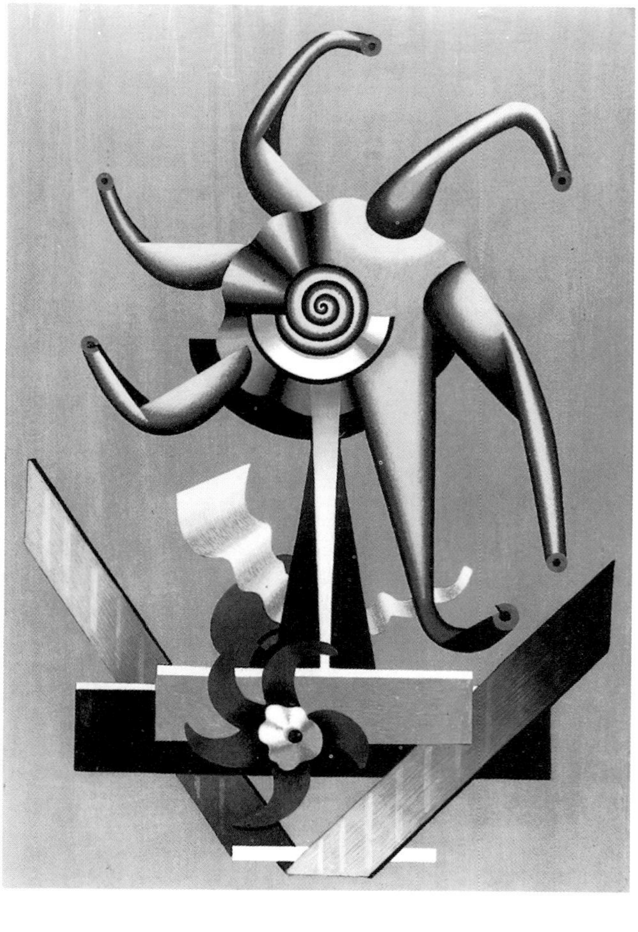

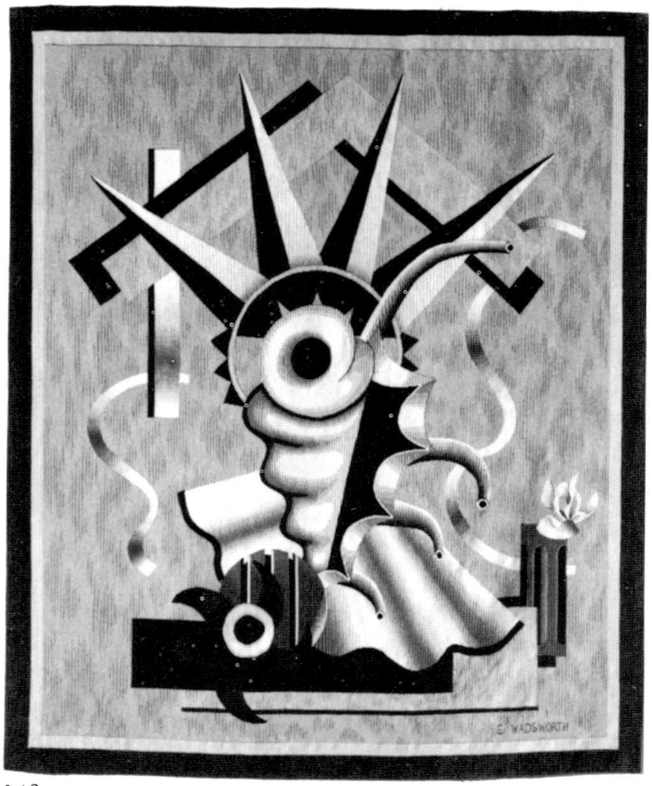

142

the issue did not centre on realism, or on the difficulty of reaching an agreed form of realism, but on a public art which would be executed on the internal and external walls of public spaces. Wadsworth himself could easily have added his signature to Léger's many statements on the subject:

> When it is based upon the object, painting takes on a social character. It becomes accessible to all, and can be used in schools, sports grounds, public monuments, etc ...
>
> The origins of the new realism are to be found in modern life itself, in its constant phenomena, in the influence of geometric manufactured objects, in a transposition in which the imagination and the real mingle and merge, but from which all literary or descriptive sentimentality, and all sensationalism, have been banished...
>
> Mural art is the great problem of the day. It is the form of painting intimately bound up with life. It will confront the crowd with everyday objects and artistic objects; it must *hold up* under every form of changing artificial light.[8]

Although Wadsworth does not seem to have been greatly concerned about coming into contact with the general public, he too passionately believed that art should relate to architecture and that the object should rule supreme. The De la Warr Pavilion was not an isolated project. Shortly afterwards, Wadsworth worked on decorative panels for the *Queen Mary* (see figs.41 and 42). Not even the war put an end to these activities, which he pursued in parallel with his easel painting.

It was not really the needs of war production which attracted him to industry. Even in his Vorticist period he had taken an interest in industrial activities and structures and in constructions like bridges and cranes. In 1941, he worked on a major series of advertisements for ICI. At the time, artists who were given commissions of this kind usually had to follow the bland conventions of representational art. Many of the sheets executed by Wadsworth are no exception. Although based upon real objects, some of them, however, come close to abstraction. When he chose to paint machine parts and metallic frames in 'Framework of the Future', for instance, Wadsworth knew very well that a viewer who was not familiar with the aircraft industry would simply see abstract forms which, with the exception of a propeller, would remind him of Wadsworth's non-figurative paintings. He seems to have been particularly fascinated by the great variety of forms that could be created with plastics. Whilst the rubber glove in 'Vinyl' is instantly recognisable and 'cocks a snook' at de Chirico who had turned it into a metaphysical sign, the other lines and spirals in the painting remain mysterious. Only the titles of 'Injection', 'Moulding', 'Extruded Tubing' and 'Nylon' allow us to see these completely abstract forms as real objects; the eye reconstructs brushes, tubes, bottle-brushes and indeterminate machine parts. Wadsworth saw that the new synthetic substances opened up new possibilities for the artist, new modes of representation which were no longer based upon the visible world. He explained the unusually abstract quality of 'Perspex' in the following terms:

> Gone are the visual certainties which the artist has so long taken for granted: the inter-relations of planes, the reflections of light and the odd accidents of surfaces in relation with these can no longer be relied upon as visual raw material. Perspex, more than any other substance, defies the traditions of appearance as hitherto known by the artists. Perspex reflects nothing but highlights and, unlike glass, it distorts nothing; its cast shadows are vague, its transparency is misleading, giving only hints to its volume ... a new medium which opens the eye of the artist a little wider.[9]

In Wadsworth's view, that was no small virtue.

In 1944, Wadsworth delivered a lecture on 'The Aesthetic Aspect of Civil Engineering Design' in which he gave an appreciation of bridges, factories and of blocks of flats and temples of all periods and from all over the world, examining each of them in aesthetic rather than pragmatic terms.[10] The lecture gave him an opportunity to restate even more forcefully convictions which applied well to architecture, painting or any other art form. In order to bring out their universal and eternal value, Wadsworth backed up his arguments with a number of quotations of which the most noteworthy is from Plato:

> Finally, we have Plato, some two thousand years ago: 'I do not intend by beauty of shapes what most people would expect – such as that of living creatures or pictures, but, for the purpose of my argument, I mean straight lines and curves and the surfaces of solid forms produced out of these by lathes, rulers and squares. For I mean that these things are not beautiful relatively, like other things, but always naturally and absolutely.'

Wadsworth's answer to Baudelaire's claim that art is a matter of mathematics or calculation is, however, somewhat disconcerting: 'It is the sensibility of the designer which gives the measure to the excellence of the work. Mathematics and calculations there must be, but calculation and feeling must always be on good terms with each other.'

These comments from 1944 mark a new departure in Wadsworth's career. Whilst the easel paintings executed over the previous decade betrayed a certain realism (magic or otherwise), his mural decorations proceeded from the basis of an abstract art and are more or less free from the conventions of perspective. His encounter with the world of industry and engineering finally convinced him that, even in his easel paintings, he should go back to abstraction, using a little or no perspective and flat grounds. As in earlier periods, there is of course a gradual radicalisation of this abstractionism.

The years 1944-5 are marked by the almost systematic presence of flowers and abstract geometric elements. Examples include the 'Rose' series of 1945 (136 and 137)

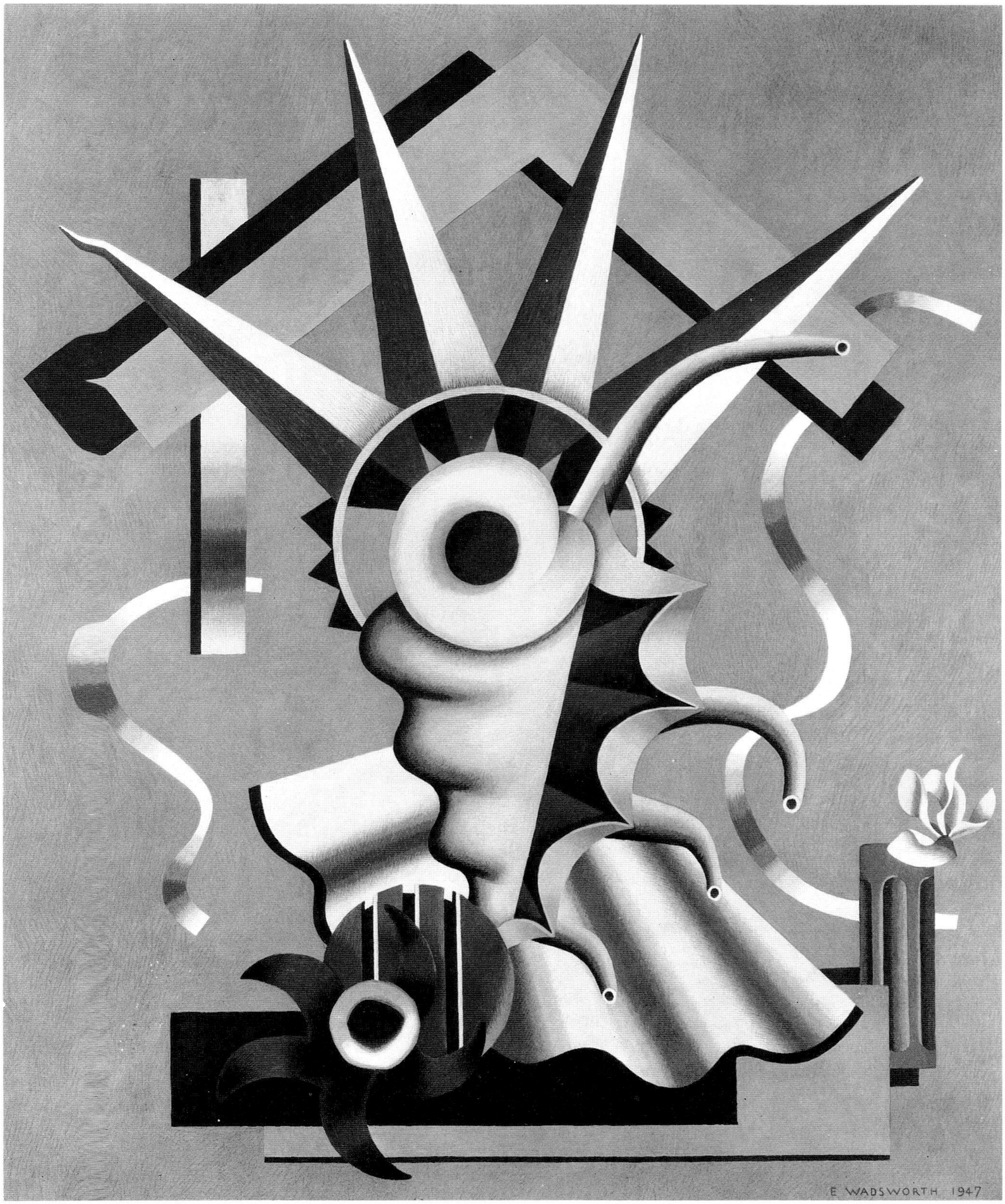

141. *Starfish and Shells/Marine Still Life* 1947

Colour p. 164

and the 'Dahlia' series of 1946-7 (138), where the flowers are juxtaposed against geometric figures and lines (one 'Dahlia' features oak leaves which remind one of Léger). Subsequently, Wadsworth was happier with marine themes like 'Starfish and Shells' 1947. This was used as the basis for both a tapestry (142) and a curious painting which is simply entitled 'Composition' 1947. The same rectilinear or undulating elements reappear but they are distributed differently. The most striking thing about 'Composition' is, however, that the star-shaped structure in the centre has been replaced by a vaguely disturbing pink object which seems to have rubbery tentacles. In the context of 'Starfish and Shells', what appears to be a squid or a distributor head seems to be a gastropod seen from the front and not from the side. In the latter painting, the abstract effect is created by the stylisation and distortion of an object which is already difficult to recognise because of the unusual angle. In 'Triangles' (143) of the following year (there are at least two versions), there is nothing to remind us of any known object, no matter how we look at it. All the shapes depicted by the painter, like the triangles or the sphere which seems to be suspended from a pipe, are imaginary and without any counterpart in the real world. They are all the more fascinating in that they appear to belong to a world which has *between* two and three dimensions.

At the time of his death in 1949 Edward Wadsworth was a completely abstract painter. Given his career and his convictions, there is every reason to think that, had he lived for another twenty or thirty years, his style would have undergone another two or three changes without destroying the internal coherence of his oeuvre, so demanding was his technique and so stubborn was his refusal to allow himself to fall into a rut.

Translated by David Macey

Notes

1. 'L'Evolution du peintre Wadsworth' in André de Ridder (ed.), 'Edward Wadsworth', *Sélection – Chronique de la vie artistique*, 13, Antwerp 1933, p.25.
2. Inner Necessity. Review of Kandinsky's book by Edward Wadsworth, *Blast No. 1*, London 1914, p.122.
3. Jean Hélion, 'A Perte de vue', unpublished manuscripts
4. *Art in Britain 1930-1940*, exh. cat., Marlborough Fine Art, London 1965, p.5.
5. 'Tendances modernes en Angleterre', *Cahiers de Belgique*, 3, March 1931.
6. Edward Wadsworth in Herbert Read (ed.), *Unit One*, London 1934, p.99.
7. Reprinted, *Unit One*, exh. cat., Mayor Gallery, London 1984, p.53.
8. *La Querelle du réalisme*, éditions Cercle d'art, collection Diagonales, Paris 1987, pp.225, 105, 33.
9. *Alphabet and Image*, 8, Winter 1948, p.69.
10. Delivered to the Institute of Civil Engineers on 31 May 1944.

143. *Triangles* 1948

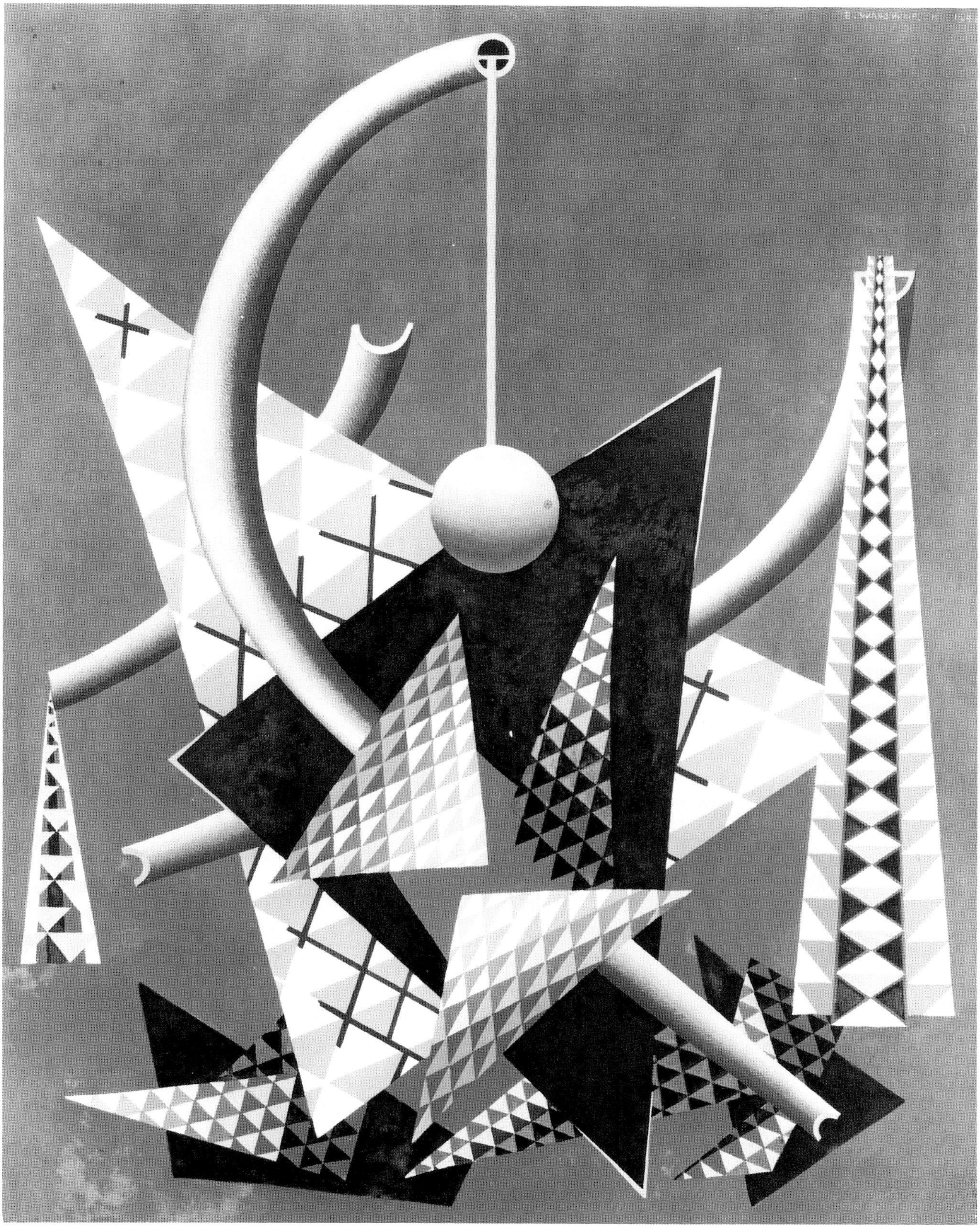

Chronology

1889
29 October
Born at Cleckheaton, Yorkshire, son of Fred Wadsworth who ran an important worsted spinning concern at Broomfield Mill. Mother died shortly after from puerperal fever.

1899
Went to Ghyll Royd School, Ilkley, Yorkshire.

1903-6
Studied at Fettes College, Edinburgh.

1906-7
Studied machine draughtsmanship in Munich and in his spare time attended the Knirr Art School on Amalienstrasse.

1908
Attended the Bradford School of Art and studied under Charles Stevenson. Won a scholarship to the Slade School of Fine Art, London.

1909-12
Studied at the Slade School of Fine Art. Won first prize for landscape composition in 1910 and first prize for figure painting in 1911. Became friendly with Mark Gertler, Adrian Allinson and Christopher Nevinson.

1912
Married Fanny Eveleigh, the violinist. Spent honeymoon in the Canary Islands, returning to England via Portugal and France.
Helped Roger Fry on restoration of the Mantegna cartoons at Hampton Court.

1913
Birth of first child, Anne.
January
Contributed to Roger Fry's *Second Post-Impressionist Exhibition, British, French and Russian Artists*, at the Grafton Galleries.
Painted Cubist landscapes.
Summer
Met Wyndham Lewis.
July
Invited by Roger Fry to carry out work for the Omega Workshops.
October
Together with Frederick Etchells, Cuthbert Hamilton and Wyndham Lewis, Wadsworth broke away from the Omega Workshops.
Contributed to the *Post-Impressionist and Futurist Exhibition* at the Doré Galleries, London.

1913-14
December to January
Contributed to an *Exhibition by the Camden Town Group and Others* (Cubist Room Section) at the Brighton Public Art Galleries.

1914
March
Contributed to *The First Exhibition of Works by Members of the London Group* at the Goupil Gallery, London. Joined Wyndham Lewis's Rebel Art Centre based in Great Ormond Street, London WC1.
8 May to 20 June
Contributed to the exhibition *Twentieth Century Art, A Review of Modern Movements*, at the Whitechapel Art Gallery, London.

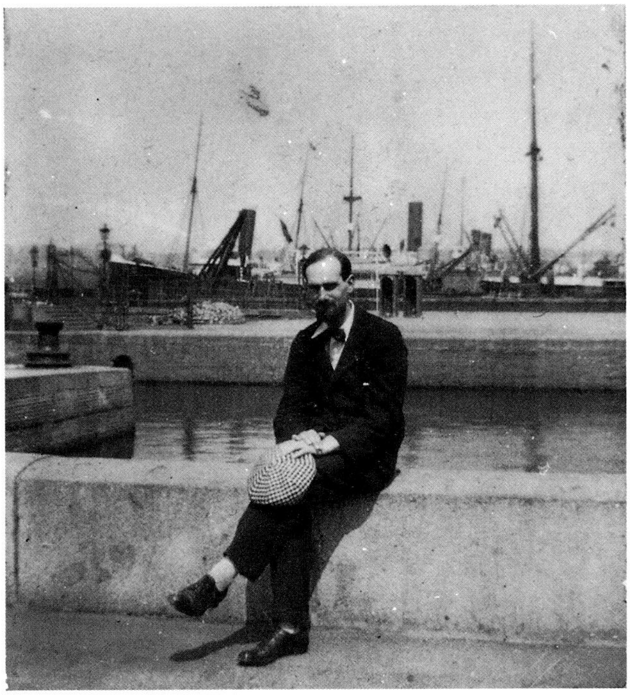
Fig.38 Wadsworth in (?)Rotterdam 1914

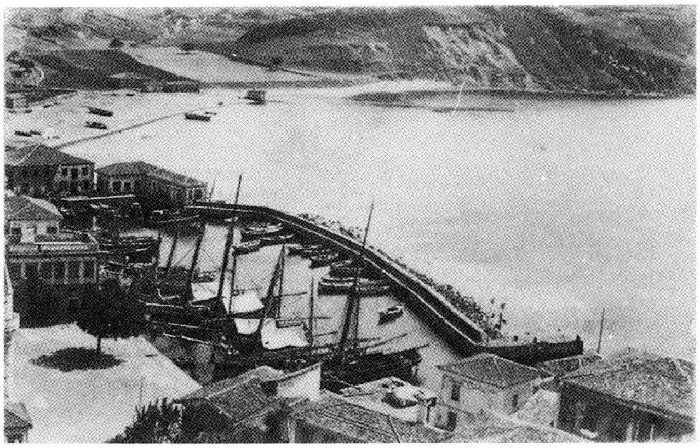
Fig.39 Kastro harbour, Lemnos c.1916-17 (photo. Edward Wadsworth)

20 June
Contributed illustrations and translations from Kandinsky's *Über das Geistige in der Kunst* to *Blast No. 1* and signed the Vorticist group's manifesto.
July
Contributed to the exhibition of *The London Salon of Allied Artists' Association Limited, Seventh Year*, at Holland Park Hall, London.

Resident at 1A Gloucester Walk, Kensington Church Street, London W8. Travelled to Holland and was in Rotterdam shortly before war broke out. Birth of second child, Barbara.

1914-15
Correspondence with sculptor Henri Gaudier-Brzeska who was serving in French army.

1915
June
Contributed to the *Vorticist Exhibition*, at the Doré Galleries, London.
August
Lewis visited Wadsworth at Hebden Bridge, Yorkshire.

1916-17
Served with RNVR as an intelligence officer on the island of Ispathio, off Mudros, in the Mediterranean.
Met the poet and art collector Bernard Windeler.
Correspondence with the American collector John Quinn who purchased works by Wadsworth.

1917
July
Invalided out of RNVR. Returned to England.

1917-18
Worked on dazzle-camouflage for ships in Liverpool and Bristol under Norman Wilkinson.

1919
Ceased to be a member of the London Group.
March
One-man *Exhibition of Original Woodcuts and Drawings by Edward Wadsworth* at the Adelphi Gallery, directed by the critic Frank Rutter. Frederick Etchells wrote preface to catalogue.
May
Moved to 76 Kensington Church Street, London W8.

1920
January
One-man show *The Black Country* at the Leicester Galleries, London.
March
Contributed as a member to the *Group X* exhibition at the Mansard Gallery, Heal's, London.
August
Walked from Cornwall to London visiting various ports and harbours including Plymouth and Portland.
September
Book of drawings, *The Black Country*, published by John Rodker's Ovid Press, with an introduction by Arnold Bennett.

1921
Joined The New English Art Club.
Inherited a fortune on the death of his father in January which enabled him to visit France regularly.
Began to paint in tempera.
Painted Cubist style landscapes.

1922
March
Travelled to Marseilles. Death of daughter Anne.
Moved to 73 Addison Road, London W14.

1923
Travelled to Italy via France and Switzerland. Visited Viareggio, Pisa, Florence, Siena, Ravenna, Bologna, Ferrara, Venice, Padua, Milan, Turin. Looked at early Renaissance art and architecture and especially tempera and fresco painting. Returned via France and Belgium in June.

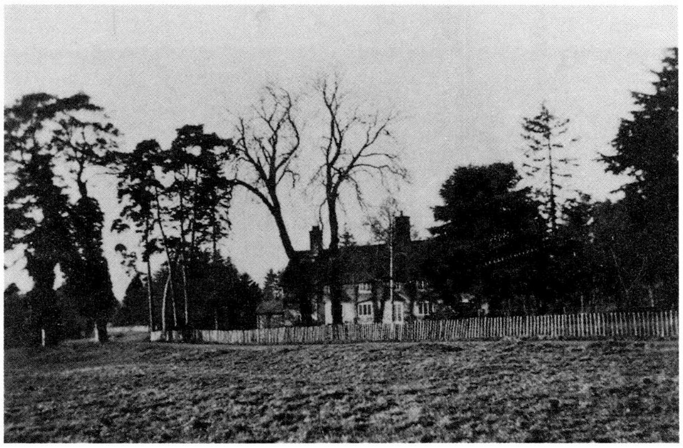
Fig.40 Dairy House, Maresfield Park

Designed 'Industrial Art of Today' poster for Board of Trade exhibition at Victoria & Albert Museum.
Met writer and painter Richard Wyndham.
Began to mix own tempera colours.

1924
Travelled to South of France and Italy with Richard Wyndham.

1925
Travelled to Italy. Met sculptor Osip Zadkine at painter and critic Michael Sevier's house by Lake Como.

1926
General Strike. Wadsworth helped authorities by driving news sheets to Sheffield at night.
Began painting marine still-lifes.
Book of copper engravings, *Sailing Ships and Barges of the Western Mediterranean and Adriatic Seas*, published by Frederick Etchells and Hugh Macdonald with an introduction by Bernard Windeler.
November
Shared an exhibition with Alvaro Guevara at the Leicester Galleries, London.

1927
February
One-man show at Galerie Barbazanges, Paris.
May-June
Exhibited at 'De Onafhankelijken' exhibition, Stedelijk Museum, Amsterdam. Stedelijk purchase 'Fruits de Mer'.
Moved to Dairy House, Maresfield, Sussex. Frederick Etchells lived nearby.

1929
One-man show at Arthur Tooth and Sons Limited, London.

1930
Satirised in Wyndham Lewis's novel *The Apes of God*.
Painted semi-abstract purist still-lifes.

1932
First of many family holidays in Garmisch in the Bavarian Alps.
Friendly with Richard Strauss and his circle in Garmisch.
Visited the Bauhaus artist, Willi Baumeister, in Frankfurt and became friends with him.
Began 'Dux et Comes' series of abstract paintings.
Became member of Abstraction-Création.

1933
Joined Unit One.
Publication in Antwerp of issue 13 of *Sélection-Chronique de la vie artistique* devoted to Wadsworth.
November
One-man show at the Mayor Gallery, London.

1934
Contributed to book *Unit One: The Modern Movement in English Architecture, Painting and Sculpture*, edited by Herbert Read and published by Cassell in London. Exhibited at *Unit One* exhibition, Mayor Gallery.
March
Daughter Barbara married J A von Bethmann-Hollweg in Munich.
May
Involved in serious road accident in Sussex. Acquitted of manslaughter at Lewes County Court.
September
Sailed to Provence.
Returned to representational painting and marine still-lifes.

1935
Contributed to the *Universal International Exhibition* held in Brussels.
18 March
BBC radio talk with critic Eric Newton.
Contributed financially to *Axis* magazine, edited by Myfanwy Piper.

1936
Designed and executed two large paintings for the Smoking Room in the new liner *Queen Mary*. Worked on this project in Maresfield Village Hall.
Produced a design for a painting for the cafeteria at De la Warr Pavilion at Bexhill, a new building designed by Erich Mendelsohn and Serge Chermayeff. Work executed by American painter Charles Howard.
November
Controversy over Wadsworth's design for advert for London Passenger Transport Board commissioned by Frank Pick. Wadsworth's design considered too 'warlike' and withdrawn.
Supported Chermayeff in planning dispute over his new modernist villa near Uckfield, Sussex.

1937
Contributed to the *Exhibition of Contemporary British Art*, held at Rosenberg and Helft, London.
Works shown in travelling exhibition of Solomon R Guggenheim Collection in United States.

1938
21 April to 14 May
One-man show at Arthur Tooth and Sons Limited, London.

1939
July 22
Visited Tristram Hillier in France.
September 4
Daughter Barbara and her husband registered as enemy aliens.

1940
17 May to 8 June
Contributed to the *Exhibition of Pictures Selected for Inclusion in the 22nd 'Biennale di Venezia'*, at the Galleries of Hertford House, London.
Moved from Dairy House, Maresfield, Sussex to Anglesey and thence to Buxton in Derbyshire. Served as a Fire Watcher and as Sergeant in Home Guard. Interrogated German prisoners.

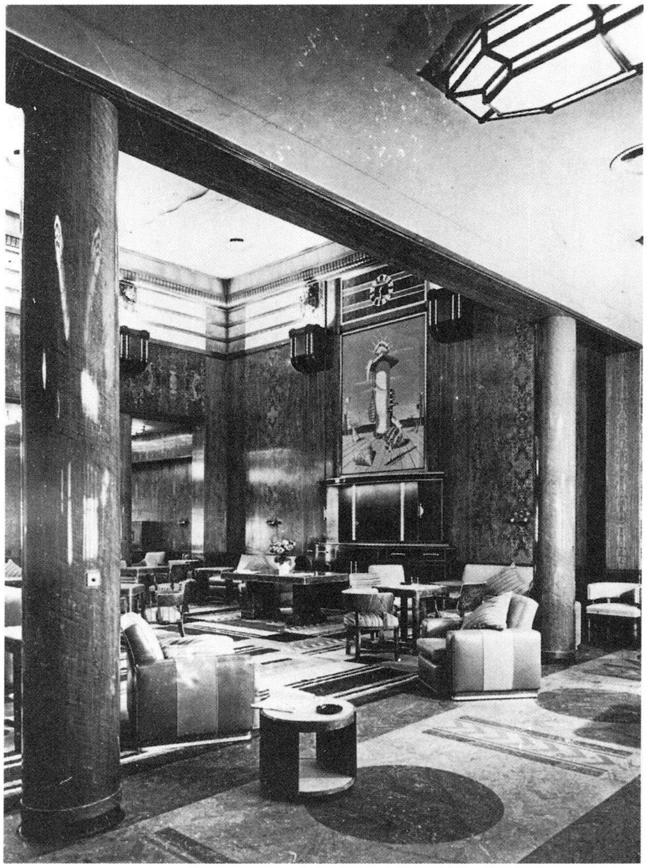

Fig.41 Interior of the Smoking Room of the *Queen Mary* with 'Dressed Overall' panel 1936 (photo. University Archive, University of Liverpool)

1941
Carried out a series of paintings commissioned by ICI Limited.

1943
Graham Sutherland visited Wadsworth in Buxton.

1944
Elected an Associate of the Royal Academy.

1945
March
Returned to Dairy House, Maresfield, Sussex.
Painted semi-abstract still-lifes.

1946
May
Contributed to the *Tempera Painting* exhibition organised by Maxwell Armfield at the Royal Water-Colour Society's Galleries, London.

1949
21 June
Died in nursing home in Cleveland Gardens, London W2.

Fig.42 Interior of the Smoking Room of the *Queen Mary* with 'Arrival' panel 1936 (photo. University Archive, University of Liverpool)

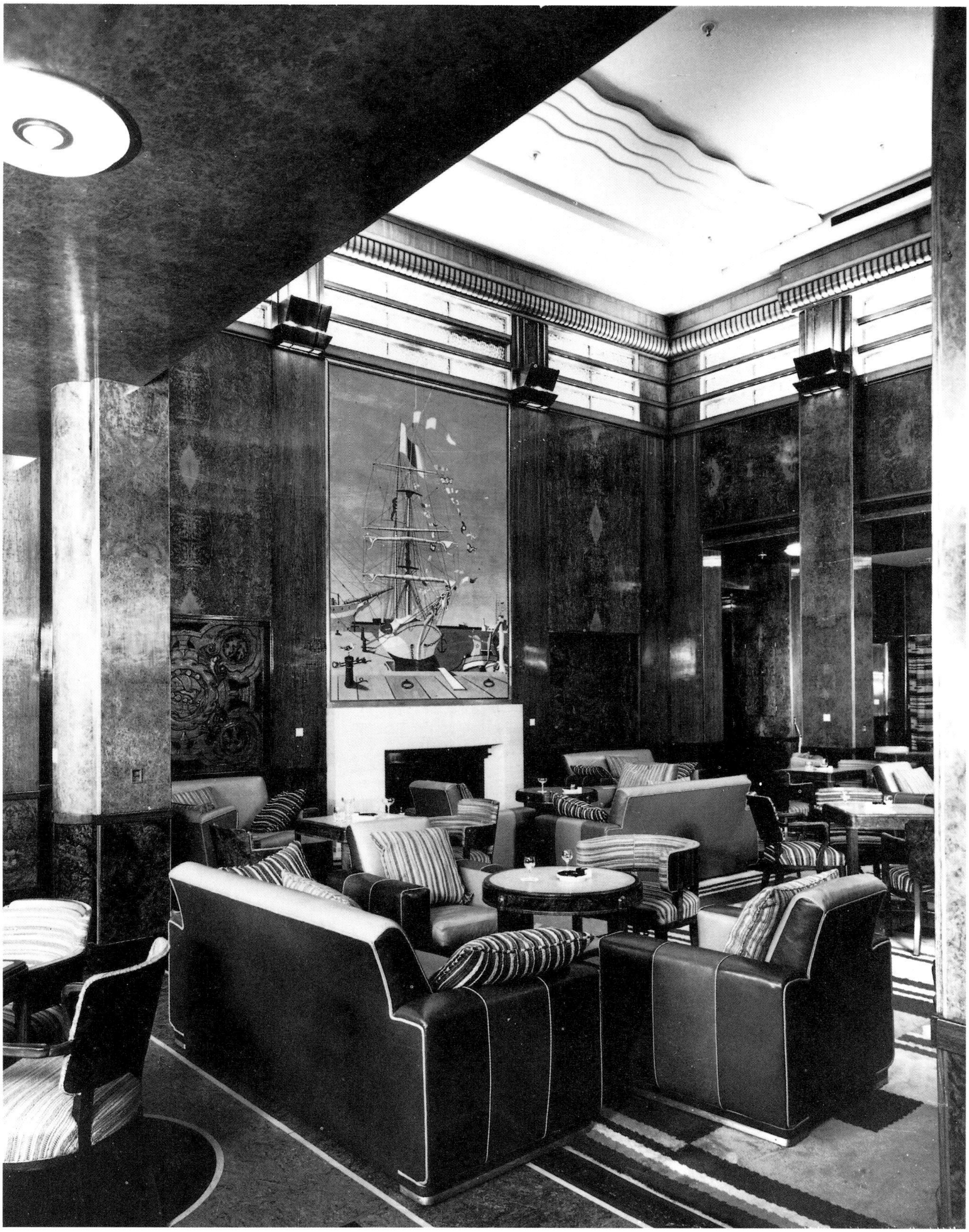

Selected Bibliography

The following list is selective and concentrates on books and articles written by and about Wadsworth. With few exceptions it does not list studies in which Wadsworth is not the principal subject.

Books and Writings by Edward Wadsworth

Contributions to Percy Wyndham Lewis (ed.), *Blast No.I*, London 1914 and *Blast No.II*, London 1915

Statement in *Watercolour Drawings of Brighton and Elsewhere by the Late Douglas Fox Pitt. Paintings in Tempera and Drawings by Edward Wadsworth*, exhibition catalogue, Leicester Galleries, London 1923

Sailing Ships and Barges of the Western Mediterranean and Adriatic Seas, with an introduction by Bernard Windeler, London 1926

'The Abstract Painter's Own Explanation', *Studio*, vol. 106, November 1933.

Statement in Herbert Read (ed.), *Unit One: The Modern Movement in English Architecture, Painting and Sculpture*, London 1934

'Problems of the Painter of 1935. A Discussion between Eric Newton and Edward Wadsworth', *Listener*, 20 March 1935

The Aesthetic Aspect of Civil Engineering, lecture delivered to the Institution of Civil Engineers 31 May 1944, Institution of Civil Engineers, London 1944

Writings on Edward Wadsworth

(Enoch) Arnold Bennett, *The Black Country. Edward Wadsworth*, London 1920

Christine Boyanoski, 'The Art of Edward Wadsworth', unpublished MPhil thesis, University of London, Courtauld Institute of Art, 1981

Richard Cork, 'Introduction', *Edward Wadsworth: Early Woodcuts*, exhibition catalogue, Christopher Drake and Alexander Postan, London 1973

Richard Cork, *Vorticism and Abstract Art in the First Machine Age*, I and II, London 1975 and 1976

T W Earp, 'Edward Wadsworth', *Edward Wadsworth Memorial Exhibition*, exhibition catalogue, Tate Gallery, London 1951

Frederick Etchells, 'A Note', *Exhibition of Original Woodcuts and Drawings by Edward Wadsworth*, exhibition catalogue, Adelphi Gallery, London 1919

Mark Glazebrook, *Edward Wadsworth 1889-1949. Paintings, Drawings and Prints*, exhibition catalogue, P and D Colnaghi and Co Ltd, London 1974

Mark Glazebrook, *Edward Wadsworth 1889-1949. Paintings from the 1920s*, exhibition catalogue, Mayor Gallery, London 1982

Stephen Hayward, 'Metaphysical Painting in England during the 1920s and Thirties: The work of Edward Wadsworth, Paul Nash, John Armstrong and Tristram Hillier', unpublished MA report, University of London, Courtauld Institute of Art, 1982

[Jeremy Lewison], entry on 'Regalia' in *Tate Gallery 1982-84. Illustrated Catalogue of Acquisitions*, Tate Gallery, London 1986, pp.347-52

Jeremy Lewison, Entry on Edward Wadsworth in *Futurismo e Futurismi*, exhibition catalogue, Palazzo Grassi, Venice and Bompiani, Milan 1986, pp.608-9

Ezra Pound, 'Edward Wadsworth, Vorticist', *Egoist*, 15 August 1914

André de Ridder (ed.), 'Edward Wadsworth', *Sélection-Chronique de la vie artistique*, 13, Antwerp 1933

Léonce Rosenberg, introduction to *An Exhibition of Tempera Paintings by Edward Wadsworth*, exhibition catalogue, Arthur Tooth and Sons, London 1929

Osbert Sitwell, introduction to *Tempera Paintings by Edward Wadsworth. Paintings of Chile by Alvaro Guevara*, exhibition catalogue, Leicester Galleries, London 1926

Barbara Wadsworth, *Edward Wadsworth: A Painter's Life*, Wilton 1989

R H Wilenski, 'Modern "Still Life". The Paintings of Edward Wadsworth', *Studio*, vol.97, June 1929

List of Works

Alternative titles are separated by / in bold.
All works are on linen stretched over board unless otherwise stated.
All measurements in cm. Measurements of woodcuts refer to image size.
Height precedes width.
Numbers in parentheses refer to appendix 2 in Barbara Wadsworth, *Edward Wadsworth: A Painter's Life*, Wilton 1989.
Works marked * are exhibited at Cartwright Hall only. Works marked ° are exhibited at Camden Arts Centre only.
Page numbers in italic indicate a reproduction of the work.

1. Christmas Card 1907
Printed paper 35 × 18
Inscribed 'Dec 1907 Edward A.W.'
Lent by Mr Jeremy Friend-Smith
(W/C 1)

2. Man Asleep 1907
Pencil 9.3 × 6.4
Inscribed 'E.A.W./1907'
Private collection
(W/B 1)

3. Edward Lowe Asleep 1908
Crayon on paper 27.9 × 26.7
Miss Gerda Sylvia Lowe
(W/B 3)

4. Cuthbert Kelly Esq. 1910
Oil on piece of miller's sacking 60 × 50.8
Private collection
(W/A 2) p.9

5. Nude in the Life-room 1911
Oil on canvas 61 × 50.8
Inscribed 'Wadsworth'
Slade School of Fine Art, University College, London
(W/A 5) p.9

6. Self-portrait in a Turban 1911
Oil on canvas 39.8 × 34.8
Private collection
(W/A 6) p.8

7. Violet Wallis 1911
Chalk on paper 25 × 20
Lent by Mr Jeremy Friend-Smith
(W/B 13) p.9

8. Grand Canary 1912
Oil on panel 23 × 40
Private collection
(W/A 12) p.9

***9. Pool with Trees and Punt** 1913
Watercolour 35 × 48.2
National Museums and Galleries on Merseyside (Walker Art Gallery)
(W/B 7) p.11

10. Landscape (1) 1913
Watercolour 27.6 × 29.5
The Trustees of the Tate Gallery
(W/B 6) p.10

11. Trees beside River 1913
Watercolour 27.3 × 35
Inscribed 'E. Wadsworth'
Bradford Art Galleries and Museums
(W/B 8) p.11

***12. Study for 'Cape of Good Hope'** 1914
Watercolour 33 × 25
Private collection
(W/B 11) p.13

13. Newcastle 1913
Inscribed 'NEWCASTLE EDWARD WADSWORTH'
Woodcut 14 × 10
Private collection
(W/D 1) p.13

14. Mytholmroyd c.1914
Woodcut 21.2 × 16.5
Private collection
(W/D 4) p.13

15. Bradford: View of a Town 1914
Woodcut 15 × 10
(a) beige/brown on cream paper
Inscribed 'Edward Wadsworth 1914'
(b) slate-grey/black on brown-grey paper
Inscribed 'Edward Wadsworth' and 'View of a Town'
Private collection
(c) grey/black on violet flecked paper
Anthony d'Offay Gallery, London
(W/D 8) *colour* p.49

16. Façade c.1914-15
Inscribed 'Edward Wadsworth'
Woodcut 17.2 × 9.5
The Board of Trustees of the Victoria and Albert Museum, London
(W/D 9) p.15

17. Street Singers 1914
Woodcut 14 × 11
(a) grey/black on cream paper
(b) grey/black on dark cream paper
(c) dark grey/black on cream paper
Private collection
(W/D 10) p.15

18. Landscape 1914-15
Woodcut 6 × 7.5
(a) blue/rust/black on cream paper
Inscribed 'Landscape'
(b) aubergine/ochre/blue on cream paper
Private collection
(W/D 12) *colour* p.49

19. Fustian Town–Hebden Bridge
Inscribed 'Edward Wadsworth/Fustian Town/Hebden Bridge'
Woodcut 10.5 × 6
Private collection
(W/D 14)

20. The Port/Untitled Vorticist Composition/Staircase with Scaffolding 1914-15
Woodcut 16 × 11
The Trustees of the Tate Gallery
(W/D 17) p.1

21. Illustration (Typhoon) 1914-15
Woodcut 28 × 25.5
Inscribed with a quotation from Joseph Conrad's *Typhoon*
The Trustees of the British Museum
(W/D 18) p.17

22. Brown Drama 1914-16
Woodcut 12.5 × 7
(a) grey-brown/black on grey paper
Inscribed 'Brown Drama'
(b) blue-grey/ochre/black on cream paper
Private collection
(W/D 21)

22a. Top of the Town 1916-17
Woodcut 10.5 × 8.1
Private collection
(W/D 22) p.17

23. Invention/Mudros 1917
Woodcut 18 × 11
(a) grey/black on cream paper
(b) dark grey/black on cream paper
Private collection
(W/D 23) p.17

24. Kt X B 1917
Woodcut 7.9 × 5.7
Private collection
(W/D 51) p.17

25. Disruption 1917
Woodcut 7.5 × 9
Private collection
(W/D 24)

26. Greek Village with Windmills 1916
Woodcut 6 × 9.5
(a) blue-black on white paper.
Inscribed 'EW 1916'
(b) brown/black on white paper.
Inscribed 'Greek Village'
(c) olive-green /black on white paper
(d) mulberry/black on white paper
Private collection
(W/D 26) p.19

27. Scene for a Fairy Tale 1916
Woodcut 7.3 × 6
Inscribed 'Edward Wadsworth'
Private collection
(W/D 29) p.19

28. Interior/Mudros 1917
Woodcut 10.5 × 7.5
Anthony d'Offay Gallery, London
(W/D 25) p.19

29. Riponelli: A Village in Lemnos 1917
Woodcut 10 × 7.5
(a) grey/black on grey paper
(b) dark grey/light grey/black on cream paper
(c) mauve/dark grey/black on grey paper
(d) pale blue/grey/black on grey paper
(e) blue/mauve/black on cream paper
(f) red/purple/black on cream paper
(g) dark grey/light grey/black on buff paper
(h) light grey/pale blue/black on buff paper
Anthony d'Offay Gallery, London
(W/D 27) *colour* p.49

30. Railway Embankment/Platelayers' Sheds 1918
Woodcut 7.5 × 7.7
Private collection
(W/D 28) p.19

31. Tugs 1918
Woodcut 8.6 × 8.9
Inscribed 'Tugs'
Private collection
(W/D 30) p.19

32. Drydocked for Scaling and Painting 1918
Woodcut 22.5 × 21
Inscribed 'Edward Wadsworth'
Private collection
(W/D 32) p.21

33. S.S. Jerseymoor 1918
Woodcut 11.9 × 21.1
Inscribed 'S.S. Jerseymoor 1918/Woodcut/Edward Wadsworth/229 Royal Liver Building, Liverpool'
Private collection
(W/D 33) p.22

34. Dazzled Ship in Drydock 1918
Woodcut 12.7 × 21.7
Private collection
(W/D 34) p.23

35. Minesweepers in Port 1918
Woodcut 5 × 13.5
(a) black on cream
(b) black on grey
Private collection
(W/D 35) p.22

36. Dock Scene 1917
Woodcut 11.4 × 17.8
Inscribed 'Edward Wadsworth 1917'
Private collection
(W/D 36) p.23

37. Turret Ship in Drydock 1918
Woodcut 20 × 14
The Board of Trustees of the Victoria and Albert Museum, London
(W/D 38)

38. Townscape 1920
Woodcut 10.5 × 9.5
Private collection
(W/D 44) p.27

39. Yorkshire 1920
Woodcut 10.6 × 14.6
The Trustees of the British Museum
(W/D 45)

40. Northern Roofscape/A Black Country Village 1920
Woodcut 15.3 × 10.2
Private collection
(W/D 46) p.27

41. Portrait of Rupert Doone 1920
Woodcut 18 × 7.5
Private collection
(W/D 47) p.27

***42. Head** 1921
Woodcut 13.5 × 7.4
National Museum of Wales, Cardiff
(W/D 49)

43. Wapping 1920
Woodcut 11.5 × 14
Private collection
(W/D 48) p.28

44. Still Life 1921
Woodcut 15.1 × 10.2
Private collection
(W/D 50) p.28

45. Theatre 1920
Woodcut 5 × 3.5
Private collection
(W/D 52) p.28

46. Alphabet of Initial Letters c.1920
Engraver's proof, each letter 2.5 × 2.5
Private collection
(W/C 6)

47. Logo for the Ovid Press c.1920
Woodcut 4.6 × 4.3
Private collection
(W/C 7)

48. Portrait of Rupert Doone 1920
Pencil 42 × 26.3
Inscribed 'Edward Wadsworth 1920'
Private collection, courtesy of the Mayor Gallery
(W/B 67) p.29

49. Head of Rupert Doone 1921
Pencil 34.3 × 21.6
Inscribed 'Edward Wadsworth 1921'
Private collection, courtesy of the Mayor Gallery
(W/B 80) p.29

50. Crouching Nude 1920
Lithograph 40.2 × 50.4
Private collection
(W/C 8a) p.29

51. *Madam Noy* c.1921-2
Printed paper 30 × 22
Private collection
(W/C 12)

52. 'Englische Graphik' Exhibition Poster 1923
Printed paper 127.8 × 90.9
The Trustees of the British Museum
(W/C 13) p.28

53. Ladle Slag 1919
Pencil, ink and bodycolour 37.5 × 51.3
Inscribed 'Edward Wadsworth 1919'
Manchester City Art Galleries
(W/B 59) p.31

54. Slag Heaps at Leeds Steelworks 1920
Ink and wash 35.5 × 50.8
Inscribed 'Edward Wadsworth 1920'
The Trustees of the British Museum
(W/B 75) p.31

55. Ladle Slag, Old Hill (2) 1919
Ink and wash 35.5 × 49.5
Inscribed 'Edward Wadsworth 1919'
The University of Leeds
(W/B 54) colour p.50

56. Netherton Furnaces 1919
Ink and wash 13.4 × 19
Inscribed 'Wadsworth'
Manchester City Art Galleries
(W/B 46) p.31

57. Blast Furnaces 1919
Ink and watercolour 28.3 × 41.1
Inscribed 'Edward Wadsworth 1919'
Manchester City Art Galleries
(W/B 34) p.31

58. Tipton/Ladle Slag, Tipton Furnaces 1919
Ink and wash 24.1 × 27.3
Inscribed 'Edward Wadsworth 1919'
Bradford Art Galleries and Museums
(W/B 28) p.31

59. Willingsworth Furnaces, Wednesbury/Smoking Chimneys 1919
Ink and watercolour 20.3 × 29.2
Inscribed 'Edward Wadsworth 1919'
Board of Trustees of the Victoria and Albert Museum
(W/B 38)

60. Factories/View of Wednesbury (1) 1919
Ink and wash 23.3 × 35.1
Inscribed 'Edward Wadsworth 1919'
Lent by the Cooper Gallery Trustees on loan from the Cooper Gallery, Barnsley Metropolitan Borough Council
(W/B 44) p.33

61. Windmill End 1919
Ink 24.8 × 33
Inscribed 'Edward Wadsworth 1919'
Manchester City Art Galleries
(W/B 35) p.33

62. Railway Embankment, Ockenhall, Gospel Oak/Slag Heap at Bilston 1919
Ink 23.8 × 34.3
Inscribed 'Edward Wadsworth 1919' on the front and 'Railway Embankment, Ockenhall, Gospel Oak' on the back.
The Mayor Gallery
(?W/B 52? W/B 64) p.33

63. Granite Quarries, Darby Hill, Oldbury (2) 1919
Ink 25.4 × 36.7
Inscribed '1919'
Whitworth Art Gallery, University of Manchester
(W/B 48) p.34

64. View near Bilston 1919
Ink 34.5 × 49.7
Inscribed 'Edward Wadsworth 1919'
Manchester City Art Galleries
(W/B 47) p.35

***65. View near Tipton, Staffs/Industrial Landscape** 1919
Ink 23.7 × 32.8
Inscribed 'Edward Wadsworth 1919'
The Trustees of the Cecil Higgins Art Gallery, Bedford
(W/B 55) p.34

66. Ladle Slag, Hingley's Furnaces, Old Hill (2) 1919
Ink and wash 25.4 × 35
Inscribed 'E. Wadsworth 1919'
The University of Leeds
(W/B 54) p.34

67. Mural Design for Leeds City Hall/Decoration for Leeds Town Hall 1920
Ink and gouache 73 × 53.4
Leeds City Art Galleries
(W/B 76) p.35

68. Blast Furnaces (1) (Netherton Furnaces) 1919
Woodcut 12 × 19
Private collection
(W/D 39a) p.37

69. Black Furnaces (2) (Netherton Furnaces) 1919
Woodcut 13.5 × 17.9
Private collection (Not exhibited)
(W/D 41)

70. Black Country 1919
Woodcut 11 × 14.5
(a) black on orange paper
(b) black on pink paper
(c) black on beige paper
Private collection
(W/D 40) p.37

71. Tarmac 1919
Woodcut 10.5 × 14.5
Inscribed 'Edward Wadsworth 1919'
Board of Trustees of the Victoria and Albert Museum
(W/D 42)

72. Ladle Slag, Old Hill (1) 1919-20
Lithograph 37 × 49
Private collection
(W/C 4) p.38

73. Ladle Slag, Old Hill (2) 1919-20
Lithograph 37 × 49
Private collection
(W/C 5) p.39

74. Kaolin/Devon Clay Pits 1920
Gouache 58.4 × 38.7
Private collection
(W/B 69) p.39

75. Fortune's Well, Portland 1921
Watercolour 55.2 × 79.5
Inscribed 'Edward Wadsworth 1921'
Manchester City Art Galleries
(W/B 83) colour p.50

76. Roofs and Bridges 1921
Pencil 25 × 39
Inscribed 'Edward Wadsworth 1921'
Board of Trustees of the Victoria and Albert Museum
(W/B 84)

***77. Broadbottom, near Glossop** 1922
Watercolour 33 × 42
Inscribed 'Edward Wadsworth 1922'
Private collection
(W/B 87)

78. Broadbottom, near Glossop/Derbyshire Village/Buxton Village 1922
Tempera 72 × 94.5
Inscribed 'Wadsworth 1922'
Bradford Art Galleries and Museums
(W/A 54) colour p.51

79. Near Marseilles/Mediterranean Town 1922
Tempera 76.2 × 101.6
Private collection
(W/A 52) colour p.51

80. The Cattewater, Plymouth Sound 1923
Tempera 63.5 × 88.9
Private collection
(W/A 56) *colour* p.53

81. La Rochelle (1) 1923
Tempera 63.4 × 88.8
Inscribed 'Edward Wadsworth 1923'
Private collection
(W/A 60)

82. La Rochelle (2) 1923-4
Tempera 50 × 58.5
Portsmouth City Museums
(W/A 61) p.43

***83. Dunkerque (1)** 1924
Tempera 63.7 × 89.2
Inscribed 'Edward Wadsworth 1924'
Manchester City Art Galleries
(W/A 63) *colour* p.52

84. Quai du Port, Marseilles 1924
Tempera 76 × 106
Inscribed 'Edward Wadsworth 1924'
Government Art Collection
(W/A 66) p.65

85. Rue Janetins, Marseilles 1924
Pencil 45.8 × 21.6
Private collection
(W/B 96)

***86. Hospice de la Charité, Marseilles** 1924
Pencil 47.4 × 20.2
Inscribed 'Edward Wadsworth 1924'
Trustees of the Cecil Higgins Art Gallery, Bedford
(W/B 94) p.47

87. Below Biot/Fortifications, Provence 1924-5
Pencil 35.3 × 25
Private collection
(W/B 111)

88. Study of Boats, St Tropez 1924
Pencil 25.8 × 39.5
Private collection
(W/B 107a) p.68

89. Tarpaulins 1925
Tempera 39.3 × 52.1
Private collection
(W/A 70) p.69

°89a. St Tropez (1) 1926
Tempera 35.5 × 51.4
Ivor Braka Ltd, London
(W/A 71) p.71

90. Quayside/St Tropez (3) 1925
Tempera 53 × 38
Inscribed 'Edward Wadsworth 1925' and 'for W.W.W. 1933'
Private collection
(W/A 73) p.72

***91. St Tropez (2)** 1925
Tempera 35.5 × 55.5
Inscribed 'Edward Wadsworth'
Private collection
(W/A 72)

92. Rue de la Reynarde, Marseilles 1926
Tempera 95.2 × 50.8
Inscribed 'Edward Wadsworth 1926'
Leeds City Art Galleries
(W/A 69)

93. Coquillages 1926
Tempera 53.5 × 39.5
Inscribed 'Edward Wadsworth 1926'
Whitworth Art Gallery, University of Manchester
(W/A 79) *colour* p.54

94. Little Western Flower/The Poet's Darling 1928
Tempera 53.4 × 38.1
Private collection
(W/A 107) p.73

°94a. North Sea 1928
Tempera on panel 86.4 × 60.9
Ivor Braka Ltd, London
(W/A 98) *colour* p.55

95. Parergon 1928
Tempera 40 × 33
Inscribed 'Edward Wadsworth 1928'
Private collection
(W/A 103) p.77

96. Regalia 1928
Tempera 76.2 × 91.4
Inscribed 'Edward Wadsworth 1928'
The Trustees of the Tate Gallery
(W/A 101) *colour* p.57

97. Bright Intervals/Song of the Sea/Dunkerque: Barometer, Wool and Floats 1928
Tempera 64.1 × 89.5
Borough of Thamesdown (Swindon Art Gallery)
(W/A 97) *colour* p.57

°97a. Still Life, Dungeness 1928
Tempera 38.1 × 53.4
Private collection
(W/A 95) p.79

98. Wings of the Morning 1928-9
Tempera 50.8 × 60.9
Private collection
(W/A 104) *colour* p.56

99. On est bien au bord de la mer 1928-9
Tempera 45.7 × 94
Inscribed 'Edward Wadsworth 1928-1929'
Private collection
(W/A 100) p.79

100. Faithful Servants/Marine 1928
Tempera 62.2 × 87.1
Leeds City Art Galleries
(W/A 108) p.81

101. Composition, Cones and Spirals (1) 1929
Tempera 62.5 × 87.5
The Board of Trustees of the Victoria and Albert Museum, London
(W/A 114) *colour* p.58

102. Cones, Spirals and Triangles 1930
Tempera on paper 23.5 × 34
Private collection
(W/B 116) p.109

103. Composition, Screwthread, Gauges and Bevel Protractor 1930
Tempera 88.9 × 63.5
Inscribed 'E. Wadsworth 1930'
Private collection
(W/A 125) *colour* p.59

***104. Composition with Shell/French Ruler and Scallops** 1930
Gouache 43.5 × 35.5
Inscribed 'E. Wadsworth 1930'
Lent by the Cooper Gallery Trustees on loan from the Cooper Gallery, Barnsley Metropolitan Borough Council
(W/B 115) p.109

105. Composition on a Pink Ground/Abstract Design with Claspknife 1930
Gouache 34.1 × 49.3
Inscribed 'E. Wadsworth 1930'
Trustees of the Cecil Higgins Art Gallery, Bedford (Not exhibited)
(W/B 118) p.109

106. Composition on a Red Ground 1931
Tempera 50.8 × 60.9
Leeds City Art Galleries
(W/A 132)

107. Composition IV 1932
Tempera 63.5 × 88.9
Private collection
(W/A 136) p.111

108. Dux et Comes (1) (Rebuff) 1932
Tempera 51 × 61
The Trustees of the Tate Gallery
(W/A 144) p.111

109. Dux et Comes (4) (Minicciando) 1932
Tempera 38.4 × 58.4
The Board of Trustees of the Victoria and Albert Museum, London
(W/A 146)

110. Dux et Comes (7) (Exhalation, 1) 1932
Tempera 38.4 × 53.3
Private collection
(W/A 148) p.111

111. World of Happy Days 1934
Tempera 27.9 × 38.1
Inscribed 'EW/1934'
Private collection
(W/A 158) p.83

112. The English Channel 1934
Tempera 50.9 × 96.5
Private collection
(W/A 159) *colour* p.61

113. Slump 1935
Tempera 76.2 × 60.9
Inscribed 'E. Wadsworth 1935'
Leeds City Art Galleries
(W/A 163) p.82

***114. Offing** 1935
Tempera 88.9 × 63.5
City of Bristol Museum and Art Gallery
(W/A 168) p.85

115. Cartoon for 'Offing' 1935
Pencil 65.6 × 44.2
Inscribed 'E. Wadsworth 1935'
Glasgow Art Gallery and Museum
(W/B 122) p.84

116. Dressed Overall at the Quay 1935
Gouache and watercolour 85 × 58.3
Ferens Art Gallery, Hull City Museums and Art Galleries
(W/B 124) p.87

117. Study-sketch for Proposed Design for Bexhill Pavilion 1935
Watercolour 18.1 × 24.5
Private collection
(W/B 121) *colour* p.60

118. Marine Set (1) 1936
Tempera 76.1 × 63.7
Inscribed 'E. Wadsworth 1936'
Laing Art Gallery, Newcastle-upon-Tyne (Tyne and Wear Museums Service)
(W/A 170) p.89

119. Horatio, Ship's Figurehead 1936
Gouache 24.4 × 20.2
Private collection
(W/B 125)

120. The Beached Margin 1937
Tempera 71.1 × 101.5
The Trustees of the Tate Gallery
(W/A 177) *colour* p.61

121. Souvenir of Fiumicino 1937
Tempera 61 × 50.9
Inscribed 'E. Wadsworth 1937'
Manchester City Art Galleries
(W/A 184) *colour* p.62

122. The First of the Ebb 1938
Tempera 89 × 63.5
Inscribed 'E. Wadsworth 1938'
Harrogate Museum and Art Gallery Service
(W/A 196) *colour* p.63

123. Airy Nothings/The Consistency of Odd Things 1937
Tempera 53.4 × 38.1
Inscribed 'E. Wadsworth 1937'
Private collection
(W/A 186) p.92

124. Cluster 1937
Tempera 53.4 × 38.1
Inscribed 'E. Wadsworth 1937'
Private collection
(W/A 182) p.93

125. Sussex By-pass 1937
Tempera 52 × 38.5
University College of North Wales, Bangor
(W/A 183) p.94

126. Imaginary Harbour 1938
Lithograph 45.3 × 61
Private collection
(W/C 26) p.95

127. Honfleur – Entrance to Harbour 1939
Tempera 71 × 62
Sheffield City Art Galleries
(W/A 211) p.96

°**127a. Bronze Ballet (1)** 1940
Tempera 63.5 × 76.2
The Trustees of the Tate Gallery
(W/A 225) p.97

128. Light Sections (3) 1940
Tempera 63.5 × 76.2
Inscribed 'E. Wadsworth 1940'
The Royal Pavilion, Art Gallery and Museums, Brighton
(W/A 221) p.99

°**128a. Requiescat** c.1940
Tempera 63.3 × 86.3
Leeds City Art Galleries
(W/A 224) p.98

129. Pendent/Punch Balls 1942
Tempera 87 × 62
Inscribed 'Wadsworth 42'
Kirklees Metropolitan Borough Council, Huddersfield
(W/A 235) p.101

130. Top of the World 1942-3
Tempera 38.2 × 53.2
Ferens Art Gallery, Hull City Museums and Art Galleries
(W/A 241) p.100

***131. Tomorrow Morning/Marine Perspective** 1929-44
Tempera 75 × 62.5
Inscribed 'Wadsworth 1929-44'
Courtesy of Whitford and Hughes, London
(W/A 111) p.102

132. Anticyclone 1943
Tempera 50 × 60.5
Inscribed 'E. Wadsworth'
Newport Museum and Art Gallery, Gwent
(W/A 243) p.103

133. Straight from the Tap (1) 1944
Tempera on paper 41.8 × 30.3
Private collection
(W/B 137)

134. Signal Station/The Jetty 1944
Tempera 106.7 × 71
Bradford Art Galleries and Museums
(W/A 244) p.104

***135. Signals** 1942
Lithograph 40 × 30
The Board of Trustees of the Victoria and Albert Museum, London
(W/C 43)

°135a. Le Havre/Harbour Entrance/ Boats in Harbour 1939-45
Tempera 76.2 × 63.5
Inscribed 'WADSWORTH 1939-45'
Private collection
(W/A 212) p.105

136. Abstract with Rose 1945
Tempera 50 × 60
Private collection (Not exhibited)
(W/A 248) p.112

137. Flowerpiece, Rose 1945
Tempera 63.5 × 76.2
Inscribed 'E. Wadsworth'
Private collection
(W/A 247)

138. Button Dahlia/Flowerpiece 1945
Tempera 66 × 78.8
Inscribed 'E. Wadsworth 1945'
Leeds City Art Galleries
(W/A 250) *colour p.64*

139. Single Dahlia 1946-7
Tempera 62 × 86
Private collection
(W/A 251) p.113

140. Composition, Invention/Flower and Shell 1946
Tempera 52.3 × 36.8
Inscribed 'E. Wadsworth 1946'
Private collection
(W/A 255) p.113

141. Starfish and Shells/Marine Still Life 1947
Tempera 74.6 × 61.9
Inscribed 'E. Wadsworth 1947'
Private collection
(W/A 257) p.115

°141a. Octopus 1947
Tempera 76 × 63.8
Private collection
(W/A 256) *back cover*

142. Tapestry of Starfish and Shells 1948-9
Tapestry 164 × 142.2
Private collection
(W/C 47) p.113

143. Triangles 1948
Tempera 75 × 62.5
Private collection
(W/A 261) p.117